WITHDRAWN
UST
Libraries

LIVING BIOGRAPHIES OF
American Statesmen

Abraham Lincoln

LIVING BIOGRAPHIES OF
American Statesmen

By **HENRY THOMAS** AND
DANA LEE THOMAS

(Henry Thomas Schnittkind and Dana Arnold Schnittkind)

Illustrations by
GORDON ROSS

Essay Index Reprint Series

 BOOKS FOR LIBRARIES PRESS
FREEPORT, NEW YORK

Copyright 1942 by
Doubleday & Company, Inc.
Reprinted 1971 by arrangement.

Library of Congress Cataloging in Publication Data

Thomas, Henry, 1886-
    Living biographies of American statesmen.
    (Essay index reprint series)
    1. Statesmen, American. 2. U. S.--Biography.
I. Thomas, Dana Lee, 1918-   joint author. II. Title.
E176.T54 1971   973'.0099   78-167412
ISBN 0-8369-2473-8

PRINTED IN THE UNITED STATES OF AMERICA
BY
NEW WORLD BOOK MANUFACTURING CO., INC.
HALLANDALE, FLORIDA 33009

Contents

INTRODUCTION	vii
ROGER WILLIAMS	3
WILLIAM PENN	19
FRANKLIN	35
WASHINGTON	53
HAMILTON	71
JOHN ADAMS	91
MARSHALL	109
JEFFERSON	125
MADISON	139
MONROE	153
JACKSON	169

CONTENTS

CLAY 187

WEBSTER 203

SUMNER 221

LINCOLN 235

JEFFERSON DAVIS 251

CLEVELAND 263

THEODORE ROOSEVELT 281

WILSON 295

FRANKLIN DELANO ROOSEVELT . . . 311

Introduction

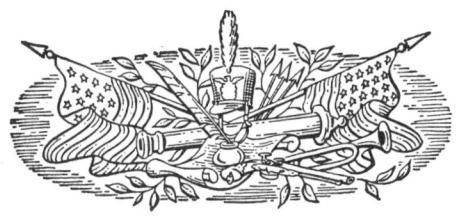

ONE OF THE MOST significant chapters in the history of America is the story of her devoted statesmen embarked upon their search for united freedom. From Roger Williams to Franklin Delano Roosevelt the great American statesmen, with the few exceptions that only emphasize the rule, have dedicated themselves to the principle that all men have an equal right to their own liberty and an equal duty to protect the liberty of others. Each of these statesmen, as we shall see in the following chapters, has contributed a definite characteristic to the composite American character of courageous and optimistic tolerance. Whether Whig or Federal, Republican or Democrat, these leaders of American political thought have worked with a deliberate bias— a bias against oppression and in favor of justice. Inspired by this American Gospel, they have gravitated toward a single objective —to transform their country into a progressive testing-ground for social and racial and religious co-operation. They have tried, each in his own way, yet all of them in the *American* way, to find the solution to the philosopher's eternal quest for the friendly fusion of mankind. Their primary concern has been to make

INTRODUCTION

the United States the first international nation in the world.

Their road toward this objective has been often difficult, at times almost hopelessly blocked. Internal bickerings, external aggressions, and occasionally the blindness and the stubbornness of the statesmen themselves—all these have at one time or another threatened to wreck their American dream. Yet in spite of their obstacles and their failings, the statesmen have at all times held tenaciously to their dream of the Great American Reunion—the reconciliation of the quarrelsome human family under the democratic form of government.

We find this American dream expressed under different forms at different periods of our history—in the *Democratic Government* of Roger Williams, in Jefferson's *Declaration of Independence*, in Madison's *Bill of Rights*, in Lincoln's *Gettysburg Address*, in Theodore Roosevelt's *Square Deal*, in Wilson's *League of Nations Covenant*, in Franklin Delano Roosevelt's *New Deal* and *Atlantic Charter*. These statesmen, and practically all the other statesmen included in this book, have envisioned the free and united states of America as a model for the free and united nations of the world.

H. T.
D. L. T.

ROGER WILLIAMS

Important Dates in Life of Roger Williams

1604—Born in London.
1627—Graduated from Pembroke College.
1629—Entered holy orders and became chaplain to Sir William Masham.
1631—Emigrated to the Massachusetts Bay Colony.
1635—Banished from the Massachusetts Bay Colony for "heretical and seditious" utterances.
1636—Founded the "first settlement for freedom of worship" at Providence.
1643—Went to England to obtain a legal charter for Rhode Island.
1654—Chosen President of the Rhode Island Colony.
1672—Held public debates with the Quakers on points of religious doctrine.
1676—Took up sword to defend colony against Indian uprisings under "King Philip."
1683—Died at Providence.

Roger Williams

Roger Williams
1604–1683

H<small>E LIVED</small> as a child in Smithfield, within the hub of London town. A mile to the west sat the tyrannical king at Whitehall with his chosen judges. But just beyond, the Thames moved in freedom. And not far from Whitehall and the Star Chamber, a Parliament of free Englishmen met and deliberated in behalf of the people. The boy was drawn by a grim fascination to play just outside the walls of the Newgate Prison. Within these walls lay the political and the religious radicals of the Kingdom. Roger had heard many stories about these dissenters. Once he had witnessed a terrible scene in the parish where he lived. Old Doctor Leighton had been put into the pillory. There had been a huge crowd gathered to see him publicly whipped. And one of his ears was cut off by the executioner and one side of his nose was split. And he was branded in the face with two searing initials—S.S. "Sower of Sedition." Many times thereafter, Roger saw these letters flaming in his sleep. "Sower of Sedition."

Gradually the boundaries of his world extended. Far beyond the parish there was a vast new continent. One day Captain John Smith had returned to London from America and had brought with him his young Indian wife, Pocahontas. And all England had been dazzled by the "prize of his pilgrimage."

But Roger had heard tales of other pilgrims—men and women who had left England and Holland and traveled across the sea. They were, like himself, people of the upper middle class. And they had gone into exile because they were martyrs of discontent and prophets of something new and better . . .

He was a quick and serious boy. He had scarcely arrived at his teens when he caught the eye of the eminent Puritan lawyer, Sir Edward Coke, who hired him as his amanuensis. Young Roger developed a marked aptitude in shorthand as he transcribed the legal speeches in the Star Chamber Courts where Sir Edward pleaded for the offenders against the Crown. From the learned mind of Sir Edward he acquired the principles of parliamentary government and of common law. And, as he grew older, he rose to comradeship with a number of influential men and women.

He entered the University of Cambridge and "hobnobbed" with the élite of Puritan society. For a time he trifled away his days and nights "breaking rules, reading forbidden books, keeping dogs and cocks, attending boxing matches and taverns." But gradually "he grew sober." As he learned to control his physical fires, the light of his mind became focused upon ever more distant horizons.

II

IN HIS twenty-sixth year Roger lived at Oates as chaplain to Sir William Masham. Here in the carved oak halls of the Tudor manor, along the terraces of the Italian garden and in the hunting grounds of the deer and the fox, he mingled with the exclusive aristocracy of England. And one "sweet spring morning" he fell in love with its fairest flower, Lady Jane Whalley. He received an instant rebuff from the lady's aunt, who asked him politely and frigidly to sum up his worldly possessions. The young preacher idealist replied: "A small library of books."

Whereupon the negotiations for the young lady's heart came to an abrupt end—so far at least as the young lady was concerned.

But Roger had not as yet lost hope as the spring advanced toward the summer. In the last throes of his romantic ardor he sent to Lady Whalley a tempest of letters, sealing them with emblems of roses and with fleurs-de-lis. To no avail.

And then he fell into an illness. He recovered slowly and convalesced under the golden autumn sunshine in the company of Sir William Masham's daughter Judith—they called her "Jug"—and her maid, Mary. The lady brought his spirits back into harmony as she played for him on the spinet. And the maid, strolling with him along the riverbank, soothed him with her silent sympathy. And then the parishioners of Oates, buzzing with the gossip of their chaplain who had been rejected by a woman above his rank, fell stunned by the thunderbolt of a new surprise. On a December day in the little parish church of High Laver not far from the village of Oates, the Reverend Roger Williams had married Judith Masham's maid, Mary Barnard.

The winter turned slowly into an English spring again.

III

As ROGER WILLIAMS held the hand of Mary Barnard and pronounced the words of eternal fidelity, he joined hands with the undertrodden throughout the world. He was a self-made middle class preacher—not good enough for the Lady Jane Whalley! Very well, he would reply to her grand rebuff in an equally grand manner. He would bring his fist down with a crash upon the myth of the upper classes. He would shatter their pretensions to bits. It was the solemn warning of an exile—he clasped Mary's hand more tightly—an exile to the ends of the earth, if need be, in order to build a better society among men. A fugitive of lost love to seek a new kind of love.

He had rebelled against the society of Charles II. There were other rebels too. Voices called him to the seacoast town of Bristol. In a crowded tavern he met the son of John Winthrop, who had gone to build a new society in America. And over his glass of metheglin his thoughts turned westward to Massachusetts Bay. Wouldn't it be a good idea to take his wife to a land where everybody got a fresh start? . . .

He embarked on the *Lyon* (December 1, 1630) in the season of hard adventure. In February the ship with its human cargo weighed anchor off the storm-ridden coast of Massachusetts. Roger Williams peered across the bay toward the wilderness. And life looked good to him. All things stared upon him "with a weather-beaten face." Here was the Promised Land.

IV

HE HAD left England to begin life anew. But he found the same old life in America. The same tyrannies and persecutions and prejudices and hates. The Puritan divines who had broken away from the Church of England and who had come to America for conscience' sake were now with heavy tyrannous hand inscribing the tablets of their own ascetic dogmas and persecuting with relentless savagery all those who would not obey. Here were the narrowness and the bigotry of the king and of Archbishop Laud displayed under different colors. Old slaveries under new skies.

At first he was silent, but then he began to speak freely and plainly. He preached from his pulpit and hoed his potatoes and marveled at the quirks of the human mind and the cruelties of the human heart. These people in Massachusetts had planted everything but freedom. But at least he, the guest among them, would never hesitate to arraign his hosts whenever he saw an injustice done. And so he gripped the spade and placed his footsteps more firmly upon the ground as he cultivated his little plot of independent soil. The government of New England was a theocracy. Why in this Promised Land, he asked himself, should a man's political rights be subjected to his religious beliefs? He refused to give the customary pledge of obedience to these church dignitaries. He would start a controversy that would shake this "Commonwealth of Saints" to its very foundations.

The eloquence of his tongue had begun to agitate the people. And the ecclesiastical princes, John Winthrop and John Cotton, had come to regard him with a hostile eye. Cotton Mather had angrily written in his books, "There is a whole country in America like to be set on fire by the rapid motion of a windmill in the head of one particular man." And the established authorities had rallied their forces to stop the preaching of this "particular man."

For, as he fanned his discontent to a flaming heat, he molded a doctrine that rang like an alarm of steel. Who were these hierophants to compel all men to live and to worship and to think and to be judged in accordance with the commandments of a few arbitrary minds? A man, declared Roger Williams, has but a single infallible judge—his own conscience. "I affirm it to be against the testimony of Christ Jesus for the civil state to impose upon the souls of the people a religion, a worship, a ministry . . . I affirm that the state should give free and absolute permission of conscience to all men." And as he spoke and developed his thought, he knew at last what it was that gave the oaks of the New England forests their living strength. It was the firmness of the roots in the rock-ribbed soil. "To persecute a man's conscience and his ways of worship is to pluck up the roots and foundation of all common society in the world."

This, declared the Calvinistic rulers of Massachusetts, was the most heretical doctrine ever heard! And so they prepared to "blot into darkness the flaming scourge who preached nothing less than an uprising of the people." With sardonic piety Cotton Mather reflected, "If the people be the governors, who will be the governed?" To him this "perplexing" question was unanswerable. His own conscience was clear. With a Bible in his hands and a prayer on his lips he came into the Newtown

Courthouse to see if the world couldn't manage another crucifixion.

V

ROGER WILLIAMS was ordered to go on trial in the church of Thomas Hooker at Newtown. It was a bleak and angry looking wooden building with scowling walls and a floor of frozen dirt. Fifty judges of the Commonwealth sat in black-robed silence. Sober, God-fearing men, Defenders of the "Rule of the Saints." The people, too, were present—a hundred of them, sitting in amazement and terror and anticipation. But they took no part in the proceedings. They had no voice.

It was a court of inquisition. There was to be neither a jury nor a written indictment. The leader of the fifty inquisitors, the prosecuting attorney and the final judge was the governor of Massachusetts. The accused man was allowed neither witnesses nor counsel. In the breathless stillness the governor announced the charge. "Dangerous opinions tending to unsettle the Kingdoms and the Commonwealths of Europe." But hold, the sentence would be stayed if the culprit confessed his error.

Roger Williams looked squarely at the judges. "I stand unshaken, sirs. I am ready not only to be bound and banished but if necessary to die for my opinions."

The governor pronounces the verdict. "Guilty . . . Deprived of rights . . . banished . . . outcast from civilized society. . . ."

Friends walked with him silently into the icy streets. The forests were trackless and waist-deep with snow—frozen tombs for the living.

"Tell the judges as a human being before God that your wife is pregnant; that you are sick in body and worn in mind. Plead with them to stay the sentence at least until the spring . . ."

The judge receives the petition. He hesitates. "Well, if he takes a solemn oath that he will cease preaching his opinions, we will permit him to wait out the winter."

Roger Williams refuses. Is one season any different from another when the truth is to be declared? The spring, too, can be hard weather for a man who stifles his voice.

The court issues a warrant for his arrest, dispatches Captain Underhill with fourteen men. But Roger Williams has left for the wilderness three days before their arrival.

A bitter, driving snowstorm. And his wife has remained behind. She will join him later with the little baby that has come—"Freeborn" they have named her.

The north wind stings like a whiplash and the blizzard blinds the eyes. He travels ninety miles from Salem, south by southwest. He seeks shelter in the wigwams of the friendly Indians and eats with them of their beaver meat and warms his hands by their fire. And he wrestles with the irony "that God's children should so persecute God's children." He looks sadly into the tongues of flame. "And we who cannot get together in this world hope to live together in heaven?"

Mile after mile he travels with his compass pointing in the right direction—to the future of decency and human rights. Ninety blood-stained miles through the heart of the winter wilderness, to the Indian island of Sowams-by-the-Sea. Here in the Narragansett territory where the Redskins raised their hands in greeting—"What cheer, friend?"—he found his Providence "northeast by a wooded hill." Upon this spot he was determined to "build a colony where all men may worship God in their own way."

VI

TWELVE FRIENDS followed him to help him build his new sanctuary of freedom. They laid foundations of flattened stones and scalped the forests of their oaks for timber. They planted their gardens and their orchards and plowed their fields and laid out their streets. And then, when they grew tired of their building, they dug out their couches for their final sleep. Five acres of working and sleeping. And no man took an inch more earth than any other man. The first settlers met together to lay the foundations of a common government. "We whose names are hereunder written . . . do with free and joint consent promise each unto the other that for our common peace and welfare we will, from time to time, subject ourselves in active and passive obedience to such orders and agreements as shall be made by the *greater number* of the present householders. . . ."

And when they had signed their names to their "democratical government," Roger Williams spoke to his fellow freemen: "I desire not that liberty for myself which I would not freely and impartially weigh out to all the consciences of the world besides . . . In this colony we shall open wide our doors so that all the number of the weak and the distressed, scattered throughout New England, may find shelter from their persecution."

In such simple fashion began the first public experiment in human liberty. To Rhode Island came a flock of refugees from oppression—anabaptists, antinomians, generalists, familists, atheists, seekers—a babel of pilgrims who expressed all sorts of political and social and religious doctrines.

To Rhode Island came Anne Hutchinson, banished from Boston for her religious "heresies." She seemed a flaming fanatic even to Roger Williams. "The Lord mercifully redeem her from her illusions," he declared. "And yet I am glad to have her for my neighbor." Here with bleeding footsteps turned Nicholass Upsall and his fellow Quaker, Mary Dyer, who had been snatched from the gallows on Boston Common. Roger Williams debated publicly with the Quakers on the tenets of their religion. He was not sympathetic to their creed. He demanded that they, in common with all the other citizens, should pay their taxes and perform their civic duties. But he never persecuted them.

Here came the Jews from New Amsterdam and Curaçao after they had been refused admission by the Dutch. In Rhode Island they were permitted to build their synagogues and to bury their dead in accordance with the demands of their own faith. All the other "civilized" communities in New England—and old

England—promptly and officially excommunicated "this plague spot of scum and castaways."

"Democracy!" growled John Winthrop of the Massachusetts Bay Colony. "Democracy is amongst civil nations accounted the meanest and worst of all forms of government." "Liberty of conscience!" declared a member of the King's government in England. "Liberty of conscience is so prodigious an impiety that this religious Parliament cannot but abhor the very naming of it."

During the years that followed, the prophet at times despaired of his experiment. As prosperity came to Rhode Island, some of its citizens forgot their heritage of suffering and quarreled with one another over corn and cattle and the distribution of land. In vain Roger Williams cried out to them to cease their haggling. "As if men and women were in great necessity and danger for want of great portions of land!" And he warned his people in his gentle way, "It was not price or money that purchased Rhode Island. Rhode Island was purchased by love."

And there were some unscrupulous demagogues who used his doctrine of civil liberty to preach civil license. They refused to pull together with the rest of the people. In the name of "individual rights" they disclaimed any obligation to pay taxes or to perform their duty as citizens under the state. Indeed, they refused to *recognize* the state.

And Roger Williams replied to these dissenters with a parable. "Sometimes it happens that both Papists and Protestants, Jews and Turks, may be embarked in one ship. None of them may be forced to come to the ship's prayer. But if any of the seamen refuse to perform their services, or passengers to pay their freight . . . if any refuse to obey the common laws and orders of the ship concerning their common peace and preservation; if any shall mutiny and rise up against their commanders and officers . . . I say, all such transgressors must be judged, resisted, compelled and punished according to their deserts and merits."

But the vast majority of the people of Rhode Island, this

population of different tongues and minds but of one spirit, refused to let their grand epic of internationalism end in failure. "When we are gone, our children after us must read in our town records, and our letters, the story of our success."

And the leader was patient to the death. In England his old master, Sir Edward Coke, and his fellow Puritans had finally overthrown the government of Charles II and Archbishop Laud. The preacher in the wilderness realized that if the ideals of his government at Rhode Island were to survive legally he must obtain a charter from his friends in London. He boarded a ship for England. And before he returned to America he took long walks with the private secretary of Oliver Cromwell—John Milton. And the author of *Paradise Lost* listened with eager sympathy to the dreamer of Paradise Found.

VII

HE WAS broken in body from his great labors. But still his eyes stood out as beacon lights for all who wandered in the night. And even now that his hair had turned winter, no enemy dared debate with him or accept his challenge to silence him with a "hanging or a burning."

Yet in spite of his vigor as a debater, he was a man of gentle tolerance. He had devoted many of his labors to the preservation of peace with the Indians. Again and again he had traveled to the Indian tribes in an effort to still their wrath against the Massachusetts Bay Colony.

And the Massachusetts Bay Colonists received the bread of his unselfish service and repaid it with stones. They formed a military alliance with the Plymouth and the Connecticut colonies against the attacks of the Indians and they allowed Rhode Island to remain defenseless and alone on the frontier without supplying her with a pound of ammunition.

But Roger Williams did not mind. He had a weapon far stronger than gunpowder. The Indians listened to his gentle words and loved him. He nursed them and fed them and closed the eyes of their warriors when their fighting was done. God in His infinite wisdom had bestowed upon the little colony two jewels. "The first jewel is liberty; the second is peace."

And then, as Roger Williams was approaching his final years, peace died a sudden violent death in New England. For the chieftain King Philip had vowed his Indians to a war of extermination against the Whites. "Iootash! Iootash! Down with the whiteskins of New England!"

The New Englanders tried desperately to make an alliance with the Narragansetts, a tribe friendly to Roger Williams. A deputation from the Massachusetts Bay Colony came to his house and implored him to intercede in their behalf.

Whereupon Roger Williams turned his tired steps into the Narragansett territory and met with his Sachem friends. Once again they listened to his words. They called him the "Quencher of our fires" and they sent him home with an assurance of their good will.

Yet even as he was preparing a report of his success with the Narragansetts, he received word that the Indians had attacked the white colonists. And then the aged peacemaker of seventy-two reached for his gun. "War," he had once said, "is the business of savages." But not war in self-defense. He had tried to be a prophet. Now he would try to be a soldier. "We will pursue them in the summer and the winter . . . until the mosquitoes and the rattlesnakes are unable to bite."

He came before the Providence Assembly and ordered the evacuation of all the women and the children. Then he remained behind with thirty men and assumed the captaincy of the band. He made an inventory of the colony's resources and found that Newport, the largest contributor to the defense, had only three barrels of gunpowder, a thousand pounds of lead, twenty-four muskets, and twelve pikes. He organized the men under his command into a fighting force and drilled them until the youngest fell from exhaustion. He fortified a stockade and started a subscription for a siege. And he pledged from his own savings the largest sum of all—fifty dollars. Thereafter he was a poor man.

In the month of March the enemy approached the outskirts of the colony. Leaning on his staff, Roger Williams dragged himself to the heights at the north of the town to meet the attack. And to reason with them. A thousand young warriors, poised with lighted firebrands, stood silently as the aged man approached.

"Massachusetts can raise thousands of men at this moment," he warned the Indian warriors. "And if you kill the men of Massachusetts, the King of England will supply their places as rapidly as they fall."

"And we," retorted a chieftain, "will kill them as rapidly as they come. But not you, Brother Williams. For you are a good man. You have been kind to us. Not a hair of your head shall be touched."

Without a word the prophet-warrior returned to his company. He preferred to die with them.

The Indians burned Providence. And Roger Williams' home fell into the flames along with the rest. Finally the combined forces of the colonists succeeded in crushing King Philip's revolt—but at the cost of much blood and many tears. Twelve towns had been burned to the ground and six hundred buildings in Plymouth, Massachusetts and Rhode Island had been destroyed. Five hundred Englishmen had lost their lives. A hundred thousand pounds in sterling had been expended.

But Roger Williams comforted his fellow townsmen as they paddled up the Seekhonk and drew near to the smoke and the ashes where once their homes had stood. "Let us set to work again with a will," he said. "Liberty does not fall like the showers and dews and manna from heaven, gratis and free, like a joyful harvest and vintage without any pain . . ."

VIII

Soon all the pain ceased for Roger Williams. With the true perspective of wisdom he had given away all his land until he had nothing left but a couch of earth in the orchard under the trees. Here lay most of his old friends and neighbors, each in a shroud of silence. One morning when the apples were redder than the dawn he took his place beside them. And the roots of the trees that canopied him reached out with every fiber of their strength and mingled with the dust of the partners who slept next to him—until all the graves were one.

WILLIAM PENN

Important Dates in Life of William Penn

1644—Born in London.
1666—Expelled from Oxford University. Went to Ireland to manage father's estates.
1668—Thrown into prison for adherence to Quaker doctrines.
1671—Wrote, in Newgate Prison, *The Great Cause of Liberty of Conscience*.
1682—Came to America and founded the Colony of Pennsylvania.
1692—Back in England. Entered politics at the Court and lost title to his colony.
1694—Title to his colony restored. Swindled by his agent. Bankrupt.
1708—Thrown into the Fleet Prison for debt.
1712—Suffered apoplectic stroke. Mind impaired.
1718—Died at Ruscombe in Berkshire, England.

William Penn

William Penn
1644–1718

H<small>IS PARENTS</small> were all-too-human. His father, Admiral William Penn, was a "good sea-dog with a bad reputation." He had a special talent—his friend and crony, Samuel Pepys, informs us—for three things: fighting, cheating and flattering. As a result of his practical ability and ethical indifference, Sir William became a rich man and a favorite of King Charles II. As for Penn's mother, she was a vain and vulgar and commonplace little plaything of a woman. Again we have Samuel Pepys for our authority. One night, writes Mr. Pepys in his *Diary,* "I went to my Lady Ballen, and there found a great many women with her in her chamber, merry; my Lady Penn . . . among others, when my Lady Penn flung me down on the bed (he was a small man) and herself and others, one after another, upon me, and very merry we were." This is but one of a number of passages in which Mr. Pepys represents himself as an eye-witness and arm-witness of my Lady Penn's jollifications.

William Penn came out of ordinary stock. And he left ordinary stock after him. His moral genius is one of the strange mysteries of life, just as strange as the intellectual genius of a

Shakespeare, who was the son of an illiterate glover and the father of an illiterate imbecile.

As a youngster, William Penn loved a good drink and a good fight. He was thoughtless, handsome, gay and athletic—a perfect specimen of the middle-class nonentities who made up the military backbone of England in the seventeenth century. His father wanted him to be a soldier, and Penn himself was not averse to the idea.

He was expelled from college, wasted a year or so in Paris, and spent another year or so in a campaign against the Irish. He had inherited the adventurous spirit of his father, and Sir William was delighted to see his son follow in his footsteps.

And then, to his father's consternation, young Penn met with the Quakers and entered upon a new campaign. He enlisted as a soldier in the Fighting Army of Peace.

II

THE QUAKERS have been among the most misunderstood people in the world. It is true that, like all other rebellious bodies, they had in their early days their lunatic fringe. Some of the hysterical members of their society walked barefoot, and at times even naked, through the city streets. One of them rushed into the Cathedral of St. Paul with a blood-smeared face and a brazier of live coals on his head. Another defiled his body with dung as a symbol of the defilement of his country. Such men, however, belonged in an insane asylum whither they were ultimately consigned. The rank and file of the Quakers were of an entirely different stamp. They were not, as is generally supposed, a drab and bloodless race of pacifists who ran away from a fight because they were afraid of being hurt. On the contrary, the Quakers were among the most valiant soldiers in history. They advocated, and they practiced, a lifelong war against all evil. They were a fearless and aggressive group who always carried the fight to the enemy. But they fought their good fight without

WILLIAM PENN

weapons. They took blows without returning them. They went to prison without offering resistance. And they died without killing.

For they had a vital idea to proclaim—the idea of justice—and they battled for it openly, fearlessly, aggressively. They stalked into the palace and declared that the "divine right" of the king must give way to the human rights of his subjects. They believed in equal opportunity and in equal dignity. All of us, they said, are the children of One God; and in His eyes the beggar is of equal importance with the king. And to substantiate this equality of all mankind, they befriended the lowest but refused to bend the knee to the highest. Even in the presence of royalty they kept their hats on their heads. "Only a slave," they maintained, "uncovers himself before his master." To the Quakers, there were no masters and no slaves.

For their daring ideas, and for their unshaken determination to express these ideas to the lords of the earth, they were whipped and imprisoned and murdered—and feared. It was the firm conviction, in many quarters, that they were in league with some strange supernatural power. On one of the occasions when their leader, George Fox, was arrested, a guard was stationed at the fireplace to prevent him from flying up the chimney!

It was this fear of their "supernatural" power that gave them the nickname of *Quakers*. "For they make people to quake and tremble at their words." The Quakers called themselves the *Children of the Light,* or the *Society of Friends.*

When William Penn joined the *Society of Friends* (in 1667), he was twenty-three years old. At that time King Charles II was on the throne. This playful Bonnie Prince Charlie had turned his palace into a gilded brothel. Nestled in the arms of his mistresses, he found no time to worry about the well-being of his people. He ate his beef and drank his beer, while many thousands of his subjects went hungry and thirsty. And when they dared to complain, he had them kidnaped on the streets and pressed into the navy. As a warning to the rest that they must obey his whims, he made it a regular practice to stick the heads of the disobedient upon the picket fence along the Thames River.

Yet he could have his occasional joke with his subjects. One day William Penn met him in the park and, as usual, refused to take off his hat. Whereupon the jovial monarch removed his own hat and stood bareheaded before the young Quaker.

"Why art thou uncovered?" asked William Penn.

"Because," answered the king, "wherever I am, it is customary for only one person to remain covered."

But in spite of his humor toward the Quakers, King Charles had no mercy for them. He packed the jails with them until there was hardly any standing room. As for the English jails of the seventeenth century, "Lord bless me, what a sight is here!" They were dank and dark and moldy, and overrun with rats and vermin. The roofing over the cells was generally rotted away, so that when it rained, the prisoners were drenched to the skin. The air was so foul with the odors of human discharges—and of rotting dead bodies—that it was almost impossible to breathe. "When we came first into Newgate (Prison)," wrote Thomas Ellwood, the Quaker friend of William Penn, "there lay . . . near the room where we were lodged . . . the quartered bodies of three men who had been executed some days before . . . We saw the heads (of these three men) when they were brought up to be boiled. The hangman fetched them in a dirty dust basket . . . and setting them down amongst the felons, he and they . . . took them by the hair, flouting, jeering, and laughing at them . . . Which done, the hangman put them into his kettle, and parboiled them with bay-salt and cummin-seed . . . to keep them from putrefaction . . . a sight both frightful and loathsome . . ."

Such were the prisons into which young William Penn was thrust again and again "in order to cool off his ardor," as the authorities expressed it. On one occasion, when he was sentenced to Newgate for several months, the judge ordered a constable to

WILLIAM PENN

take him to the prison. "Thank you for the escort," said Penn, "but I know my way to Newgate by this time."

The charges on which he was committed were of the most curious kind—such as his insistence upon his "hat honor," his defense of the poor, and his declaration that God was merciful rather than revengeful. At times he was sent off to the Tower without any charge whatsoever. And without any trial. But the admiral's son was a fighter. One day he was arrested and sent to prison for having "conspired" at a Quaker meeting. He demanded a jury trial—and got it, with the cards stacked against him. When he tried to testify in his own behalf, he was dragged off to "the Hole"—a place, Penn informs us, "not fit for pigs." The Lord Mayor then charged the jury, in the prisoner's absence, to find a verdict of "Guilty of conspiracy against the King."

The jury retired and after careful deliberation returned with a verdict of "Guilty"—not, however, of conspiracy, but merely "of speaking in Gracechurch Street."

"I insist upon a verdict as outlined in my charge!" shouted the Lord Mayor and sent the jury back to their deliberations. Half an hour later they returned with the selfsame verdict: "Guilty of speaking in Gracechurch Street."

Whereupon the Lord Mayor turned furiously upon the foreman of the jury. "If you fail in your duty, sirrah, I will slit your nose open!"

"My lord," replied the foreman, "I will do my duty."

Again the jury retired. For two days and two nights they were kept locked up without any food or drink, and then the foreman sent word that they had changed their verdict.

The jury filed into the courtroom. The judge turned to the foreman. "Have you reached a verdict?"

"Yes, my lord."

"What is your verdict?"

"Not guilty!"

III

At twenty-eight William Penn married Gulielma Springett, a Quaker girl of extraordinary charm and gentle character. For the next nine years he devoted his time to preaching the Quaker doctrine and writing about it and going to prison for it. And then, in 1681, there came to him a great vision—to build a united brotherhood in America as a model for the united brotherhood of mankind.

He called his American project the "Holy Experiment." In order to carry out this experiment, he received from King Charles a large tract of land on the Atlantic seacoast. The king gave this land to Penn for two reasons: in the first place, to discharge a debt of £16,000 (worth about $160,000 in present-day money) which he owed to Penn's father; and in the second place, "to get rid of Penn and his troublesome companions." At that period the kings and the nobles of Europe had very little use for America. They looked upon it as a dumping ground for "the undesirables and the riffraff—the Puritans, the Catholics, the Quakers, the rogues and the jailbirds." And so the "Merry Monarch" presented Penn with his land grant and his charter and his "good-riddance" wishes, and with a sigh of relief snuggled back into the arms of his mistresses.

At the insistence of the king, William Penn's land was named Pennsylvania—not in honor of William, but rather as a monument to his father, a crony whom Charles esteemed as a rascal after his own heart.

It was in October, 1682, that William Penn arrived in America and received the customary deed of turf, twig, water and soil as the symbol of his ownership of the New Land.

Immediately after his arrival he established the famous "Great Law"—that is, the legal right of every man to worship his God in his own way. And then he proceeded to plan his City of

WILLIAM PENN

Brotherly Love (Philadelphia) and his Christian Government of Peace.

The external form of the government did not greatly concern William Penn. What interested him especially was the internal substance—the soundness and the fairness of the laws. "Any government," he maintained, "is free . . . where the laws rule and the people are a party to them." A good *governor,* he said, is more important than a good *government.* He believed in liberty, but not in license. "Liberty without obedience," he wrote, "is confusion." Yet obedience must not be blind. For "obedience without liberty is slavery." His idea of freedom, in other words, was a wise application of the law on the part of the governor, and a sensible observation of the law on the part of the people. He was unable to divorce himself entirely from the "divine right" idea. But he modified and refined this idea into something new. All authority, he said, is invested with a twofold divinity. It possesses not only a divine right to rule, but a divine duty to rule righteously. The governor must always be obeyed if just; but if unjust, he must be criticized and corrected. To summarize his idea of government, he compared it to a clock which must be regulated by the people whom it guides. "Governments rather depend upon men than men upon governments. Let men be good, and the government cannot be bad."

With this political theory as a foundation, William Penn set up a state that was half paternal and half democratic. It consisted of a governor, a governor's council, and an assembly of freemen. The governor was the guide, but the people held the power. They had the right, through their assembly, to make, to alter and to repeal the laws; to appoint constables and judges; and to elect commissioners, or executives, who were responsible to the people. It was a government of free speech and of free worship; a state without an aristocracy or an army; a commonwealth dedicated to the ideals of friendship, justice and mercy. Having personally experienced the horrors of prison life, he did away with the penal system of the Old World. Instead of the

English prisons, he built American houses of correction. For he was interested not in punishing the crime, but in reforming the criminal. Of the two hundred offenses that in England were punishable by death, he retained only two—treason and murder.

His sense of justice tempered with mercy extended to his relations with the Indians. "William Penn," writes Mrs. Preston, one of his Quaker contemporaries, "made himself endeared to the Indians by his marked . . . acquiescence to their wishes." And by his democratic spirit of camaraderie. "He walked with them, sat with them on the ground, and ate with them of their roasted acorns and hominy." The Indians respected him not only for his moral grandeur but for his physical prowess. One day, writes Mrs. Preston, the Indians "began to show how they could hop and jump; at which exhibition William Penn, to cap the climax, sprang up and beat them all!" They gave him the pet name of *Onas*—the Indian equivalent of *Pen* or *Quill*—and they declared that this man, in spite of his pale skin, must have the Indian spark of the Great Spirit within him. "Your skin may be white, but your heart is red."

And Penn, on his part, respected his "Red Brothers." He made it not only a moral offense, but a legal crime, to cheat an Indian. One of his first official acts in America was to draw up the great Shackamaxon Treaty—a covenant of mutual friendship between the Whites and the Indians. "This," said Voltaire, "was the only treaty in modern history that was never ratified by an oath and that was never broken." During the seventy years of Quaker sovereignty in Pennsylvania, not a single Indian was ever cheated by a white man, and not a single white man was ever murdered by an Indian. "To William Penn"—again we quote Voltaire—"the world owes the inauguration of the Golden Age."

IV

ALTHOUGH William Penn had received his American possession as a grant from Charles II, he repurchased it from the Indians to whom it rightfully belonged. And then, having acquired the land and formulated its laws, he invited the persecuted and the oppressed to come and make their home there. Not only from England, but from Germany and Scotland and Sweden and Ireland and Holland and France, the Quakers flocked to this new refuge in Penn's Land. To all these "foreigners" he granted equal citizenship with the English. It was an embryo League of Nations that he set up in Pennsylvania, with himself as its moral and political guide. Going about with his blue sash—this quiet little Quaker was somewhat vain of his appearance, a characteristic inherited from his mother—he dispensed justice, reproved mischief and laid down in Pennsylvania the "foundation for the perfect state." He was "much pleased," he wrote to his family in England, with his "place and fortune . . . The land is good, the air clear and sweet, the springs plentiful, and provisions . . . easy to come at . . . In fine, here is what Abraham, Isaac and Jacob would have been well content with, a land of promise, and service enough for God . . . How sweet is the quiet in these parts, freed from the anxieties and troublesome solicitations, and hurries and perplexities of woeful Europe!"

Yet he returned to Europe after only a few years in Pennsylvania. And this brings us to a chapter in his life which is hard to understand. It is a chapter in which the uncompromising Quaker became the flattering courtier. He joined the court of James II, the new king of England, he found his way into the inner circle of the king's friends and he allowed himself to become implicated in the tangled meshes of imperial politics. His detractors made the most of this "apostasy" on the part of William Penn. Even among the Quakers there were those who called him a renegade. He himself maintained that whatever he did, he did for the benefit of the Quakers. Accusations and explanations flew back and forth. In interested circles the controversy has been raging to this very day. The truth of the matter seems to be somewhere between the two contending parties.

William Penn was a sincere Quaker and a great statesman. He was a superior type of man but he was not a superman. He had his weaknesses as well as his virtues. He loved humanity but he also had a measure of love for himself. He was fond of pomp and ceremony and he was not averse to the enjoyment of personal glory—provided, however, this glory came to him as a reward in a good cause. It was a great triumph for him to become the intimate confidant of the king. But, on the other hand, he realized that his friendship for the king meant freedom for the Quakers. Again and again he prevailed upon the king to release the Quakers from prison. That was his job—to secure the freedom of conscience. He courted the king in order that the king might court justice.

For William Penn was a man with a practical head and a gentle heart. He was that rare combination of character—the politician and the prophet rolled into one. And it was a lucky thing for the Quakers that this leader of theirs could be a smiling flatterer as well as a sincere friend. Thanks to his influence with the king, he received from him a charter of religious indulgence for the "Children of the Light." In the so-called "apostasy" of William Penn there was perhaps less of the sinner than of the saint.

V

It was a dangerous thing to meddle in the politics of England. Indeed, it came near to costing Penn his life. King James II, who was a Catholic, had been expelled from England, and the Protestant William III had come to the throne. But William Penn, with the indiscretion of a reckless friendship, persisted in his correspondence with the exiled king. Some of his letters were intercepted, and he was arrested on the charge of being "a traitor to his country and a papist in disguise."

William Penn denied the charge, but frankly admitted his friendship for the unfortunate exile. "I have loved him in prosperity," he confessed, "and I cannot hate him in adversity.

WILLIAM PENN

I love him for the favors he conferred on me, and would reward his kindness by any private office in my power, but only as far as my duty to the Government permits . . . I have never had the vanity to think that I could restore the crown."

The enemies of the Quakers cried out for Penn's blood, but King William ordered his release. "I respect his honesty, and I believe in his innocence."

Another trip to America, and another interlude of idyllic peace. "Divine pleasures," he wrote, "are to be found only in a free solitude." He enjoyed his spacious Pennsbury Manor, his six-oared barge, his occasional glass of Madeira, and the friendship of his white and his Indian subjects. "We are all," said the Indians, "the children of Onas." They came to his banquets in their feathers and paints, and he received them as his honored guests.

And he still loved, as of old, his little pageants and pomps and ceremonies. At all state meetings a man marched before him with an ivory wand in his hand. And in front of his gate stood a footman holding a ten-foot pole with a silver head.

A few years of this peaceful pageantry, and then Destiny once more laid a heavy hand upon him. His wife Gulielma had died. And his son, Springett. Another of his sons, William, had turned out to be a wastrel. For these sufferings he had found a measure of consolation in the love of his second wife, Hannah. But now, in the decline of his life, he was overwhelmed with a tempest of misfortune. The success of his "Holy Experiment" was threatened by the king, who wanted to remove him from the governorship and to terminate the independence of Pennsylvania by transforming it into one of the "royal plantations" of America. Together with his family he returned to England, to petition the king's favor in behalf of Pennsylvania.

Shortly after his arrival in London, King William died and Queen Anne came to the rescue of Pennsylvania. "Mr. Penn, I promise . . . that both your friends and yourself may be assured of my protection."

Penn's province was safe. But not so William Penn. He had lost the bulk of his fortune in the interest of his American colony and in the payment of his son's gambling debts—these debts amounted to about £10,000. And now there fell upon him the greatest blow of his life. He had left the balance of his estate in the hands of a steward, Philip Ford. This man was capable but dishonest. He prepared papers for Penn's signature; and Penn, relying too much upon the man's integrity, signed the papers without reading the contents. One day he was amazed to receive from his steward a demand for £14,000. Without knowing it, he had signed away his property to the designing scoundrel, Philip Ford.

Unable to pay the extortionate debt, William Penn took a final trip to prison. He stayed there for nine months before his friends were able to liquidate the debt and to rescue the remnants of his property.

The remainder of his life was a hide-and-seek game with his creditors. In the door of his house he had ordered a peep-hole to be made, so that he might observe the visitors before they entered. One day a creditor sent in his name. Fifteen minutes, half an hour passed, and no sign of life. Finally the creditor knocked for the servant. "Won't your master see me?" he asked.

"Friend," replied the servant. "My master *has* seen you, and he doesn't like your looks."

VI

HIS HEALTH had now given out. One day, as he was writing a letter to a friend, he was seized with a paralytic stroke. His mind became a blank. In his *Mysterious Stranger* Mark Twain tells us that those whom the gods love they make mad. For in this way they save them from the ugly spectacle of man's inhumanity to man.

For several years Penn lingered on in this twilight indifference

WILLIAM PENN

that followed his mental sunset—and then he passed quietly into the night.

When the Indians heard of the passing of their beloved Onas, they sent his widow a present of warm skins to be made into a cloak. "This cloak is to protect you through the frosty wilderness now that you are alone and without your guide."

FRANKLIN

Important Dates in Life of Benjamin Franklin

1706—Born in Boston, Massachusetts.

1723—Broke away from his printer's apprenticeship in Boston and set up for himself in Philadelphia.

1730–44—Established the *Pennsylvania Gazette*, the Philadelphia Library, the American Philosophical Society.

1732–57—Published *Poor Richard's Almanac*.

1746–52—Investigated nature of lightning.

1753—Appointed Postmaster-General of the Colonies.

1754—Introduced a project for uniting the thirteen colonies under a central government.

1766—Aided in bringing about the repeal of the Stamp Act.

1775—Appointed to the Continental Congress.

1776—Served on committee to draw up the Declaration of Independence.

1776–85—Minister to France.

1782—Negotiated together with Adams and Jay, the treaty of peace with England.

1785–88—President of the Supreme Council of the State of Pennsylvania.

1787—Delegate to the Constitutional Convention.

1790—Died at Philadelphia.

Benjamin Franklin

Benjamin Franklin
1706–1790

THE YANKEE "Thunder-Master" was on one of his official visits to England. Everywhere the people looked with open-mouthed astonishment at this magician who, with his electrical wand, had snatched the lightning from the heavens. He was rated among the famous enchanters of history—Moses, Merlin, Paracelsus, Cagliostro, King Solomon, the Devil himself. And just now he had offered to perform a trick which even the Devil would have found beyond his power. "I shall repeat one of the miracles of the Bible," he said with a quiet smile. "With this walking stick I shall calm the raging waters."

They were standing on the edge of the lake at Bowood, the palatial estate of Lord Shelbourne. Among the guests on that occasion were famous scientists, clergymen, poets, statesmen, scholars, and a handful of cynics who "believed in the gospel of disbelief." One of these cynics turned to Dr. Franklin. "You're just trying to diddle us, sir, are you not?"

"On the contrary, I'm quite serious," rejoined Franklin, raising his cane above his head. "Look."

Thrice he whirled the cane over the water whose surface was

being plowed up by a spanking breeze. As he did so, he muttered a "magic formula." The cynics laughed as they looked on at this childish farce. But suddenly their laughter was changed into a cry of amazement. "By Jove, he has done it!" With the waving of his cane, Benjamin Franklin had smoothed the ruffled waters although the breeze was blowing as lustily as ever.

"How did you manage it?" asked the Abbé Morellet a few minutes later, when they were alone.

"By filling my hollow cane with oil," remarked Franklin simply. "I just scattered the oil over the water, and the water became calm." And then, with a twinkle in his eye, he added: "Almost every problem can be solved if you know how to go about it."

This was the secret of Franklin's success. Throughout his life he made it his business to know how.

II

FRANKLIN WAS BORN with a good physical and mental endowment. On his father's side he came of a race of blacksmiths, and from them he inherited his iron constitution. His grandfather on his mother's side was a poet, and from him he derived his fine feeling for words. As for his humor, he must have extracted it from his native soil. For it was flavored with the pungency of the pine grove, and it crackled like a fire over a bundle of evergreens.

He rode into the world on the wings of a northeaster in the winter of 1706. It required a tough constitution to survive in that primitive little city of Boston, "squeezed between the Atlantic and the marshes." But the new Franklin baby was equal to the job. He "learned to walk on frozen toes" and liked it. And he liked the wrangling and the tangling companionship of his brothers and his sisters—there were sixteen of them. From infancy he was well trained in the art of getting along with people.

His father, the candle-maker Josiah, preferred Benjamin to all his other children. He was such a precocious little tyke. At five he could read the Bible, and at seven he could already interpret it in his own way. "Father," he said once at the dinner table, "why waste all this time giving your daily blessing? Why not give one general blessing once and for all? I think this would save your time and the Lord's time." He would make a good clergyman, thought Josiah.

And so he sent him to the Boston Latin School for a classical education. But after a while Josiah realized that it was beyond his purse to indulge his son in a "gentleman's" career. He transferred him from the Latin School to George Brownell's School, an institution which specialized in the practical rather than in the liberal arts. But even this sort of education proved to be too expensive for Benjamin. No use trying to cultivate a Franklin mind when there were so many Franklin mouths to feed. Two years of schooling were enough. Let Benjamin be a toiler instead of a tattler. Josiah took his son out of school and into his candle shop.

But Benjamin disliked the smell of the tallow. He looked around for an apprenticeship at a more congenial trade, and found it in his brother James's printing shop.

At this early age (twelve) Ben Franklin was already somewhat of a personality. He wrote poetry and printed it and sold it in the streets of Boston. He played with the boys and generally beat them at their games. And he discussed books with his elders and generally beat them at their discussions. He was an excellent swimmer, a handy mechanic, a voluminous reader and a skeptic. He argued about everything and he took nothing for granted. He stopped going to church on Sundays, because he wanted to spend the day in reading. A good book, he said, is more educational than a bad sermon. Yet he was not irreligious. Throughout his life he showed a deep reverence for God —the Creative Power of the World and the Father of Mankind.

His apprenticeship in his brother's shop kept Franklin busy

and out of mischief. For, in accordance with the contract which he had signed with his brother, he had indentured himself body and soul to his job—not only *during* but also *after* his working hours. "Taverns, inns, or alehouses"—thus ran the contract—"he shall not haunt. At cards, dice, tables or any other unlawful games he shall not play. And"—continued the curious document—"matrimony he shall not contract."

In return for these prohibitions his brother had promised to keep him until his twenty-second year, to "teach him the art of printing," and to supply him with "meat, drink, washing, lodging, and all other necessaries during the said term." As for salary, there was to be none.

But Franklin wanted ready cash. And before long his ingenious mind hit upon a plan which would not only provide him with the necessary cash but would also supply his brother with extra funds. It was his brother's custom to take his meals, together with his workmen, at a neighbor's boarding house. "Suppose you let me eat by myself," said Benjamin, "and pay me only half of what my meals cost you."

His brother, like a regular Franklin, jumped at the idea. And thus both James and Benjamin saved money—James through his complacency, and Benjamin through his frugality. For, by changing his former diet of roast beef and cider to a strict regimen of vegetarian broth, the young apprentice was able to lay aside many a pretty penny for future use.

He enjoyed his vegetarian food—for ideal as well as for practical reasons. It soothed his conscience at the same time that it filled his pocket. "To eat meat," he had read in a book by a certain Mr. Tryon, "is a crime. For animals have souls. When you kill the body of a living creature, you do an injury to its soul." Throughout his life the son of the Yankee chandler maintained a double objective for his conduct: he tried to achieve moral purity and financial security. His motto was—a life full of good deeds and of good dollars. He was a perfect child of New England.

Yet he was unhappy in his New England surroundings. He couldn't get along with his brother. "This place isn't big enough for the two of us." And so on a September night in 1723, while the Bostonians were busy entertaining a delegation of Indians; the seventeen-year-old apprentice slipped quietly out of the city and boarded a sloop bound for new scenes and new services.

He disembarked at New York; but after surveying the "little village" of 7000 inhabitants and finding it not at all to his liking, he fared on and finally landed in Philadelphia.

He was hungry and dirty and ragged, and he had used up all his capital with the exception of a single Dutch dollar. But he had a more important possession—the capital of a tenacious perseverance and a penny-counting thrift. Money, he said, is the most prolific thing in the world. A dollar married to a dollar results in healthy offspring. And it didn't take him long to prove the validity of this motto in his own case. He worked for some years as a printer in the Quaker City, saved his pennies, went to London for more capital and experience, and finally returned to Philadelphia to open a printing shop of his own. Some of his friends tried to discourage him. "We are in the midst of a Great Depression," they said. "The country has stopped growing. Everything is going to the dogs." But while these people sat idly *bewailing* conditions, Franklin worked steadily to *improve* them. He familiarized himself with every phase of his business—typesetting, presswork, engraving, binding. He even learned to make the type. And, above all, he learned to make friends. Friendship, he said, is the most precious thing in the world. Both spiritually and financially, *it pays*.

His friendships really did pay. He organized a club—the *Junto*—whose members exchanged ideas and brought business to one another. Franklin was now sufficiently prosperous to think of marriage. He became engaged to a charming young lady—and broke the engagement because she couldn't bring him a dowry. And then he married a rather uncharming but homelike and motherly young woman, and gave her one of his illegitimate children as a wedding present. He continued to increase his family both by legitimate and by natural means, and to attend to his printing, and to multiply his friendships, until he was ready at forty-one to retire from business with an assured and comfortable income for life.

And then he really began to live.

III

FRANKLIN'S business activity was the least important aspect of his many-sided personality. The character of Franklin is a veritable kaleidoscope of dazzling colors. The eighteenth century produced only one other man of that universal type—Voltaire. But Franklin, though perhaps the less talented of the two, was the more versatile. He interested himself in almost every phase of human activity. And in everything he undertook, he became a master: It seemed as if Nature, having experimented on every possible type of American, decided at last to combine them all into one and created Benjamin Franklin. He was a journalist, statesman, philanthropist, philosopher, scientist, inventor, humorist and ambassador. And for a time he even thought seriously of becoming the founder of a new religion.

His career in journalism had begun at sixteen. At that time he was engaged as a printer's apprentice on his brother's paper, *The New England Courant*. One morning, when brother James opened his office, he found an article that somebody had slipped under the door. The article was signed—*Mrs. Silence Dogood*. "Sir," began Mrs. Dogood, who described herself as the modest widow of a country parson, "it may not be improper . . . to inform Your Readers that I intend once a Fortnight to present them, by the help of this Paper, with a short Epistle, which I presume will add somewhat to their Entertainment . . ."

This was the beginning of a series of letters, written in an unassuming style that sheathed many a subtle sting at the follies of the day. Each of these letters arrived at the office of the *Courant* via the selfsame crack under the door. In vain the editor published a request that Mrs. Dogood bring the articles in person, so that "he might have the pleasure of her acquaintance." It was not until all the articles had been published that the "moralistic old lady" revealed herself to be none other than young Ben Franklin.

These cynical letters of Mrs. Dogood were the beginning of a cataract of political and social satires that tumbled from his laughter-loving pen throughout his life.

He wielded his pen in the service of his politics. Benjamin Franklin was one of the shrewdest of American politicians. And one of the noblest of her statesmen. He entered upon his public career at thirty, when he was elected clerk of the Pennsylvania Assembly. A few years later he became a member of that body. His constituents liked his forthright honesty in the declaration of his principles. Years before the Revolution he was the incarnation of the American spirit of independence. As early as 1737 he wrote in his *Poor Richard's Almanack:* "An innocent plowman is more worthy than a vicious prince"—a sentiment which the plowmen and the pioneers of America found after their own hearts. He advocated (1753) the confederation of the American colonies into a political union. He wrote an article— which was published in nearly all the newspapers of the colonies —representing the disunited colonies by the picture of a serpent cut into wriggling but helpless segments. Under this symbol he inscribed the words—"Join or Die." He tried to interest not only the American colonies but the English government in this Confederated Dominion of the New World. But at that period both the American and the English politicians were too shortsighted to accept his plan.

Having failed in his national plan, the philosopher-statesman proceeded to look after the local interests of his people. The proprietary colony of Pennsylvania was going through a stormy crisis. The question of taxation was threatening to scuttle the Holy Experiment of the Quakers. The king demanded his taxes from Pennsylvania as well as from the other colonies. The people of Pennsylvania were willing to pay these taxes provided the proprietors of Pennsylvania—the two sons of William Penn who had inherited their father's colony but not his character—would contribute their proportional share. This the proprietors refused to do. Whereupon Franklin shouldered the responsibility of teaching the proprietors their lesson. He went to England, presented to the king the case of the people versus the proprietors, and won his point. From that time on, the sons of Penn as well as the sons of penury were obliged to pay their share of the taxes.

As a member of the Assembly and later as Postmaster General, Franklin devoted himself as usual to a double service—to extend his own glory and to further the interests of the people. He had learned early in life the important fact that kindness is a profitable investment. "It is good business to do good." And thus he accumulated his dollars and his honors through the simple device of accumulating his friends.

Yet his motives were not altogether selfish. There was a strange admixture of idealism in the character of this practical Yankee. He was the first of the modern Americans—that delightful combination of sentimentalism and common sense. He promoted the happiness of his fellows because in this way he promoted a happy feeling in himself. He used his politics as a soil for the growth of his philanthropy. As a result of his influential position he was able to institute a police force, to inaugurate a fire department, to organize a street cleaning division, to open an academy which later developed into the University of Pennsylvania, to improve the postal system, to build a lecture hall for free political and religious discussion, to establish one of the earliest colonial hospitals and to create the first public library in America. Franklin was justly proud of these practical achievements—especially of the part he played in the education of the people through the library system. "These libraries," he tells us in his *Autobiography*, "have made the common tradesmen and farmers as intelligent as most gentlemen from other countries, and perhaps have contributed in some degree to the stand so generally made throughout the colonies in defense of their privileges." Through all his public career Franklin made it his business, insofar as he was able, to eliminate the physical and the mental imperfections of mankind. He regarded himself as an apprentice—God's apprentice. God had created the world, and Franklin tried to add the improvements and to keep the machinery in running order.

His interests were speculative as well as practical. He was one of the foremost philosophers and scientists of his day. Unschooled though he was in formal knowledge, he received honorary degrees from Harvard and Yale as well as from several of the leading universities of Europe. His Junto Club—a "modest gathering of artisans for mutual self-improvement"—developed later into the American Philosophical Society. Franklin's own achievement as a philosopher was second only to that of Voltaire. He was a Yankee Socrates. His philosophical papers, like the dialogues of Socrates, were marked by a forthright honesty and homespun simplicity. Like the Athenian sage who had made it his purpose to bring wisdom down from heaven as an everyday tool for his fellowmen, the Yankee philosopher made it his business to interest himself in the human rather than in the divine problems of the world. He liked to speculate on the needs of men rather than on the nature of God.

Franklin's philosophy, in other words, is utilitarian. It takes a practical turn. His primary concern was to make the world a better place to live in—materially as well as morally. Accordingly he interested himself in all sorts of scientific experiments with a view to improving and to prolonging human life. He lived in an age when everybody was excited over that "new mysterious substance—electricity." People wrote texts of polysyllabic pretentiousness in which they discussed the theoretical question as to whether there is any analogy between electricity and lightning. Franklin read none of these texts—he probably wouldn't have understood their Greek and Latin terminology if he *had* read them. Instead, he resorted to the only simple and direct treatise which dealt with the question—the lightning itself. In the midst of a thunderstorm he went out with a kite in his hand to seek the answer to the problem. And the answer came flashing down from the heavens by way of the metal key attached to the end of the kite: *Lightning and Electricity are one.*

Always he tried to reduce the mysteries of nature to their simplest equations. And in revealing these mysteries to his fellows he employed no subtle formulas but presented plain facts. And he made these facts *interesting*. While the pedants huddled in their dusty rooms, Franklin invited his friends to an "electrical picnic" on the banks of the Schuylkill. At this picnic, he announced, "spirits are to be fired by a spark sent from side to side through the river, without any other conductor than the water ... A turkey is to be killed for our dinner by the electrical shock and roasted by the electrical jack, before a fire kindled by the electrical bottle ... And the healths of all the famous electricians in England, Holland, France and Germany are to be drank in electrified bumpers, under the discharge of guns from the electrical battery."

But Franklin didn't confine his experiments to electricity. His investigations extended into the fields of pathology and anatomy, he studied the nature and the velocity of the winds and the current and the temperature of the Gulf Stream. Blessed with skillful hands as well as with a versatile mind, he developed several of his experiments into practical inventions. Even as a boy he had devised a pair of hand paddles which enabled him to outswim his playfellows. When he was an assemblyman in Pennsylvania, he invented a street lamp which turned the narrow lanes of Philadelphia into "great white ways" as compared with the dimly-lighted thoroughfares of metropolitan London. Aiming always, as he did, at the comfort of his fellows, he invented an iron stove which consumed less fuel and gave greater heat. And—here is an interesting phase of his personality—this

FRANKLIN

"greatest inventor of the colonial period" refused to take out a patent on any of his inventions. The human race, he said, is one brotherhood; no one should receive pay for the presents he gives to his brothers.

Franklin was not only the leading scientist of the colonial period, but he was its greatest humorist as well. In his humor he was the forerunner of Mark Twain. Like Mark Twain, he told some of his best stories orally, for men's ears only. But even in his written work we can frequently observe the hearty flavor and the unrestrained laughter of the outdoors. It is the humor of a pioneer country. Practically all his writings are sprinkled with the spice of his pointed aphorisms. He is at his best in his *Poor Richard's Almanack*. To be sure, many of the adages contained in this *Almanack,* like many of the stories in Shakespeare's plays, are not original. They are, as Franklin himself confesses, "the gleanings . . . of the sense of all ages and nations." But Franklin took this universal wisdom and whittled it into something distinctly American. He expresses the deepest truths in the fewest words. As a rule, Franklin's aphorisms deal with the homely virtues—such as duty, thrift, industry, honesty and common sense. Every American school child is familiar with Poor Richard's truisms that *honesty is the best policy,* that *God helps them that help themselves,* that *there are no gains without pains,* and that in order to succeed, *you must keep your nose to the grindstone.* These, and many others like them, are mixed like tasty raisins into the pudding of our everyday American thought. But not all his maxims are of the type that inculcate the simple constructive virtues. Many of them are as cynical as the darts of Voltaire's or of Swift's destructive satire. Again and again Franklin expresses his contempt for courtiers and kings "and other such useless trash." *He who would rise at court,* he tells us, *must begin by creeping.* He is amused at the endless royal squabbles over petty causes. *Children and princes,* he observes, *will quarrel over trifles.* He is disgusted with the extravagance of the kings at the expense of their subjects. *The king's cheese,* he writes, *is half wasted in parings*. But, adds Franklin sarcastically, this is of no concern to the king. For his cheese *is made of the people's milk*. With a hearty American disdain, he laughs at purple blood, or blue blood, or "ancient ancestral" blood. *All blood,* he points out, *is alike ancient*. Ancestry, aristocracy and royalty have no place in the democratic philosophy of his American humor.

Franklin's disdain for royalty was equaled by his dislike for war. To the colonial American, war was a distasteful business—sometimes necessary, perhaps, but always disgusting. The American settlers had more important jobs to attend to. They were interested not in destroying but in building. Yet the American frontier had to be protected—and Franklin was above all a realist. Accordingly he was active in the organization of an American militia. When General Braddock came with his British soldiers to defend the colonies against the French and the Indians (1755), Franklin not only raised a large sum of money for his army but helped to supply him with guns and wagons. Civilian though he was, he had the military foresight to advise Braddock that his European manner of fighting in close ranks would only be playing into the hands of the Indians, accustomed as they were to shooting from behind the shelter of trees and rocks. Unfortunately Braddock disregarded this advice—with disastrous results.

Franklin's military experience was not confined to giving advice. For several months during the French and Indian War he commanded a division of troops in defense of the northwestern frontier. He engaged in no actual battles but he won the respect and the discipline of his men. He restrained them with a witty tongue rather than with an iron fist. On one occasion the chaplain of the division complained that the soldiers refused to come to the prayer meetings. "I have a good remedy for that," said Colonel Franklin. "Offer them rum after their prayers." The remedy worked. From that time, the prayer meetings enjoyed a perfect attendance.

FRANKLIN

Franklin, however, felt more at home in the diplomatic arena than in the military camp. In 1765 he was at the British court as the unofficial ambassador of the American colonies. The Stamp Act had just been passed against America. This act provided that all bills, legal documents, marriage certificates and the like were to be written only on stamped and taxed paper. The colonists were indignant, and Franklin undertook to point out to Parliament the injustice and the folly of such an act. It would prove to be an excessive burden, he argued, to the people of the American frontier, who had become impoverished as a result of the French and Indian War. The English government, he insisted, had no right to impose taxation without representation.

"Do you think," he was asked, "that the people of America would submit to pay the stamp duty if it was moderated?"

"No, never," replied Franklin. "The people of America would never submit unless compelled by force of arms."

The British Parliament heeded Franklin's words. The Stamp Act was repealed, and for the time being the Revolutionary War was averted.

At first Franklin was not favorable to the American Revolution. He was afraid it might fall into the hands of the unthinking mob. "A mob," he had written in *Poor Richard's Almanack*, "is a monster—heads enough but no brains." What he aimed at for his country was a confederation that would be a peaceful, free and integral part of the British Empire. Franklin hated war. But when, against his advice, the war was declared, he threw himself heart and soul into the American cause. For he realized at last that America was compelled to choose between foreign rule and freedom. Franklin's love for freedom proved to be greater than his regard for England. Once more he urged upon his people a confederation—this time, however, not as an integral part of the British Empire but as an independent unit. "If you do not all hang together, you will be hung separately."

During the course of the Revolution he was inspired to some

of his most pungent satire. In his attitude toward the conduct of the (German) Hessian leaders in the British army—King George III himself, it must be remembered, was a German—Benjamin Franklin outswifted even Swift himself. He directed a satirical pamphlet against the brutality of the German princes who sold their Hessian soldiers to the British army. The pamphlet is written in the form of a letter directed by a petty German prince to his Hessian general in America, urging him not to spare the lives of his men, since England gave him thirty guineas apiece for each soldier killed, and he needed this money for his coming opera season:

"I am about to send you some new recruits," writes the prince. "Don't economize them. Remember glory before all things. Glory is true wealth. There is nothing that degrades the soldier like the love of money. He must care only for honor and reputation, but this reputation must be acquired in the midst of dangers. A battle gained without costing the conqueror any blood is an inglorious success, while the conquered cover themselves with glory by perishing with their arms in their hands. Do you remember that of the 300 Lacedaemonians who defended the defile of Thermopylae, not one returned? How happy should I be could I say the same of my brave Hessians!"

At the time when he wrote this denunciation of the military-minded brutality of the Prussians, Franklin was serving as the American ambassador in Paris. When Congress had elected him to this post he had said, "I am old and good for nothing; but, as the storekeepers say of their remnants of cloth, I am but a fag end, and you may have me for what you please." Yet this "fag end" of a precious personality succeeded in performing a double service in Paris: he enlisted the aid of the French in the American Revolution, and he helped to sow the seeds of the French Revolution. Thanks to Benjamin Franklin, the New World was the teacher of the Old World in the experimental science of self-government.

Throughout his stay in Paris, Franklin was the sensation of

the day. Everybody flocked to see the strange son of an American tallow chandler who looked like a peasant and talked like a god. The populace cheered him, the ladies lionized him, and even the king addressed him with respect. And Franklin, as of old, took his cheers and his honors with his tolerant smile and his whimsical humor. One day a gushing old lady congratulated him on the beautiful spectacle the "fighting Americans" were giving to the world. "Yes," replied Franklin dryly. "It's a beautiful show, but the spectators haven't paid the price of admission."

His person, like his style, was simple and unadorned. On only one occasion—when invited to a royal function—did he condescend to go shopping for a wig, since a wig was the absolute rule at Court. But he was not able anywhere to be fitted. "It isn't that the wigs are too small, sir," remarked a clerk at one of the stores, "but your head is too big."

One day the "biggest head in America" met the "biggest head in France." This encounter between Franklin and Voltaire was, in the words of a contemporary journalist, "the event of the eighteenth century." The two old philosophers—Franklin was seventy-one and Voltaire eighty-four—shook hands and then impulsively embraced, while the spectators "burst into tears." Franklin had his grandson with him at the time. Voltaire placed his hands upon the child's head, and in a voice trembling with emotion said: "My boy, dedicate yourself to God and Liberty."

IV

WHEN Franklin returned to America (1785), he was nearly eighty years old. Yet his work was not yet over. At eighty-two he attended the Constitutional Convention. He was too weak now to stand long on his feet, and so his speeches were read out by a friend while he sat and nodded his wise white head in approval.

When the Convention was over, he felt that he had outstayed his welcome in a world that had proved so hospitable to him.

"I seem to have intruded myself into the company of posterity," he said, "when I ought to have been abed and asleep."

But there was one more thing to do before he went to bed. He must inaugurate one more crusade before he could lay down his trembling pen. A crusade against human bondage. He gathered enough strength to finish his *Plea for the Abolition of Slavery*—and then the summons came.

His last hours—he was suffering from pleurisy—were painful. When one of his attendants tried to turn him on his side so he could breathe more easily, he observed, "A dying man can do nothing easy."

Yet he was cheerful to the end. "These pains will soon be over." And after that? "I cannot suspect the annihilation of souls . . . I believe I shall in some shape or other always exist."

WASHINGTON

Important Dates in Life of George Washington

1732—Born in Westmoreland County, Virginia.
1748—Became surveyor in the employment of Lord Fairfax.
1752—Received from Lieutenant-Governor Dinwiddie commission as major in colonial forces.
1754—Defended Fort Necessity against an attack by the French.
1755—Fought under Braddock in disastrous battle at Turtle Creek.
1759—Married Martha Custis.
1774—Delegate to the First Continental Congress.
1775—Chosen Commander-in-Chief of the Continental Army.
1776–83—Led Continental Army to victory.
1783—Bade farewell to army and returned to private life in Virginia.
1787—Chosen President of the Constitutional Convention.
1789—Inaugurated as the first President of the United States.
1792—Re-elected for a second term.
1797—Retired from the Presidency.
1799—Died at Mount Vernon.

George Washington

George Washington
1732–1799

WE BEGIN our story of George Washington with three scenes:
First scene, shortly after Brandywine:
Washington has been riding furiously all day. A lashing rainstorm has arisen. Washington has taken shelter in a farmhouse. He is about to change into dry clothes when the farmer knocks at the door. "Pardon me, sir, but would you mind stepping into the parlor when you are ready? My little daughter is anxious for a peep at our great visitor."

"Glad to oblige," laughed Washington. And without waiting to take off his rain-drenched clothes he proceeded to present himself to the little girl.

"Well, my dear," he said, "you see a very tired old man in a very dirty shirt."

* * *

Second scene, just before Trenton:
The American cause is on the brink of disaster. A member of the Philadelphia Congress is waiting upon Washington. "The general appeared much distressed," writes this Congressman, "and he lamented the ragged and dissolving state of his army

in affecting terms. I gave him assurances of the disposition of Congress to support him ... While I was talking to him I observed him to play with his pen and ink upon several small pieces of paper. One of them by accident fell upon the floor near my feet. I was struck with the inscription upon it. This inscription was—'victory or death.' "

* * *

Third scene, at Valley Forge:

For weeks now his half-naked men have eaten no meat. The Congress at Philadelphia has taken no steps to supply the army with food or clothing or shelter. The rank and file are ready to desert. Even Washington has come to the reluctant conclusion that the case is hopeless. He has just written his resignation as commander-in-chief. He sits toying with his white-handled pen-knife as he discusses his resignation with General Knox. "This pen-knife," observes Knox, "is the best argument against your resignation."

Washington looks at Knox with a puzzled expression in his eyes. And then he remembers. The pen-knife is an old present from his mother. Years ago, at the age of fifteen, he wanted to enlist in the navy. His kit had already been taken aboard and he himself was on the point of following when his mother, in a final plea, induced him to remain. As a reward his mother ordered a "good pen-knife" from England; and when it arrived, she presented it to him with the words, "Always obey your superiors."

Washington's friends have often heard this story from his lips. And now, when he is about to resign from the army, General Knox reminds him of his knife as the symbol of his duty. Always obey your superiors. "Congress has commanded you to lead the army. Nobody has commanded you to lay down this leadership."

"You are quite right," agrees Washington. "It is not for me

to make the decision." And picking up the resignation from the table, he tears it into pieces.

* * *

These episodes represent three of the outstanding facets of Washington's many-sided character. When we try to pierce through the legendary mists that surround his figure, we see him stand forth as a man of simplicity, determination, duty.

But this is only a small part of the living picture that is George Washington.

II

OF ALL the great men of the past, George Washington is perhaps the most difficult to visualize in the living flesh and blood. He stalks like a shadow through the pages of history. The fault, we believe, lies with two of his earliest biographers: Parson Weems and Professor Sparks. The parson depicted him as a bundle of Sunday School maxims, and the professor displayed him as a glorified wax dummy. Both of them made the unwise attempt to deify him and only succeeded in dehumanizing him. Most of his later biographers, taking their cue from their earlier models, have pumped the hot red blood out of his veins and refilled them with a cold preservative fluid. They have even mutilated his own words and transformed them from living tones into dead echoes.

For example:

One day, when aroused over the conduct of Edmund Randolph, he declared: "A damneder scoundrel God Almighty never permitted to disgrace humanity." His editors changed this to, "A greater scoundrel never disgraced humanity."

On another occasion, when he discussed a proposed appropriation by Congress, he observed: "One hundred thousand dollars will be but a flea-bite." His editors expurgated this into, "One hundred thousand dollars will be totally inadequate."

And thus his early biographers edited not only Washington,

by their invention of words that Washington never said, but they also edited God, by their creation of an image that God never made. If we are to understand Washington as a living personality, we must at the very outset recognize the fact that he was human and not divine. He had human faults as well as human greatness. He was not a paragon of virtue. On occasion he lied, he swore, he flirted, he gambled, he lost his temper and he whipped his unruly slaves. And he did not look, as he is almost universally pictured, like a flawless ancient statue dressed in a Continental uniform. As a matter of fact, his jaw was somewhat out of shape as the result of a poorly-fitting set of false teeth. And—a point which most of his painters and his sculptors have tried to conceal—his face from early youth was disfigured with pockmarks.

He was a poor looker and a poor speller. He rarely got his e's and his i's correct in such words as *believe, receive, ceiling*. The color *blue* he always spelled as *blew*. The word *lie* generally appeared in his papers as *lye*. He referred to London as the great *matropolis*. And once, when he was disappointed in love, he wrote that he would *eliviate* his sorrow by staying away from the ladies.

Yet all these blemishes, far from belittling the father of our country, only tend to make him more approachable, more lovable, more human. Knowing Washington as he really was, we shall stop adoring a manikin and begin to admire a man.

III

As a boy he was shy, reserved and unprecocious. His early acquaintances remembered him as a gangling youngster with a gawky nose. "His nose," remarked his mother, "seems to grow faster than all the rest of his body." As a result of this defect he always felt inferior in company. And determined. "Some day, somehow, I'll make them like me in spite of my nose!"

WASHINGTON

At eleven he lost his father. And now he was more determined than ever. In accordance with the inheritance laws of the day his brother Lawrence, the oldest of the Washington children, had received the bulk of his father's estate. Young George would have to carve out his own fortune. And he meant to do it! "For all my handicaps, I must get people to respect me."

But in the meantime, he must get through with his education. A practical education, fit for a youngster who meant to live a practical life. Reading, writing, arithmetic—especially arithmetic. Two acres plus two acres equals four acres. Four plus four equals eight. When he grew up, he would add acre to acre, house to house, plantation to plantation. He would be a rich man. *That* was the way he would get the respect of his neighbors. He would take after his brother Lawrence. This young man, George's senior by fourteen years, was already one of the most respected citizens of Virginia. A landowner, an aristocrat, a soldier. A shining hero for a shy but energetic and proud and ambitious young fellow.

At his brother's invitation he went to live with him. Here, at the spacious estate of Mount Vernon, he met all the fine gentry of Virginia. They treated him as one of them. He rode with them after the foxhounds, rode at breakneck speed, and they applauded him for his horsemanship. He was glad now he had given up his momentary impulse to go to sea. He was too fond of the land, of galloping through the pathless forests, of dancing over the polished floors of the drawing room.

Yet it wasn't often he got an opportunity to dance. He was too awkward—over six lanky feet of bones and sinews and knuckles, with size thirteen shoes and "the biggest hands in the colony of Virginia." And he was too bashful. Instead of speaking boldly to the girls he wrote verses to them, hinting—in a manner that would delight the modern psychoanalysts—at conquests and flirtations that he dared not bring to fulfillment.

"In deluding sleepings let my eyelids close
    That in an enraptured dream I may

> In a rapt lulling sleep and gentle repose
> Possess those joys denied by day."

He soon gave up his poetry, however, and returned to the field in which he was much more adept—mathematics. He took up surveying. As a preliminary to *owning* land he would learn to *measure* land.

And at this point a stroke of good fortune came to him in the guise of Lord Thomas Fairfax. This nobleman owned an estate amounting to the almost incredible figure of five million acres. He hired young Washington to survey this land. The job, with interruptions, lasted about two years—a period, to a penniless youngster, of "lavish" earnings. "A Dubleloon," wrote Washington, "is my constant gain every day that the weather will permit my going out and sometimes Six Pistoles." A doubloon was worth about $7, and six pistoles amounted to about $21.

When finally he returned from his surveying, he felt "comfortable in purse and rich in experience." It was his first protracted contact with the hardships of the wilderness. On the first night out, he tells us, he was put up at a farmhouse where he was surprised to find his blanket "with double its weight of vermin, such as Lice, fleas, and so forth." On several occasions, "after Walking a good deal all the Day, I lay down before the fire upon a Little Hay, Straw, Fodder or Bearskin . . . with Man, Wife and Children like a Parcel of Dogs and Catts, and happy is he that gets the Birth nearest the fire." After experiences such as these he "made a promise . . . to sleep in ye open air."

IV

IN 1751 George Washington accompanied his brother Lawrence to the island of Barbados, in the West Indies. His brother had contracted tuberculosis and had decided upon this trip to the "flowery garden of the tropics" in an effort to rid himself of the disease.

The trip did neither of them any good. Lawrence came home

WASHINGTON

a dying man, and George a marked man. He had caught the smallpox at Barbados, and his face remained disfigured for life.

When Lawrence died he left his Mount Vernon estate to his little daughter, with George as her manager. In the event of his daughter's death, Lawrence had provided, George was to inherit the property. Within a short time the child died, and George had become the owner of a sizable plantation and a flock of slaves.

But he was not satisfied. In order to gain the respect of his fellows it was necessary not only to *own* things but to *do* things. His brother Lawrence had been a soldier. George, too, wanted to be a soldier. He possessed a stronger body than Lawrence's—indeed, one of the strongest in the colony. "I have a constitution," he wrote to Governor Dinwiddie, "hardy enough to undergo the most severe trials." And he enjoyed the dangers of an exposed life. Once as a surveyor in the wilderness he had met a company of Indians returning from battle. And instead of terror he had experienced, to quote his own words, "an agreeable surprise." He had mingled with them and asked them "to give us a War Daunce." George Washington was insensitive to fear.

His reputation as a fearless explorer of the wilderness had reached the ears of Governor Dinwiddie, who appointed him as a messenger to warn the French away from the British territory in America. His mission was unsuccessful, but it gave him an invaluable lesson in the taming of an ice-filled river. "There was no way for getting over but on a Raft," he writes. "We set about building it with but one poor hatchet . . . Before we were half way over we were jammed in the Ice . . . The Rapidity of the Stream . . . jerked me out into ten feet of water . . ."

A prophetic rehearsal for the crossing of the Delaware, many years later.

Shortly after his return from his mission to the French he was appointed aide-de-camp to General Braddock. He considered it a rare privilege "to attain some knowledge in the military profession . . . under a gentleman of General Braddock's abilities and experience."

He was disappointed, however, in his commander's abilities and experience when he witnessed Braddock's European methods in fighting an American war. In vain he pointed out to the general that in attacking the Indians you must adopt the backwoods style of fighting—that is, you must scatter your ranks and take advantage of the sheltering rocks and trees. But Braddock, a man "devoid of both fear and common sense," disdained the "skulking cowardice" of his American soldiers. He would meet the enemy in regular battle order, platoon formation, mass attack and full face!

Such was his order at Turtle Creek (1755). His army was almost annihilated. How Washington escaped alive from this massacre is one of the miracles of history. Three horses had been shot under him. His uniform had been punctured with several bullet holes. But his body had received not a scratch.

And, in spite of his chagrin at the disaster, he had thoroughly enjoyed the fight! "I have heard the bullets whistle," he wrote to his brother Jack, "and believe me, there is something charming in the sound."

He reveled in the whistling of the bullets, but he shrank from the sound of applause. For he had not yet overcome his bashfulness. In 1759, as a reward for his "coolness under fire," he was elected to the Virginia House of Burgesses. Mr. Robinson, the Speaker of the House, greeted the new member in words of glowing praise. In answer to the cheers that followed, Washington rose, cleared his throat, blushed, and sat down in embarrassed silence. "Mr. Washington," said the Speaker gently, "we quite understand. Your modesty is equal to your valor. And both are beyond the power of words."

WASHINGTON

V

Washington was jilted by several young women because of his pockmarks and the length of his nose. Finally, however, he succeeded in winning the affections of Martha Custis, a personable young widow who possessed an enormous estate and two little children. Their marriage was one of the social events in colonial history.

George Washington's time was now divided between the management of his Mount Vernon plantation and the care of his wife's estate (which was called the White House). He took his place among the Virginia gentry, he raised fine horses, he followed the foxhounds, he bought his slaves—but he didn't sell them, for fear that they might fall into the hands of an unkind master—and on the whole he seemed to be a safe and sane exponent of British Toryism in America.

But somewhere within him there flickered the spark of rebellion. Just when and where this spark had entered his heart we don't know. Perhaps it was during his adolescent days of surveying among the pioneers that he had learned to understand and to pity the lot of the underprivileged. Perhaps it was in the French and Indian War that he had come to despise the superciliousness and the cruelty of the British officers in America. He was a man of few words and he rarely made a display of his emotions. Yet once or twice, in his campaigns with the British against the French, he had expressed his resentment at the arrogance of the British officers toward their American soldiers. "Captain Mackay," he wrote to Governor Dinwiddie, refuses "to oblige his (British) men to work upon the road . . . whilst our (American) soldiers are laboriously employed." On another occasion he wrote that it irked him, a colonel in the American army, to swallow the insults of the majors and the captains in the British army—men inferior to him "both in rank and in courtesy." The British, he felt, looked upon themselves as a master race, and upon the Americans as their slaves.

And so he went about his business and observed much and thought much, but said little. He read about the British atrocities in Massachusetts and kept silent. He read the fiery speeches of Patrick Henry and went back in silence to his plantation. And when, on June 15, 1775, he was appointed commander-in-chief of the American army, he went silently to place himself at the head of the rebels. He had little confidence in himself as a military leader. "I do not think myself equal to the command I am honored with," he wrote at the time of his appointment. But he had the greatest confidence in the cause he was fighting for and the most implicit faith in the ability of his soldiers to win the war. At the Battle of Turtle Creek he had learned that the British soldiers knew how to run. And now he learned that the American soldiers knew how to stand. While he was on his way to Boston to take command of the army, he heard of the Battle of Bunker Hill. "Did the militia fight?" he asked.

"Yes," was the reply.

"In that case," said Washington, "the liberties of the country are safe."

VI

ONE of the chief characteristics of Washington as a military leader was his ability to outsmart his opponents. It was not without reason that they called him the Old Fox. The enemy was never able to guess at his plans, or to calculate the time or the place of his next attack, or to ascertain the size of his army. And, in order to keep the British in a continual state of befuddlement, he didn't *withhold* information but fed them with *wrong* information. He prepared false reports about his army, and deliberately allowed the enemy to capture the messengers who carried these reports. And thus the British were always acting upon "certainties" that turned out to be illusions.

WASHINGTON

Yet let us not be unfair to the British. Their army was compelled to struggle under three disadvantages: a set of officers who didn't believe in their cause; a mob of Hessians who had been shipped to fight in America against their will; and a military campaign whose general outlines were planned not by the experienced commanders in the field but by the clerks of the War Department in London.

The officers of the British army did not care to fight against the Americans. They wanted to conciliate them rather than to kill them. Had their hearts been in the war, they might have won it on several occasions by a decisive blow. For, in spite of Washington's brilliant maneuvers, they had the American army trapped over and over again. But they never could find the energy to spring the trap. There was too much unnecessary danger on the battlefield, and too much fun in the cities where they were so comfortably stationed. They believed they could *starve* the Americans, instead of *shooting* them, into submission. In the meantime, let the American rebels suffer while they themselves were living literally "on the fat of the land"—good food, jolly parties, pretty women, fine music and excellent wine. To the Americans the Revolutionary War was a tragedy. But to the British officers it was a comic opera. It was a splendid show while it lasted; and, for all they cared, let it last forever.

Added to the heedlessness of the British officers was the listlessness of their Hessian troops. These Hessians had been sold by their German princes, like so many slaves, to fight for a nation whose language they didn't understand, and for a cause in which they hadn't the slightest interest. Their princes got about fifty dollars apiece for selling them, but all that the Hessians got for their fighting was danger and sickness and death. Accordingly they developed their strength in their legs rather than in their arms. The Hessians in the British army were among the best runners in military history.

But the greatest obstacle against which the British army had to contend was the stupidity of the War Department which insisted upon mapping out in England the campaigns that were to be fought in America. It was a case of absentee generalship. The Englishmen in London knew nothing about the geography of the American wilderness, with its swamps and hills and gullies, its pathless forests and its impassable rivers. Accordingly they planned out a preposterous campaign (in the summer of 1777) whereby General Burgoyne, General Howe and Colonel St. Leger, each one starting from a different point, were to meet at a certain date at Albany. The Tories were exultant. At last there would be a consolidation of the British forces, and the American army would be crushed.

But things didn't work out as planned. The British commanders lost their way in the American bogs—a contingency unforeseen by the British War Department—and General Burgoyne, as he tried to find his way out again, was attacked and decisively defeated at Saratoga. Obliged to surrender, he agreed to ship his entire force back to England.

One of the English armies was now gone. But the other two still remained in America, and to Washington the situation looked as desperate as ever. For he, too, was beset with seemingly insurmountable difficulties and handicaps. The Congress, whenever he requested help, kept "nibbling and quibbling" and ended by refusing his requests. Neither in the Congress nor in the country was there a united consecration to the cause. The national crisis, like all other national crises the world over, had daily become the more critical through the obstructionism of the ill-disposed traitors and the well-disposed fools.

The Revolution, in other words, far from being the divine vision of "rosy pillars and patriotism" was in reality a very human mixture of grandeur and graft. Within the army, as in the Congress, there was backbiting, incompetence, dissension and fraud. And the low ebb in this morale, both within and outside of the ranks, was reached at the Valley Forge period. Again and again during this period Washington complained of the desertions of the soldiers and of the "speculation and the

WASHINGTON

peculation" of the profiteers. "Shall a few designing men . . . to gratify their own avarice, overset the goodly fabric we have been rearing at the expense of so much time, blood and treasure?" On another occasion: "General Fry . . . has drawn three hundred and seventy-five dollars, never done one day's duty, scarce been three times out of his home." And still again: "Different regiments were upon the point of cutting each other's throats . . . Many of the soldiers are deserting . . . Such a dearth of public spirit I never saw . . . and pray God I may never be witness to again."

But—and here we have Washington in his most admirable mood—"we must bear up . . . and make the best of mankind as they are, since we cannot have them as we wish."

And so he took his soldiers as they were and transformed them into a conquering army. They called him the "Necessary Man." As time went on, he became to them more precious than their very lives. Again and again they begged him not to expose himself to the bullets of the enemy. But he laughed off their fears. *Their* danger, he said, was *his* danger; and *their* suffering, *his* suffering. He insisted upon sharing their risks, just as he insisted upon their sharing his triumphs. And even his very food. "One day," writes the Chevalier de Pontgibaud, "we were at dinner at headquarters. An Indian entered the room, walked round the table, and seized a large joint of hot roast beef. We were all much surprised, but General Washington gave orders that he was not to be interfered with. 'Gentlemen,' he said, 'let him be. He too, it seems, is a hungry man.'"

The comfort of his soldiers was always a thought nearest to Washington's heart. An aide-de-camp, who had come down with a heavy cold, lay coughing in his cot, unable to fall asleep. Suddenly he became aware of a towering, night-clad figure approaching his cot. It was General Washington, who had got out of his bed to prepare a hot bowl of tea for his suffering "comrade."

VII

AT LAST George Washington, the "Old Fox" to the enemy, the "Gentle Father" to his own people, defeated Cornwallis (Yorktown, 1781) and won the freedom of America. And then, like the ancient Cincinnatus, he took off his military uniform and became once more a private citizen. His zest for battle was over. He wanted to be left alone, to end his days in the peaceful retreat of his Mount Vernon plantation, to raise his crops, to look after his slaves, to entertain his guests—"a glass of wine and a bit of mutton are always ready." He was old now, and his sight was impaired. "I have not only grown gray but blind in your service," he had said to the soldiers upon his retirement from the army. But he asked for no reward, and he refused to speak of his conquests. A guest remarked about his "thoughtful silence, with lips moving, as if wrapped in an inward isolation." It was in this mood of thoughtful silence that he met his friends and rejoiced in their joys and helped them in their sorrows. He dispensed his favors and distributed his charities with the request—as Bishop White informs us—"that this be done without ostentation or mention of my name." The noblest kind of charity, said the great Jewish philosopher, Maimonides, is to give without revealing the identity of the giver.

And thus George Washington lived in peace, enjoying his declining years under his "vine and fig tree," as he expressed it, when unexpectedly his country drafted him once more into the turmoil of public life. His old "modest diffidence" was still upon him when he was elected to the Presidency. "I wish," he declared in a public address, "that there may not be reason for regretting the choice." And in a private conversation with General Knox he remarked: "My movement to the chair of Government will be accompanied by feelings not unlike those of a culprit who is going to the place of his execution."

But he accepted his duty and like a good soldier fulfilled it to the best of his ability. He was not, as he himself readily admitted, among the greatest of statesmen, just as he was not among the greatest of generals. But he had one of the most solid characters in history both as a statesman and as a soldier. He was that rarest type of individual who could win the admiration of his enemies as well as of his friends. He was *wholesome*, a *whole* man—just the sort of leader necessary in an infant republic. His personality was like a healthy mortar which cemented all the separate states, with their conflicting local differences and interests, into a national unit. His attitude toward national and international questions was conservative and, for that day, sound. The reactionaries thought him too liberal; and the liberals, too reactionary. But he wisely selected a middle course and persisted in that course to the very end of his administration. For his cabinet he appointed conservatives like Hamilton and radicals like Jefferson; and between the two extremes he was able to watch the pulse of the normal thought and temper of the people. He signed a treaty with England and he was charged with being an Anglophile. He refused to endorse the Reign of Terror in France and he was accused of being a counter-revolutionist. But in everything he did he had a single definite aim—to keep his nation independent and respected and *at peace*.

Throughout his two terms in the Presidency there was a hysterical fear in many parts of the country that he wanted to become king. Washington made repeated attempts to dispel this "insane" fear. "I would rather be back on my farm," he said, "than to be seated on the throne of the *entire world*."

And he meant it. At the end of the second term he flatly refused to be re-elected. "Although I have abundant cause to be thankful for the good health with which I am blessed, yet I am not insensible to my declination in other respects. It would be criminal, therefore, in me . . . to accept an office . . . which another would discharge with more ability."

And so John Adams took the presidential oath and George

Washington, "his gray hair streaming in the wind," stepped down from the public gaze. As he passed through the cheering crowd, "his eyes were bathed in tears"—this picture comes from the lips of one of the bystanders, as quoted by Washington Irving—"his emotions were too great for utterance, and only by gestures could he indicate his thanks and convey his farewell blessing."

He had finished his job. "With God's help I have lived to see the United States as one great whole . . . *a nation which may bid defiance in a just cause to any power on earth.*"

HAMILTON

Important Dates in Life of Alexander Hamilton

1757—Born in West Indies.
1769—Entered the counting-house of his uncle, Nicholas Cruger.
1772—Came to New York.
1774—Entered King's College.
1777—Became Washington's aide-de-camp.
1780—Married Elizabeth Schuyler.
1782–83—Served in the Continental Congress.
1786–87—Delegate to the Constitutional Convention.
1787–88—Interpreted the Constitution in a series of articles, the *Federalist Papers*.
1790—Appointed Secretary of the Treasury.
1795—Resigned to practice law in New York.
1800—Blocked attempt of Aaron Burr to become President of the United States.
1804—Killed in duel with Aaron Burr.

Alexander Hamilton

Alexander Hamilton
1757–1804

It was a hot, haze-ridden morning when he crossed the Hudson River in his boat. Mr. Pendleton, his second, was peering anxiously from the bow at the gleaming outlines of the Palisades on the Jersey side. Dr. Hosack, the surgeon, was quietly inspecting his bandages. Alexander Hamilton looked at Dr. Hosack and his first-aid kit. The good old surgeon would be very busy in just a few minutes, trying to staunch the blood from a mortal wound. No question that it would be mortal. Hamilton's lips moved as if to say, "This will not be a duel, it will be a suicide." But instead he merely murmured, "Isn't the Hudson beautiful today?"

He had first seen the Hudson thirty-two years ago, in 1772, when he had reached New York after a passage from his native island of Nevis in the West Indies. How broad and tranquil the river had seemed in contrast to the surging waves of feeling in his own heart! It was the heart of a lad of fifteen, pounding like a hurricane at his venture into the New World. And now at forty-seven he was preparing to pass to another world. His hair was streaked with gray, and his lips were compressed with the sadness of a man who had lived too long and who refused any further extension of life.

He turned one more glance toward the city he was leaving just as the boat was beached on the red clay soil of New Jersey. Back toward the island where he had waged the most exciting battles of his political career, where his wife and his children were now asleep. That was his magic city. For fifteen years he had held it in the palm of his hand. Hamiltonopolis! The capital of his Empire. He had shuffled the destiny of its people like dice. No guardian deity of any ancient Greek citadel had exercised a more absolute power or compelled a more profound reverence than he. But now he had left his sanctuary. He was traveling in the dawn to a duel of honor at Weehawken. He had determined that he would die under Colonel Burr's fire. He would point his gun to the sky. There would be no uncertainty about his death just as there had been no uncertainty about his life. He had planned out every conscious hour, from the moment he had realized the strength of his will. It was no small satisfaction for him to dictate to the destinies just how and when he, Alexander Hamilton, would end his career. It was no small triumph to flaunt the gift of life right back into the face of the gods who had bestowed it upon him. He disdained their gift. At forty-seven he was ready to die. Let Aaron Burr live on.

The haze lifted as Hamilton, together with his party, reached Weehawken in the Palisades. Colonel Burr and Mr. Van Ness, his second, were already clearing the brush. Burr nodded to his antagonist in a warm friendliness. And Hamilton replied with a stiff bow—as if he had made a gallant little speech and was now awaiting applause. "I feel it is my religious duty to oppose his political career," he had repeatedly told his closest friends.

Mr. Pendleton handed him a pistol. Mr. Van Ness marked off ten paces.

What in the world had the final quarrel been about? Oh, bother! There was a breath of expectancy in the air. It warmed his blood. It was going to be another hot day, another day of life and women and wine.

"No quarrel," he muttered as he allowed himself to be carried gently to the boat. He felt his head growing light and he heard the whisper of Dr. Hosack. "A mortal wound." Overhead the blue of the sky had broken into a rainbow of colors through the prism of his tears.

II

WHEN Alexander stood in the tropical sunset of his last night on the island of Nevis and bade farewell to his aunt, there were no tears in his eyes. Tears do not come readily to a proud, ambitious lad of fifteen fired with the expectation of conquest. He was leaving the store at Christianstadt and going to America for a college education. He had no regrets at parting company with his uncle and his job. He had shed his last tears over his mother when they had buried her four years ago. He might have clasped the hand of a father with something of a lump in his throat. But his father, having suffered financial misfortune, had left his family to the care of wealthy relatives and had sought employment on another island. Alexander knew that while his mother lived, his father had occasionally corresponded with her. But after her death he was heard from less frequently until finally he became somewhat of a legend.

There had been tears in the voice of his mother just before she died. But they had been chilled by a look of cold determination in her eye. "No matter what anyone may say to you, Alexander, your father is a good man." And when she had gone, he heard ugly mutterings about himself from his acquaintances. "Illegitimate. Born out of wedlock." And he had come to his aunt, his cheeks on fire, demanding to know.

"Your mother and your father loved each other very deeply, Alexander. But they were never married in the eyes of the law. In the eyes of God I'm sure they were forgiven!"

And then she went gently on with her story. "You see, Alexander, your mother was a very sad and beautiful lady, compelled by her parents when she was little more than a child to marry a wealthy old landowner whom she detested. And before she was out of her teens she separated from him. But she was unable to get a divorce. The Parliament in England was too busy passing budgets to listen to the pleadings of a woman's heart . . ."

And his eyes glistened with pride as she continued with the story of his origin. "Your father was a Hamilton. James Hamilton, of the Scotch aristocracy. When he came adventuring to the island, he was only a year older than your mother. They made a bonny handsome couple, those two."

A fierce sense of grandeur stirred the fires of his spirit as he heard this story. So he was no common boy! He would wear his irregular origin as a badge of distinction and not as a mark of shame.

He had formed his plans to go off adventuring like his father. When a close friend of his had left the island to get a college education in America, Alexander knew that he too must acquire this most powerful weapon for social mastery—a trained mind. He worked ever more assiduously at the hateful business of piling up money for his uncle and dreamed of the day when he too would be able to leave for America.

At times, when he wrote to his friend in college, his hand trembled with the impatience of his desire to get away. ". . . For to confess my weakness, Ned, my ambition is prevalent, so that I contemn the grovelling condition of a clerk, or the like, to which my fortune condemns me . . . I would willingly risk my life . . . to exalt my station."

His relatives knew only the outside of him. What they knew they liked. Hair a glorious shade of red just like his mother's. Patrician nose. Determined chin. A dandified little gentleman. Quite the finest breed of the rich tropics. Why not send him away to college? He had written a very fine descriptive essay on the hurricane that had lately swept the islands. A newspaper in St. Kitts had published it. Let the winds blow him westward to America. He had been born of a tropical passion. Let him rise to success through a hurricane.

III

IN THE glittering parlors of New York he lost much of his sensitivity. He had arrived with the best of credentials from his uncle and he met the most promising people. "Born of a plantation aristocracy in the West Indies," the Schuyler, Livingston and Witherspoon families were told. The result of an irregular affair. But an affair of the finest blood. Mother, a Huguenot; father, a Hamilton of the old Scottish clans.

The ladies, Kitty and Judith and Sarah and Susan, made much of a fuss over him. What an interesting eye! Like a violet half frozen in the spring. And what an enviable complexion! "My dear Hamilton," breathed Kitty Livingston, "have a care. You are far too fortunate. You will rise rapidly to the highest places. And the jealous gods will smite you."

He bore himself correctly. The boys at King's College where he studied for his degree envied the unerring grasp of his mind. And Hamilton was quite comfortable, for he envied no one. When his fellow students fancied themselves swept away in a crusading spirit against the British Parliament, it was Hamilton who found the most fitting arguments with which to plead their case from the college steps. He had been in America only three years, and he already had a more comprehensive understanding of the controversy between the colonies and England than "these heathen," as he contemptuously called the native students.

In the moments when he rested from his law books he wrote pamphlets on the problem of taxation without representation, adding the reflections of his eighteen years to the wisdom of the leading patriots and scholars of America.

He had not forgotten his studies in Demosthenes. "As a general marches at the head of his troops, so ought wise politicians, if I dare use the expression, to march at the head of affairs." He would take more and more of an active part, even join the army if open rebellion was decided on. No question, he had concluded, that the inhabitants of America had the right to the disposal of their own lives and property, without being imposed upon by a Parliament sitting three thousand miles away. And moreover—he calculated—those who stood solidly by their guns, though now they were in the minority, would some day become the very saints of the people. There was a mob of hare-brained patriots, to be sure, men who were ready to risk their lives for emotional slogans. "A reliance on pure patriotism has been the source of many errors," he reasoned. Well, he would take up arms on a calculation that had nothing of the heart's voice in it. The financial classes in America were bound by every right of the history of financial groups everywhere to free themselves from the domination of foreign capital. There was only one issue in doubt. Could the British force the colonies into subjugation? Hamilton thought not. And so with remarkable shrewdness he joined a company of "rebels," and shortly received a commission as captain of artillery. It was in the skies of a free America that his star would rise.

"Dear Hamilton will never look natural in a military uniform," declared Kitty Livingston. "And his cheeks are too rosy to be stained in the smoke of battle."

"You do not know your soldier," whispered one of her friends. "His lips are severe. He will get along."

The battle of Long Island. The retreat to Jersey. Grime, sweat, blood, tears, despair. Hamilton marched beside his cannon with his cocked hat pulled down over his brilliant eyes, lost in thought.

The American cause in the deepest shadow. George Washington was strolling along the ranks on the lookout for an aide-de-camp. He saw Hamilton digging at a breastwork. Their eyes met. "I will have you."

The members of Washington's family were fascinated by the

new aide-de-camp. He sat at the General's table along with Lafayette. He spoke little, looked silently at his food, blushed on occasion when he was complimented. Washington valued Hamilton's services highly. He got out more letters and attended to more business than any dozen of his other aides. "He is my high-priest of energy," Washington often told his friends.

And Hamilton sat writing the General's dispatches and learning much of the inside detail of the American campaign for independence. He had a genius for campaign strategy. Not only on the battlefield but in the terrain of the hearts of those who suited him. Which was the greater battle—the fight of the Continental army, or his own fight? To his friends in the West Indies with whom he corresponded regularly he gave an account of the army's military policy. "We are retreating step by step in the face of superior numbers. We are avoiding a general engagement with the enemy. Our hopes are not placed in any particular city or spot of ground, but in the preserving of a good force, furnished with proper necessaries, to take advantage of favorable opportunities, and to waste and defeat the enemy by piecemeal. Every new post they take requires a new division of their forces. In the end we will be successful." But to no one did he reveal the tactics of his own advance.

On official duty he was sent to General Schuyler, the head of one of the wealthy patroon families in New York and one of the leading politicians of the country. Schuyler admired Hamilton's businesslike manner. And Schuyler's second daughter, Betsy, completely lost her heart to him.

"I must have a wife," Hamilton had declared to a fellow aide, "who believes in God and hates a saint." And in his effort to secure his wife, he dispatched to Betsy letters of love in a handwriting of legible beauty. Everything about him was so neat and precise. And calculated. Before the British had surrendered, the Schuylers were united with the Hamiltons.

But the war had not reached its end when Hamilton suffered a minor disagreement with Washington and resigned from his desk to go into the field. He received the command of an infantry company and distinguished himself in battle. He played the role of a conscious hero. "Two nights ago," he wrote to his wife, "my duty and my honor obliged me to take a step in which your happiness was too much risked. I commanded an attack upon one of the enemy's redoubts; we carried it in an instant and with little loss."

At the cessation of hostilities he was regarded as a soldier who had offered himself wholly to his country. There were few who could go back to civil life—and politics—boasting a more distinguished record of patriotic service.

IV

DURING the months following the treaty of Yorktown, Hamilton became a father and a lawyer. "I have been employed for the last ten months," he wrote, "in rocking the cradle and studying the art of fleecing my neighbors." His efficiency in matters commercial as well as in matters political had won him the eye of the financier of the Revolution, Robert Morris, who asked him to draw up a financial account for the State of New York. And within a short time he had become prominent enough in state politics to be appointed as a delegate to the Convention of the States at Annapolis held in 1786.

At this Convention he became the leading proponent of a federal constitution for the thirteen states. In his advocacy of a firm and centralized machinery of government by a few men, he confessed candidly that "our prevailing passions are ambition and self-interest." And, he continued, "it will ever be the duty of a wise government to avail itself of those passions."

In order to explain and to "sell" the new constitution to the people of New York, he wrote a series of *Federalist Papers* under the pseudonym of *Caesar*. And he bit his lip in anguish when he realized the blunder he had committed. Caesar! His political opponents had caught up the name and the blunt philosophy it

HAMILTON

expressed, and had hurled it back at him in a thousand different ways.

"Why, this dapper little fellow possesses the very subtlety of a Caesar. His perfumed glove conceals an iron hand. Come to think of it, it was he who first proposed a centralized government—in other words, a tyranny—even before the end of the war." Could this sort of agitation please the people who had just waged a war to rid themselves of *another* tyranny?

And Hamilton stood before the mirror powdering his hair and tying it into a queue. Why should he be ashamed? A man must always advocate the politics that *benefit* a country, not the slogans that *please* it. He carefully placed a flower in his lapel. Was that the reason for the continual whispers about him? "Beware of Alexander Hamilton. He is an exotic flower who will poison the soil into which he has been transplanted." He frowned. How poetic! And how silly! He would far rather be called a tyrant—if he *must* be called names—than a flower. There was nothing static or flowerlike about *his* genius.

The State of New York had finally voted to accept the constitution. But only with reluctance. And only after Alexander Hamilton had spoken briefly but effectively in its favor at the Convention Hall. He had played his game well. With his pen and with the assistance of his able political lieutenants he had won the city folk of Manhattan over to his cause. And then he had faced the "die-hard" residents of upper New York. "I therefore announce to you, gentlemen, that if you do not ratify this constitution without further talk, then Manhattan, Westchester, and Kings counties shall withdraw from the State of New York and form a state by themselves, leaving the rest of you without a seaport for your commerce." That was sufficient. New York entered the union.

To be sure, Hamilton was not completely satisfied with the constitution he had saved. He had desired a President and a body of Senators modeled after the British Monarch and the House of Peers, and elected on the basis of their property holdings to serve for the duration of their life. Yet, "with all its imperfections," he regarded the adoption of this constitution as a personal triumph. Some of his friends dared to call him "Alexander the Great." The city whose political opinion he had swayed was his very own "Hamiltonopolis." He stood at the window in the sunset and watched the parade of thousands of demonstrators in the street—celebrating the victory of the new national government. Shipbuilders and blacksmiths and stone masons marched singing through the streets. He felt pleased —and yet annoyed at the same time. What were these commoners celebrating for? He hated mobs and their celebrations. Did these masses of humanity think that *they* were going to rule the new government? He laughed outright at this "amusing" thought. "Poor heathen!"

V

IT WAS NOT in the hands of the people he would place the future security of his country, vowed Alexander Hamilton as he came to his desk. He had just been appointed Secretary of the Treasury in the administration of President Washington. This was no time for shilly-shally sentiment. The monarchies all over Europe were looking with expectant and greedy eyes upon this "foolish" experiment of the United States of America. If it failed to survive, the day of kings had only just begun.

Ill-wishers abroad predicted that this government would die in an excess of simple and childish idealism. But Hamilton thought differently. "No, we shall outwit you as we have outfought you. This is no attempt at a Utopia—to perish in a day. We realize that all men unfortunately are *not* created equal. We shall build a government that will appeal to the one stable element in human society—the self-interest of influential men. Our country will outlast your hopes."

He sat fourteen hours a day preparing a report for Congress on the new financial system of the nation. This nation would

HAMILTON

survive through the law of the survival of all the strong nations. "This government, like all (solid) governments, shall be an administration of the few." But the few in America are not, as in Europe, an aristocracy of *land* owners; they are an aristocracy of *money* owners. The past has been with you, your kings and your warriors; the future is with us, our merchants and our bankers. "I shall attach the money owners so closely to the government that the success of all their *personal* fortunes will be identical with the success of the *national* fortune."

During the Revolution, many of the rank and file had invested all their savings in government certificates. But as the fortunes of the government seemed to wane and the investors found themselves in need of ready cash, they sold their bonds to speculators at a fraction of their original value. When Hamilton came into the Cabinet as Secretary of the Treasury, he decided that it was "a matter of principle and honor, in laying the cornerstone of our financial policy, to redeem these bonds at their full original value." This full value, however, was to be paid not to the first purchasers of the bonds, but to their present owners. "It is true that a great proportion of the poor people's money has passed into the hands of adventurers and that we shall therefore by a stroke of the pen create a new class of rich men. But we must compromise with the evil. Government must always depend upon a group of faithful retainers. And the new class of financiers will be our strongest supporters."

Thus reasoned Hamilton. "I will propose also that the Federal Government take over every dollar of the debts contracted by the states during the war and that it share the total obligation directly and equally with all . . . In this way I shall create for each a stake in the national government, a common revenue and a common obligation to see the Union through to the finish. I shall get the necessary votes for this measure in Congress even if I have to transfer the capital from New York to the South . . . I shall recommend the creation of a national bank. This shall be a business man's government, a government of buying and selling and investing. It is a disgrace the way our poor heathen hoard their goods in their cellars and hide their money in their stockings. Out into the open with all the citizens' assets. A citizen with savings invested in a national bank will never be a *rebellious* citizen."

And Hamilton went on with his reasoning. "When I have thus assured the allegiance of the bankers and the speculators, I shall broaden the basis of our wealth. I shall introduce a system of protective tariffs that will create a new class of manufacturers and owners of merchandise. I shall increase the numbers of the ruling classes. For in numbers alone there is security."

Security created by measures of finance. Security sealed by the creation of an army and the rigid enforcement of the law.

He rose in the subdued splendor of his library to his full height.

VI

SIDE BY SIDE with Alexander Hamilton in the Cabinet sat Thomas Jefferson, the Secretary of State. As the plans of the "little Treasurer" unfolded, a volcano of feeling blazed through Jefferson's pale blue eyes. The hand that had written the Declaration of Independence trembled and curled into a fist. "This man would be Monarch of America," he told his lieutenants in Congress, Madison and Monroe. And Alexander Hamilton measured his opponent coolly. "This man shall be the monarch's fool." Methodically he rallied his followers for the life-and-death struggle to come.

Never was his pen more desperately needed. The Jeffersonians had organized a newspaper which sounded the key for a mass campaign to force Hamilton from the Cabinet into private life. And Hamilton hurled pamphlet after pamphlet into the battle for the defense of his financial policy. Finally the Jeffersonians, in their effort to oust him, engineered a Congressional resolution compelling him to make a public accounting of his treasury expenses. "Jefferson has raised the devil," he blazed to his friends. "He has become a colossus of hate." Yet he submitted his accounts to the public scrutiny—and cleared himself to the satisfaction of everyone.

In the meantime, ill winds were blowing from abroad. The French Revolution! Here was Jefferson's faith in the nobility of the people being put to the test. The streets were slippery with the blood of those who, like Hamilton, disagreed with the philosophy of liberty, equality, fraternity. "What philosopher," argued Hamilton, "ever meant sincerely that the voice of the people is the voice of God?" Hamilton walked triumphantly into the "parlors of the elect" as the news of the French Reign of Terror reached America. "Your people, Sir, is a beast." At bottom, he admitted, the masses are no more beastly than the classes. But they are *hungry, exploited, bruised* and *beaten* beasts, and therefore when they are let loose they are more dangerous than the sleek and the well fed. "The vices of the rich are far more congenial to good government than the vices of the poor."

But Jefferson stayed away from the "unwholesome brilliance" of society. He sat by his dim candle-light and refused to lose his faith in the people. A stubborn fanatic!

They met again at a Cabinet session when the ambassador from the French Republic arrived in Washington and asked that the American people take definite sides with the French people in their struggle against the counter-revolutionary forces of the world. Hamilton insisted that America, as a neutral nation, must refuse to take part in foreign quarrels. But, Jefferson wanted to know, had not France taken part in the American quarrel by sending Lafayette over to our aid? "The people's fight against dictatorship is not merely a European or an American issue. It is a *world* issue."

Hamilton jumped to his feet. "You have no business, Sir, to sit in this Cabinet by day and hire henchmen by night to fill the press with scurrilous attacks against constituted order!"

"Why, Sir, do you despise the common folk?" retorted Jefferson. "Why do you endeavor to turn our dream of organized justice into a nightmare of organized wealth?"

When Washington supported the foreign policy of the Secretary of the Treasury, Jefferson resigned from the Cabinet in a white wrath. And all "Hamiltonopolis" applauded. The "little lion" had won a mighty victory. "You have driven this dangerous rabble rouser from the government into the streets where he belongs!"

The Secretary of the Treasury remained in the Cabinet. And he turned with an iron hand to domestic affairs. He recommended a direct tax on liquors. The farmers of Western Pennsylvania stormed into rebellion. At a series of mass meetings they determined to resist rather than to pay the tax. President Washington hesitated. "Call out the army," demanded Hamilton, "and permit me to march at its head."

Hamilton marched. The farmers quickly dispersed and paid the tax. And Hamilton smiled once again in the parlors. "To perpetuate the United States of America there must always be a man on horseback."

"But if you are to play the role, my dear Alexander," said Kitty Livingston, "you must remember this: the man on horseback must sooner or later face a hostile army. And more often than not he falls to earth."

"Have no fear about my future. I am resigning from the government. I am going back to my private law practice. For my family." He chuckled mournfully. "I suppose my enemies do not realize how much money I have sacrificed by giving up my practice and taking a thirty-five hundred a year government job. I have made a fortune for my country—and I have impoverished myself."

He retired to private life. But events skidded rapidly on the greased wheels of irony. He was still recognized by the rank and file of his supporters as the creator and the very personification of the Federalist Party. And yet there was one man who challenged his supremacy in silence, who refused to take the second place in the party hierarchy. This man was John Adams, delegate to the old Continental Congress, signer of the Declaration of Independence, minister to England under the Confederation. In Washington's first administration he had been elected Vice-President of the United States. And now upon Hamilton's retirement to private life he became the President of the United States. In silence he had watched the development of Hamilton's control over the party. He knew that the Secretary of the Treasury had tried to pull every wire to block his election to the Presidency. And he suspected—with good reason—that every member of his own Cabinet was sworn to the "little lion" in New York. With a touch of malice he wrote in his private notes: "Hamilton is commander-in-chief of the Senate, of the House of Representatives, of the heads of departments, of General Washington, and least, if you will, of the President of the United States."

Clearly the Federalist Party was not big enough for two such men. And a series of political skirmishes led to a final break between them.

This final quarrel grew out of the international position of the American government. In spite of Washington's declaration of the country's neutrality in foreign affairs, American relations with France had become strained to the breaking point. Preparations were being made to raise a large army against the possibility of a Franco-American war. Hamilton had applied for a commission second to that of General Washington. But Adams, venting his spite, appointed his Secretary of War instead of Hamilton to that commission.

The Franco-American war failed to materialize. But war to the finish had been declared within the ranks of the Federalists. Hamilton retaliated to Adams' rebuff by writing a pamphlet in which he attacked the character of the President more scurrilously than he had ever attacked Tom Jefferson. It was a fatal blunder, for the attack had been made on the eve of a national election. He had bitten off the nose of the Federalist Party to spite the face of his personal enemy. In the picturesque words of Hamilton himself, "For the first time I have taken off the head of a statesman and assumed the ears of an ass."

The Federalists, having already aroused the resentment of the public with their restrictive laws against the freedom of the press, now split themselves wide open with their foolish fratricidal strife. The Jeffersonians were quick to seize their opportunity. Into the split they thrust a wedge and widened the gap still further. At the polls their two candidates—Aaron Burr and Thomas Jefferson—had received the highest number of votes for the Presidency. The two were deadlocked with an identical number of electoral votes. According to the law of the land the election would be decided by a poll of the House of Representatives. But the majority in the House was still in the hands of the Federalists. And therefore Hamilton, as party director, controlled the election.

When the leaders of the House of Representatives called on him for his decision he remarked graciously: "Is there any doubt as to what my vote will be? I have nothing against Aaron Burr except that he is a political demagogue with unlimited personal ambition, completely unfit for high office. I have nothing in favor of Thomas Jefferson except that he is an honest man. I charge you to make him President of the United States."

VII

THE BOAT carrying the man with the mortal wound slowly crossed the Hudson in the morning.

Dr. Hosack looked down. "From the day of Jefferson's election," he remarked to Pendleton, "Alexander Hamilton was marked for death. Two years later he stopped Aaron Burr from becoming Governor of New York. And Burr, who wouldn't hesitate to kill on far slighter provocation, just waited for the opportunity to shoot it out. A strange and compelling man, this Hamilton."

HAMILTON

They were approaching the New York landing. "For many years he knew Burr's domestic and political life intimately. He was thoroughly convinced that Burr was an unscrupulous demagogue, a Caesar who would destroy the country. Well, Mr. Pendleton, we may agree or disagree with many of Hamilton's ideas. That's an American privilege. But here is an action that speaks much louder than any philosophy. This was an American duty."

Duty. . . . The air was wringing wet. The heat burned slow madness into the veins. Mr. Pendleton drew his snuff. "He was a little hard on the people, Sir. He believed they had taxes to pay before they could receive their liberties, duties to perform before they could claim their rights." He looked lengthwise down the peaceful river. "This country will be a going concern as long as we pay our debts *his* way."

JOHN ADAMS

Important Dates in Life of John Adams

1735—Born at Braintree, Massachusetts.
1755—Graduated from Harvard College.
1758—Commenced practice of law.
1766—Published essays on *Colonial Rights*.
1768—Moved to Boston.
1770—Counsel for the British soldiers on trial for the Boston Massacre.
1774—Elected delegate to the Constitutional Convention.
1775—Entered motion for appointment of George Washington as Commander-in-Chief of Colonial Army.
1776—Moved for Jefferson to write the Declaration of Independence.
1778—Appointed Commissioner to France.
1780—Commissioned to negotiate treaty of peace and commerce with Great Britain.
1785–88—Minister to England.
1789—Elected Vice-President of the United States.
1792—Re-elected Vice-President.
1796—Elected President of the United States.
1799—Averted, by patient negotiations, a war with France.
1800—Defeated by Jefferson for re-election to the Presidency.
1826—Died at Quincy, Massachusetts, on the Fourth of July.

John Adams

John Adams
1735–1826

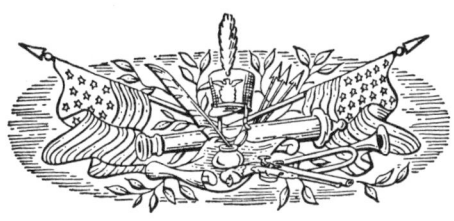

THE BOY was born with an instinct for resistance and an acid tongue. "For generations," wrote his grandson, Henry Adams, "his predecessors had viewed the world chiefly as a thing to be reformed, filled with evil forces to be abolished." For generations the family had learned to make crusading a pleasure.

He spent his boyhood in the New England climate—under the caress of the June sun and the lash of the December wind. His character, like the New England weather, was a paradox—a fusion of two conflicting lives in a single body. He had been born with "three eyes—two to look without, and one to look within." And the inner eye gradually grew blind with too much staring.

His father was a Braintree (Massachusetts) farmer, honest and conservative. He sent John to the Latin School to acquire the antiquities of culture. And then he sent him to Harvard College where John at the early age of nineteen completed his studies leading to the School of Divinity.

As a young man, he informs us with a grim sense of duty, he was somewhat overfond of two things—"the cup that cheers, the caress that endears." As for the details of his youthful indiscretions, "I shall draw no characters, nor give any enumeration . . . It would be considered no compliment to the dead or the living." Perhaps, after all, he was not lost. "This I will say: they were all modest and virtuous girls, and always maintained their character." Could he live the life of a Puritan, as his family and his tradition expected? "I have an ungovernable tongue, an uncontrollable temper." And other "disturbing" and "unpuritanical" instincts. "I am thrown into a transport when I behold the miracles of nature." The transport of a romantic poet and not of an austere prophet.

Yet the austere ancestors within him refused to give up without a struggle. His conscience tortured him mercilessly. Time and time again he wrote in his diary: "Rambled about all day, gaping and gazing . . . Not one new idea all this week . . . Dreamed away the time as usual . . ." And once he observed passionately, "What is the reason that I cannot remove all papers and books from my table, take one volume into my hands and read and reflect upon it till night, without wishing for my pen and ink to write a letter, or to take down any other book, or to think of the girls?" And all this while he had been reading, writing, and studying no less than sixteen hours a day! "I believe," he remarked with a wry sense of humor, "I am a *passionate Puritan*."

When he had completed his studies, he received an appointment as teacher in a grammar school at Worcester. But he disliked the work of instructing "a large number of little runtlings, just capable of lisping A B C, and troubling the master." There was only one profession that encouraged the development of the most precocious element of his nature—his sarcastic tongue. And that was the law.

He entered Colonel Putnam's firm and chewed tobacco over his law books. He married Abigail Smith, the daughter of a Weymouth clergyman. He read aloud Ovid's *Art of Love* to a neighbor's wife and wrote remorsefully in his diary, "I think it's high time for a reformation, both in the lawyer and in the man."

The summer and the winter in his soul had entered upon their lifelong struggle. "Summer," wrote his grandson, Henry Adams, "was a tropical license; winter, a desperate effort to live."

II

JOHN ADAMS was a busy lawyer. The people of his home town, harsh and aggressive and disputatious, had become immortalized in a New England proverb—"As litigious as Braintree." The little courthouse rang incessantly with claims and counter-claims, until John Adams observed wearily, "The very earth groans and the stones cry out." He was overwhelmed with paltry lawsuits. His colleagues in Boston looked at him disdainfully. "He's nothing but a twopenny lawyer."

Adams revenged himself upon his critics by moving to Boston and taking away from them a good part of their practice. The brilliance of his tongue and the soundness of his mind brought him the clientage of the "Big Business" interests in the Colony. He understood and sympathized with their grievances against the Big Business interests of their motherland.

His Boston clients phrased their complaints against England somewhat as follows: "The English colonies in this part of the world have increased so much in wealth and population that they vie with European England. But the English, to maintain their own commerce and power, have passed a series of Navigation Acts by which the colonies are forbidden to establish any new manufactures that might compete with them . . . by which the colonies are forbidden, with the exception of a few places, the liberty to trade in any ports not belonging to the British Empire . . . by which the colonies are forbidden to accept the commerce of any foreign power . . ."

The American businessmen were insistent upon their right to free trade, even if they must resort to smuggling in order to maintain this right. At the same time they deeply resented the

Writs of Assistance issued by the royal court in Massachusetts, permitting the King's officers to search the houses of the colonists on suspicion of smuggled goods.

Adams, while he fought for his clients, at the same time saw the humor of their plight. One of their chief efforts at free trade was the smuggling of molasses. "As every gallon of molasses yields, by distillation, a gallon of rum, and as every gallon of rum is sought after by the four million inhabitants of the colonies, I devoutly pray—the Lord have mercy on us!"

When the British expanded their system of revenue imposts to include definite excise taxes such as the tax on stamps, the complaints in America had risen to a crusade for a principle. These taxes, maintained the colonists, amounted to a confiscation of property. What right had a parliament in England to confiscate the property of Americans across the sea? What right had *any* legislative body in England to pass laws for the colonies in America when not a single American sat as a representative in that body?

And so the colonists resisted the Stamp Act, and for a time it seemed as if all business would come to a stop. John Adams had fallen into the deepest gloom. "The probate office is shut, the custom house is shut, the courts of justice are shut, and all business seems at a stand . . . I was but just getting into my gears, just getting under sail, and an embargo is laid upon the ship."

He didn't want to have any part of the trouble. He was interested in getting bread. He was therefore not a little shocked to learn that the town meeting had appointed him as counsel to petition the Governor to remove the Stamp Tax. The aristocracy of the colony was overwhelmingly English. So, too, was the magistracy of the courts. Should he, John Adams, associate himself with a rebel movement?

He entered upon a crisis of thinking. In his diary he recorded: "Sunday. At home with my family, thinking." And on a Christmas morning, "At home, thinking, reading, searching, concerning taxation without consent."

JOHN ADAMS

But Hutchinson, the royal Governor of Massachusetts, had also been thinking. Through one of his assistants he sent Adams a cautious proposal. "Would you care to accept the office of advocate general in the court of admiralty?" The implication was clear. The position was "a sure introduction to the most profitable business in the province, a first step in the ladder of royal favor and promotion." In plain words, a simple bribe. John Adams declined the offer.

It was a dangerous move on Adams' part, and he knew it. Daily, as he looked out through the window of his home on Brattle Square, he saw the Redcoats whom Governor Hutchinson had summoned to "keep order" in Boston. "My reflections for two years at the sight of those soldiers before my door was serious enough. The danger I was in appeared in full view before me." It was a red badge of oppression. "I very deliberately and very solemnly determined at all events to adhere to my principles in favor of my native country, which indeed was all the country I knew, or which had been known by my father, grandfather, or great-great-grandfather." Yet at the same time he refused to attend, much less address, the town assemblies of the people who were agitating against the King. It was better to hold one's self in sober restraint.

In the meantime, the American "independents" were preparing for the inevitable fight. Every evening the martial strains of the British regiment were answered by the pipes and drums of a volunteer brigade—the "Sons of Liberty"—who paraded boldly before Adams' window. But one frosty night in March, 1770, all music had suddenly stopped. Instead, the sound of shots and the shouting of an infuriated mob.

A scuffle had taken place between the soldiers and the civilians. In the confusion, some of the Redcoats had lost their heads and fired. Five Bostonians had been killed; six others lay wounded. The bells tolled. The streets were filled with raging men and women. "Massacre!" The British regiment stood silent and with fixed bayonets. Finally Governor Hutchinson arrived on the scene and made a solemn promise that the soldiers guilty of the aggression would be arrested and duly punished. Only then did the crowd disperse.

The following day Captain Preston and eight of his regulars were indicted for murder. But who would be their counsel? It seemed that no Bostonian would plead in court for them.

An influential citizen entered the law office of John Adams. "I have come with a very solemn message from a very unfortunate man. Captain Preston wishes for counsel and can get none. I have waited on Mr. Quincy, who says he will engage if you, Mr. Adams, will give him your assistance; without it, he positively will not. Even Mr. Auchmuty declines unless you will engage."

John Adams measured him with a steady eye. "In a free country, Mr. Forrest, counsel ought to be the very last thing that an accused person should want. The prisoners have the right for an impartial hearing. We Americans are fighting for the rights of all human beings, our enemies as well as our friends. I shall take the case."

Captain Preston was acquitted of the charge of murder, for the evidence had failed to show that he had given the order to fire. Six of the eight regulars were likewise set free because of insufficient evidence to prove their guilt. The remaining two soldiers, who declared they had fired the shots in self-defense, were convicted of manslaughter and escaped with their lives.

Years later old John Adams wrote, "Not the battle of Lexington or of Bunker Hill, not the surrender of Burgoyne or of Cornwallis, were more important events in American history than this battle of King Street, on the fifth of March, 1770."

III

THE PEOPLE of Boston had so far regained their sobriety as to realize the wisdom of Adams. They elected him by a popular majority as Representative of the General Court of Massachusetts.

As he rode around the circuit of the court, he heard the voice of the people in the taverns, around the tables at the wayside inns, at the blacksmith shops where they stopped to shoe their horses. Once, as he alighted at a crossroad, a man rushed over to hold his stirrup and surprised him by calling his name. "Mr. Adams, as a man of liberty, I respect you; God bless you! I'll stand by you while I live."

Yet he was still undergoing his old struggle—the conflict between his love for America and his loyalty toward England. And this struggle was wearing down his health. "I am tired," he one day remarked to James Otis, that fiery patriot who knew no diplomacy of the tongue but who could speak only the language of the heart.

Otis gave him a withering look. "Tired, are you? Tired with one year's service, dancing from Braintree to Boston, moping about the streets of this town like an old gaffer of ninety, and intent upon only one solitary thought—how to get enough money to carry you smoothly through life!"

Money? That was not it. He was not greedy. It was just that he couldn't make up his mind. Couldn't understand the drift of his own life. "I wander alone and ponder. I muse, I mope, I ruminate. I am often in reveries and brown studies. The objects before me are too grand and multifarious for my comprehension . . ."

But when His Majesty's government closed the port of Boston and threatened a slow blockade of starvation unless the colonists yielded utterly, the call came at last to Adams. And he understood the call and answered, though with a heavy heart. Appointed as one of the Massachusetts delegates to the Continental Congress in Philadelphia (1774), he accepted the duty with an expressed fear of his inability to fulfill it. "I feel myself unequal to the task. All of us are unequal. We are deficient in genius, in education, in travel, in fortune—in everything—to have allowed the business to approach this stage of calamity." And then he added: "May God give us the wisdom to see it through!"

In the month of August he parted from his family and set out for Philadelphia. It was the first time he had journeyed beyond the borders of New England. He looked with interest at the scenes and the people on the way. "I have been treated well," he wrote to Abigail from New York City, "but I have not seen one real gentleman, one well-bred man since I came to town." And in return he heard many uncomplimentary remarks about the "Quaker-murderers" and the "Witch-hunters" of New England. There was, he noted with a pang, an utter feeling of disunion among the colonies. And of irresponsibility. When he arrived in Philadelphia, he discovered that the momentous deliberations of the Continental Congress were to be introduced by a "splendid conviviality." Wine was to unlock the gates to wisdom, while the war clouds gathered for one of the world's greatest tempests.

"We drank toasts till eleven last night," wrote Adams to his wife. "Lee and Harrison were very high." And in another letter: "A most sinful feast again. Turtle, flummery, jellies, twenty kinds of sweetmeats, whipped sillabubs, floating islands, custards, tarts, creams, almonds, pears, peaches, Madeira, Bordeaux, Champagne, Burgundy, Sherry, Alicant, Navarre, and Vin de Cap." The motto of those colonial rebels, according to John Adams, was—"Drink, and show yourself a man. And let them hang you if they can!"

IV

THE CONTINENTAL CONGRESS has come down to us—and justly so—as one of the most momentous deliberative bodies in history. We judge it today not by its imperfections but by its achievements. This Congress appointed one of its members, George Washington, as Commander-in-Chief of the American armies,

JOHN ADAMS

and voted one day in the summer of 1776 "that these United Colonies are, and of right ought to be, free and independent states." This body financed and governed and kept in unity the sorely bleeding country during the long hard years of battle.

But men are seldom prophets to their own contemporaries. The usually caustic pen of John Adams dripped with gall as he wrote to Abigail about his impressions of the various debaters. "Rutledge has an offensive habit of shrugging his shoulders, distorting his body, wriggling his head, rolling his eyes, and speaking through his nose." Sherman of Pennsylvania is "stiffness and awkwardness itself, rigid as starched linen or buckram, awkward as a junior bachelor or sophomore." Most of the other members "have a remarkable want of judgment." They are "the very reverse of grace."

The blunt, red-faced New Englander was shocked at the "pusillanimous attitude" with which most of the delegates viewed a struggle with England. Stubborn to the very marrow of his bones when once he had made a decision, he could not sympathize with those who disagreed. After much hesitation and misgiving, he had decided at last that the colonies must fight for independence. "The vast majority of the delegates shudder at the prospect of blood," he growled. "And yet they are opposed to submission." He thundered and threatened and grew purple in the face as he listened to the longwinded arguments for conciliation.

And then the time for conciliation was past. Blood had been shed in the faraway lanes of Concord and Lexington, and the Congress found itself suddenly faced with the fact that America was at war. "We can not force events," remarked Adams grimly. "Events force us."

Yet there were those who still wanted to temporize. One of those men who "feared to take the final step" was John Dickinson, of Pennsylvania. "Dickinson's mother," wrote John Adams to Abigail, "is continually sending him letters in hysteria. 'Johnny, you will be hanged; your estate will be forfeited and confiscated; you will leave your excellent wife a widow, and your charming children orphans, beggars and infamous.' "

"Thank Heaven for *my* wife!" thought John Adams. "If Abigail had expressed such sentiments to me, they would wholly unman me."

And so he sat thinking and observing while the Congress debated and the farmers spilled their blood at Lexington and Concord and Bunker Hill. Good Lord, these delegates must make *some* final commitment. This struggle *must* be raised from a sectional squabble into a national crusade.

Finally he rose from his seat. Seven years earlier he had been the only man in Boston to arrive unerringly at the truth of a situation. Against the public clamor he had defended the lives of the British soldiers. And once more he grasped the historic essence of a moment. For some time there had been a desultory discussion as to who should be elected Commander-in-Chief of the army quartered in Cambridge. This army was composed of New Englanders, officers and men. The general feeling prevailed that John Hancock of Massachusetts should be given the commission.

John Adams made a motion that the New England troops be commanded by a Virginian, Colonel George Washington. The effect was electric. John Hancock, who presided over the session, fairly leaped from his chair and the entire Massachusetts delegation stared at Adams in amazement. In an assembly of party jealousy and of sectional quarrels it was nothing short of a miracle that a Virginian should be proposed by a New Englander. And that this Virginian should finally be approved by the majority of the delegates. With a single bold stroke the shrewd Yankee lawyer had drawn the colonies, into a coöperative unit. "This fight," he wrote, "is no longer the fight of Massachusetts alone . . . The whole country is now as deep in the business as we are . . . We shall live or die—united."

Yet Adams refused to regard himself as a rebel. "I chafe at that name. I want to be called a free citizen and a patriot."

JOHN ADAMS

It was the Tories who were the rebels—for they rebelled against the interests of the country in which they lived. "John Dickinson is a rebel. John Adams is an American."

The American patriots had decided to write some form of a declaration. Adams looked about for a man to draft the words. He had picked one Virginian to lead with the sword. Why not pick another Virginian to lead with the pen? "Tom Jefferson, you are the man to draw up the declaration. It will perpetuate your name."

"But you yourself should do it," returned the scholar.

"Nonsense. I am obnoxious, suspected and unpopular—and you can write ten times better than I can."

The night of July 3, 1776. John Adams sat in the sultry shadows and peered over his pen in a thimbleful of candle-light. "Yes, Abigail, yesterday we decided the greatest question which was ever debated in America . . . You ask how the delegates (who signed the document) acted?" He hesitated for a moment and then went on with the grim truth. "For months there were majorities constantly against it. And to the very last there were many members torn with doubts . . . when the moment came to sign—ah, could I but see their hearts!—a number of our worthy gentlemen lifted their hands trancelike and cried out in horror to heaven."

V

JOHN ADAMS, born with the instinct for resistance, had completed his share in the destruction of the British empire in America. From now on, he must face the acid test—his ability to share in the building of a new American society. While the last battles were being fought in the field he was sent as commissioner to France and he negotiated a loan from Holland. And when the military contest was decided he served on the peace commission with Benjamin Franklin and with John Jay. And irony of ironies! The arch rebel of the Revolution was now selected as the first American minister to the court of George

III! It was a role John Adams reveled in. "I am the most unpopular man in all England." He walked the streets through rows of staring eyes, presented himself stiffly to His Majesty and flushed with pleasure while the King reddened with pain.

But when he returned to his country he found himself in a curious situation. He was too big for a provincial law practice. And there was no longer any revolution. He found himself in a decidedly uncongenial atmosphere of tranquillity. Moreover, he discovered that there were names in America greater than his. George Washington's, for instance. The irascible New Englander fell from a squinting into an outright shutting of the eyes. Hadn't he made George Washington? What was all this fuss about a military hero? Hadn't his own politics won the war? *He,* and not George Washington, was the father of his country. The old trouble, the struggle of the seasons, awoke once more in his soul. The fortunes of his country seemed to be emerging into spring. Well, he too would put away the snow shovel and enjoy the flowers. The people had chosen Washington President of the new government and had given him, John Adams, the second place. He would show them how splendid a pageant a Vice-President could put on! While the capital awaited the arrival of Washington, John Adams sat under his canopy of velvet "and grew giddy with his own magnificence." Unfriendly tongues had dubbed him "His Rotundity." His vanity was indeed ridiculous. This new country must be a Grand Republic. He and the President must surround themselves with pomp and finery, chamberlains, aides-de-camp, stewards and ushers of the black rod. When the news reached him that George Washington would be addressed, not as *His Most Serene Highness,* but simply as *Mr. President,* he was dumfounded. "Good Lord, but this is how the president of a fire company or a cricket club is addressed!"

He learned more things in his sadness. His drab duties, for example, as the Vice-President of the United States. With his eyes the gloom of cypress and his tongue as caustic as ever,

JOHN ADAMS

he remarked, "My country has in its wisdom contrived for me the most insignificant office that ever the invention of man contrived or his imagination conceived." He had reveled in his debates on the assembly floor. And now he had been reduced to a sanctimonious silence as referee in the Senate over the debates of other people.

But if he couldn't exercise his oratory, he continued to find solace in his pen. The Federalist Party was passing legislation and establishing institutions that fitted exactly into his own conservative outlook. In his pamphlets and his letters he made it known that he was no less cynical of "mob-rule" than Hamilton himself. During the following years he rose with Hamilton to the leadership of the Federalist Party, lending the mind of a lawyer to the soul of a financier. "To place property at the mercy of the majority who have no property," he wrote, "is to entrust the lamb to the wolf. My *fundamental* maxim of government is: never to trust the lamb to the custody of the wolf." To this conservative credo Alexander Hamilton could only say, *Amen*.

VI

WHEN Washington had completed his two terms, the Federalists were strong enough to elect John Adams to the Presidency. But Adams was dissatisfied. George Washington had been the *unanimous* choice of *all the people*. But he, John Adams, was merely the *not-altogether-acceptable* candidate of *one of the parties*. Even within the party, he knew, there were men who had strenuously opposed him. Alexander Hamilton, for instance. "How dared he fight against *me!*" shouted Adams, his volcanic temperament rising to an explosive heat. The eye of his philosophy had become inflamed with too much staring upon a single object—himself. He had come to look upon himself as the indispensable man. "If the project to defeat me had succeeded," he wrote to a friend, "our Constitution would not have lasted four years." He could no longer understand his own faults, or anybody else's virtues. In the midst of his greatest honors he had begun to experience a cold hostility toward all men. And the cold hostility of all men toward himself. As he rode to the inaugural ceremonies he felt "like a patriot going into his exile."

He journeyed through the term of his Presidency in a great pilgrimage of loneliness. He was the target of everybody's abuse. The Jeffersonians attacked him for his "too shackled mind"; the Hamiltonians, for his "too unshackled tongue." Never had he shown a greater genius for making enemies than now. The very men he named as members of his Cabinet were his secret foes. They kept his political opponents informed about his most confidential Cabinet secrets.

And the international situation, too, was trying enough for anyone even less irascible than John Adams. France, offended that her generous contribution to American independence had been repaid with an "inexcusable American aloofness" in her own struggle for independence, was ready now to fight America on the slightest provocation. Nor did she leave the provocation to America. On the contrary, she took the initiative herself. She preyed on American commerce and insulted American ministers. And when Adams had sent commissioners to Paris in order to negotiate a truce, Talleyrand had shamelessly demanded a bribe as the preliminary price of the negotiations. It seemed that the United States, the peace-loving republic which had proclaimed its neutrality in European affairs, would have to go to war in the defense of its right to stay neutral. It was a time for a stout heart and a cool head. But the "Anglophile Federalists" had neither. They saw the impending war as a political opportunity to crush the Jeffersonians who had French leanings. Adams was a Federalist. Yet he realized that a war, coming so soon after the titanic struggle with England, could end only in a national disaster. He therefore persisted in looking for a peaceful solution. He dismissed his belligerent Cabinet and sent to France a commission of his own choice with instructions to avert the catastrophe, if possible.

JOHN ADAMS

The commission was successful, and the Federalists branded him as "a coward, a renegade, a pacifist, a Francophile and a Jeffersonian"—just because, as he bitterly remarked, he had served his country better than he had served his party. No tongue spoke a word of encouragement—or even of wonder—for the amazing discipline which this choleric old statesman had been able to display once again in a crisis.

Adams was undismayed at the abuse of his enemies and at the silence of his friends. For he was a man who sought justification not with the masses, but within the humble chapel of his own conscience. At each great crisis in the life of his country it had been his destiny to stand alone against the crowd. As his Presidency came to an end, he realized that he had assassinated his own last hope—the honor of re-election to the highest office. His party had been so widely split by his independent action that Jefferson, his rival candidate, had won the election "almost without a struggle."

VII

HE SAT in the chambers of the last long night. Outside, a nation was busy preparing for the inaugural welcome of the new President. Thomas Jefferson was the popular man. But never John Adams.

And yet—"was it not I who put the pen into Jefferson's hand to write the Declaration of Independence? . . . And was it not I who gave a leader to our people?" His eyes grew bright as he recalled that assembly of heated and bickering delegates in mid-July of 1776, when he, John Adams, had risen from his seat to nominate what then was only a name—George Washington—to the supreme command of the American army. And both these children of his choosing had become the saviors of America. But never John Adams. He alone sat in the blackest night.

But before the clock struck midnight, he would have time to

create one more great American. John Marshall of Virginia. "I shall make him head of the Supreme Court." He smiled. "The Supreme Court will become a mighty instrument for justice in the hands of the right man." Always choosing the *right man*. He, John Adams, was not a *savior*, but a *maker* of saviors. *That* was his mission in life—to proclaim the coming of the redeemer and then to step humbly aside.

Early the next morning, as the multitudes gathered to see their new President, the aged, irascible, Puritan John the Baptist stole home to dream of new Messiahs.

MARSHALL

Important Dates in Life of John Marshall

1755—Born at Germantown, Virginia.
1776—Lieutenant in the Continental Army.
1778—Captain in the Continental Army.
1781—Admitted to the bar.
1782—Elected to the Virginia Assembly.
Married Mary Ambler.
1788—Member of the Federal Convention appointed to discuss the ratification of the U.S. Constitution.
1797-98—Special Envoy to France, to adjust commercial relations between France and United States.
1798—Elected to the United States House of Representatives.
1800—Appointed Secretary of State under President Adams.
1801—Appointed Chief Justice of the Supreme Court.
1804-07—Wrote five-volume biography of George Washington.
1831—His wife died on Christmas Day.
1835—Died at Philadelphia.

John Marshall

John Marshall
1755–1835

His father was a soldier and a pioneer. He could display no emblazoned coat of arms or match his plebeian origin with the pedigreed aristocracy of Virginia. But his wife could boast a family tree whose bark was coated with silver and whose leaves were ingots of gold. She was descended from the Earls of Scotland —a clan of fighters who had served under some of the greatest military heroes in British history. It was a strange and powerful union—this marriage between the red blood of the New World and the blue blood of the Old.

When John was ten years old, his parents moved from their dank log cabin in Virginia to the heart of the Blue Ridge Mountains. It was a terrifying place where "the weeds of disease and the wiles of the Indians" lay in ambush for the white settlers. But Mary Marshall spoke reassuringly to her children, especially to the eldest who would be able to understand. "Don't be afraid, Johnny. The pioneers of the past have shown us the way. And, God helping us, we will show the way to the pioneers of the future."

II

Young Johnny loved his mother, but he simply adored his father. Tom Marshall, a flame of defiant courage, had served his community successively as vestryman, sheriff and member of the Virginia House of Burgesses. His heart had leaped high on that never-to-be-forgotten day when Patrick Henry had stood up to denounce the injustice of the British king against the American colonies.

On his return home, Tom Marshall had gravely considered the issue. He had heard rumors that the Bostonians had sent a shipload of British tea to the bottom of the harbor. And that a handful of farmers in Lexington had chased the British regulars twenty miles. Soon these rumors were confirmed. American blood had been spilled. Massachusetts was at war. There was no doubt as to where Virginia would stand.

One day he spoke to John, who was now twenty years old. "Son, they tell me you're one of the best shots around here."

"Well, I guess I have a *little* bit of skill."

"You'll need it, son." He handed him the rifle which he had taken down from the wall. "There's war with England."

"Thanks, Father, I will march with you."

III

Together the two militia men, Lieutenant John Marshall and his father, helped to hold the bridge over the Elizabeth River against the charge of Governor Dunmore and his Virginia regulars. Together they enrolled in the Third Virginia Regiment and threw aside their homespun shirts and bucktail caps for the Continental blue and buff. Together they marched north to help the hard-pressed Washington. And together they starved and froze at Valley Forge.

Many fathers and sons had enlisted as partners in this uncertain adventure for freedom. Fathers of the colonial past, sons of the republican future, comrades in the hard-fighting moments of the present.

When John Marshall resigned from the service, the war was not quite over. But he was the hero of a dozen tales of glory. Among the fashionable Virginians everybody knew that old Tom Marshall's son had proved himself an exemplary soldier. His stoical conduct at Valley Forge had been a model for all his fellow soldiers. His coolness under fire had won the praise of all the officers. The young ladies of Yorktown talked about his exploits with heightened pulses and flushed faces.

Especially the three Ambler girls, the daughters of the treasurer of the colony. They could scarcely sleep when they heard that young Marshall was coming to town—"resplendent in his gold braids and epaulettes, and carrying a dazzling sword."

What was their chagrin when they were introduced to a tall, gangling youth in ill-fitting homespun clothes, a "country bumpkin" who stumbled in his speech and shambled in his walk! And yet there *was* an undeniable charm about him. He came often to see the girls. He read them poetry in a pleasant, "soulful" voice while the two older girls knitted with lowered eyes. But Mary, the youngest of the Ambler sisters—a pert little hoyden of fourteen—looked boldly upon him as he read. "I will marry him," she decided.

She set her cap for him with the clever audacity of a young woman who had made up her mind. And poor John, for all his experience in war, was no match for her attack. The tall young oak tree fell at the stroke of a wisp of a girl. He found himself desperately in love.

But she was too young. They would have to wait for marriage. Moreover, it was high time he looked around for something to do in the way of a career. The soldiers at Valley Forge had told him he was born with a legal mind. They had laid their squabbles before him, and never once had they dissented from his decisions as they sat on their straw mattresses and munched their "firecakes" and listened to those masterpieces of logic that came out of his untutored mouth. "Anybody can tell you were cut out for a lawyer."

Ah, wouldn't his Mary's eye glow with pride when, in the presence of the learned Jurors, he pitted his mind against the minds of the most distinguished lawyers in Virginia!

It was love that gave the final spurt to law. He entered the College of William and Mary, a school with a fine tradition and congenial customs. "No liquor shall be furnished or used at table," read one of the regulations, "except beer, cider, toddy, or spirits and water." In hot weather the students attended classes without their coats, shoes, or stockings. For John Marshall it was always hot weather. He came to his classes regularly, and with many notebooks. But hardly a page did he fill with the wise utterances of his professors. On every line appeared the name of Mary Ambler. "Miss M. Ambler," written upside down. "Miss Mary A.—J. Marshall," scrawled on the margins. And sketches of her face from a hundred different angles graced the covers.

Finally he could stand it no longer. He was certain she would give her heart and her future to someone else unless he really got down to making a living. His studies at William and Mary were a waste of time and energy. Bother the *theory* of law. He knew enough already of the *practice* of law to get his license and begin to hunt up clients.

He applied for admittance to the bar and—such were the standards of the time—his application was successful. American jurisprudence directly after the Revolution was a field not for scholars but for pioneers. A tough intellectual fiber, a sympathetic insight into human emotions, and a dauntless energy—these rather than scholastic learning were the requirements for a legal career in 1783. And John Marshall possessed, in addition to these requirements, a fourth asset not infrequently to be found among the pioneering folk who spent many hours around the campfire telling tall stories—the gift of an eloquent tongue.

MARSHALL

There were many claims and much business for the struggling young lawyer—but no cash. Cash was a scarce commodity and men paid for their services in land and in durable goods. For three years Marshall collected his goods. And then he joined hands with his beloved. He was twenty-seven. The bride was seventeen. When he had finished paying the minister, he had one guinea left in his pocket.

IV

JOHN MARSHALL'S rise to prominence was rapid. By his marriage he had become allied to one of the most powerful families in Virginia. But the deep respect he commanded in his profession was due to his native genius and not to his acquired family connections. Within a short while his reputation for controversy was known throughout the state.

A distinguished visitor from another part of the country had come to Virginia to appeal a lawsuit in her courts. He looked around for a suitable attorney. The landlord of the hotel where he was staying recommended young John Marshall. "There comes young Marshall himself," added the landlord as they were chatting on the piazza. The client looked down the street. The lawyer strode slowly by. He was dressed carelessly in a black blouse and unpressed trousers. His hair was disheveled and his shoes were untied. He carried his hat in one hand and nibbled at a bag of cherries which he held in the other. So this was "the famous" Mr. Marshall! The guest had been introduced to another advocate—a venerable patriarch of the law, dressed in a powdered wig and a fashionable cloak. There was no doubt in his mind as to which man he would choose. But before his case was called he had an opportunity to be present when both the "aristocrat" and the "roughneck" argued before the judge. "Mr. Marshall," he said right after the latter had finished his argument, "I have made a dreadful mistake. I have already given my lawyer half of his fee. I will give you the remainder if you stay away from the courthouse and eat cherries until my case is closed."

But the unfortunate visitor was not alone in his initial estimate of John Marshall. The learned members at the bar, long used to judging all manners of men, confessed that their young colleague defied analysis. "Without a commanding presence in the courtroom, with a dry, hard voice and clumsy gestures, possessing not a single ornament of the orator, John Marshall is one of the most eloquent men in the world." And the reason for this eloquence was not far to seek. John Marshall possessed one original and almost supernatural faculty—the power to encompass a subject by a single glance of his mind. "His genius is not forensic. Nor is it artistic. It is the charm of his intellect that casts forth a potent spell." No matter how complex and confusing a subject, "though ten times more knotty than the 'gnarled oak,' the lightning of heaven is not more rapid or more resistless than his astonishing penetration." Folks responded to the logical development of his pleadings with a fervor that was almost evangelical. The stuff of his genius was no less scientific than that of Euclid's. His brain cut away at a fact with a series of swift, simple, energetic strokes. "The audience is never permitted to pause for a moment . . . Every sentence is progressive; every idea sheds new light on the subject." The dawn advances. One by one the salient features of the argument take shape until the entire body is touched into flame by the sudden sunburst of a magical phrase. And the audience, spellbound, is witness to a new miracle—the lifeless word transformed into living flesh.

John Marshall's genius was bound to make itself felt not merely in the courtroom but in the entire life of the newly awakened nation. The principles for which he had fought against the British were still (in 1788) in abeyance. His countrymen had thrown off the burden of the British government, but they had not as yet assumed the responsibilities of a national government of their own. The states were zealous of their sovereignty

MARSHALL

and refused to yield any essential rights to a central power. While they loudly insisted upon their independence from foreign slavery, the American people were allowing themselves "to sink into a galling domestic bondage"—the bondage of anarchy, and impotency, and disunion. George Washington, the patriarch who had given up all considerations of personal freedom in order to lead his countrymen to Canaan, had declared for a strong national government as the only instrument for the realization of a people's true liberty. "For men are truly free only when they have the courage to surrender voluntarily as much of their private rights as is commensurate with the public good."

Yet when Washington and Madison and Jefferson and the other students of political science drew up a Constitution for the "public government" of the United States, the majority of the people at the outset were strongly opposed to accepting it. It required the combined brilliance and persuasiveness of the greatest minds among the supporters to win over the necessary nine states for the ratification of this Constitution.

Foremost among the Virginians in pleading the cause of the Constitution was John Marshall. To the incessant fulminations of the opposition he entered a lucid and classic argument: "What are the objects of the national government? To protect the United States and to promote the general welfare. Protection in time of war is one of its primal objects. Until mankind shall cease to have avarice and ambition, wars shall rise . . . The honorable gentlemen say that we need not be afraid of war. But look at history . . . Look at the great volume of human nature. They will both tell you that a defenceless country cannot be secure."

Finally the Virginia delegates accepted the Constitution by a majority of ten votes—and Marshall returned to the business of making a living at the bar. But he no longer practiced in the comparative privacy of a local reputation. He had become a national figure. With the formation of a republican government and the election of a President and a Congress of the United

States, the necessity arose for a new type of American—a man who could rise to the stature of statesmanship. And John Marshall proved to be the man. The Federalist Alexander Hamilton, committed to the philosophy that the men of solid property alone should rule the state, had found in John Marshall a fellow Federalist. For Marshall was a lawyer whose mind tended naturally to honest and solid conservatism—not the ostentatiously elegant conservatism of the Boston, New York and Philadelphia Federalists, but the "homespun stability" that fitted into a slack attire and uttered words of wisdom in a rustic vernacular.

Marshall was still a man of rustic sensibilities. He loved his common neighbors of the countryside. And he was eager for their happiness. Even now he awoke nights with a moan as he felt the chill of the winter at Valley Forge seep through his veins. And he resolved that he would do his part to build a solid and substantial nation in which this terrible catastrophe of ice and blood must never happen again.

V

JOHN MARSHALL'S sun was rapidly climbing to its zenith. He had been a strong supporter of President Washington's foreign policy, and he was appointed by President John Adams to a commission whose job it was to keep the hotheaded revolutionary government of France at peace with the United States. When the members of the French foreign office brazenly demanded a bribe of good American coin before they talked business, Marshall replied by demanding his passports back to the United States.

He came home in a halo of martyred glory, served a term in the House of Representatives and accepted the portfolio of Secretary of State in the final Cabinet of President Adams.

And then fate played her familiar role of irony. The Federalists who had held the reins of power for ten years, ever since the formation of the government in 1789, now saw themselves rapidly slipping into the discard. In the fall of 1800 Thomas Jefferson,

MARSHALL

the candidate most obnoxious to all men of property, was elected President over John Adams. It was a complete victory for the party of "farmers and day laborers." For they had won not only the Presidency and the Vice-Presidency, but the Congress as well. To the Federalists it was tantamount to a revolution. There was one branch of government they might still retain in the face of the avalanche, however, and that was the judiciary. As Adams' term of office neared its end, he frantically signed permanent appointments for his "old guard Federalists" to the principal judgeships of the nation. In the arms of the law, at least, the principles of property would be protected.

And then, at the last moment, Adams produced his masterstroke. Looking around for someone of his own persuasion to be selected as the final guardian of the American Constitution, he decided there was one man in the country pre-eminently suited for the office—John Marshall.

And so at forty-five, still robust, still fond of his game of quoits, John Marshall found himself Chief Justice of the Supreme Court—an institution new in the history of government and of law. There was no precedent for his office, no guide for his action. What good would all the learning of Blackstone and all the experience of Mansfield do him? Until this appointment he had never even held a judicial office. And now as he donned the judge's robes, he felt the same nameless fear that had paralyzed him as a child when he moved from the comfortable log cabin in the Tidewater into the Western Wilderness through the paths of the Unknown. Once again he was called upon to take an unknown road, to break new ground. This was the scourge—and the sublimity—of being an American.

After all, what a man needed was merely a deep sense of justice. Here was the Constitution of his government. Interpret its definitions as to the rights and the duties of four million Americans not with subtlety nor with sophistry, but with justice.

In 1789, when the Constitution became the supreme law of the land, many people predicted openly—and some of them with malice—that it would fail within a decade. These shortsighted Americans had never understood the serious purpose of the Constitution-makers—not to present the substance of a dogma, but to preserve the spirit of an ideal, the soul of human independence resurrected out of the scarred body of the American Revolution. And Marshall, as he sat down for the first session of the Supreme Court held under his leadership, was conscious of the great creative task before him. For the Constitution would become potent only through the interpretative genius of the philosopher-judge who could transform its *written words* into *living thoughts.*

One of John Marshall's shrewdest associates on the bench, Judge Story, looked at him inquisitively as the Chief Justice donned his robes. "He will see the law through honest eyes," he decided. "I love his laugh; it is too hearty for an intriguer."

VI

For thirty-four years John Marshall saw justice and made it into American constitutional law. In his major decisions he gave full affirmation to the ties that solidified the great and efficient family of the United States. Opponents argued loudly that the United States was a government of *enumerated powers.* Marshall answered, "It is a government of great *national purposes."* And such it has remained by the verdict of the Supreme Court.

In the first major case presented to him, Chief Justice Marshall set a precedent for calling his court *Supreme.* For he proclaimed the *final right* of the judiciary to pass on the constitutionality of an act of Congress. In a subsequent decision he extended the powers of the federal government by affirming the right of the Supreme Court to pass on the constitutionality of a measure enacted by a state legislature. In still another historic instance he further broadened the basic power of the central government when he declared that the establishment of a national bank was quite in accord with the spirit of the

Constitution. There were those, indeed, who charged that ninety percent of his decisions were marked by "a Federalist bias," and that he had deliberately turned away "from the democracy of the individual to the autocracy of the state." But this was a fault (if fault it was) of his nature, not of his morals. The particular shape of his personality had stamped him as an *honest Federalist*.

Yet in one instance, it must be confessed, he allowed himself to yield to the flames of prejudice. It was at the trial of Aaron Burr, whom the Jeffersonian administration had labeled as a traitor endeavoring to carve a Mexican empire out of the Western territories of the United States.

Marshall presided at the trial. He was completely impartial in his feelings toward the defendant. But he was a lifelong political enemy of Thomas Jefferson, the President who, as the Federalists alleged, had engineered the trial. Marshall had received his appointment as Chief Justice from John Adams just before the inauguration of President Jefferson—in order, ran the Republican gossip, "to entrench federalism in those regions where the long arm of the people can not reach." Ironically enough, the new President and the Chief Justice were cousins by birth. And during the course of the trial, Marshall proceeded to make things "very hot" for Cousin Jefferson. Burr had asserted that some of the evidence necessary to his defense was in the hands of the President. And he had demanded that the President be subpoenaed as a witness in the trial. Marshall sustained the plaintiff and thus bade fair to set a pretty precedent. "Only the King of England is exempt from giving evidence in common law," he asserted. "The American President can claim no exception to the rules." And he ordered a subpoena to be served on Jefferson. The country waited to see what would happen. Would Titan bend the knee to Titan? The issue was not long left in doubt. The President wrote a stormy reply to the subpoena. "The Constitution enjoins the President's agency in the concerns of six millions of people. Is the business paramount to this which summons him as witness in the behalf of a single one?" He threatened among his friends to arrest Marshall and to throw "the whole meddling court" out of the country. He fumed and fulminated. "Yet in spite of all this," one of Marshall's friends remarked to the Chief Justice, "I am sure your subpoena is constitutional."

"Yes," replied Marshall with a wry smile. "But read the Constitution again. I am compelled under its authority to *issue* the order. But there is no authority in the land that can compel the President to *obey* this order."

VII

FOR the rest of his life the stalwart descendant of the Earls of Scotland and of the carpenters of America brought his decisions to every man's fireside. And in this way he sealed a glorious verdict "on his property, his reputation, his life, his all." Every morning, with republican simplicity, the distinguished Federalist walked on foot to market and fetched home a basket of vegetables under his arm. In the rainy season he carried a faded green umbrella; and on sunny days he paused a bit by the wayside, placed his bundles on the ground, and rolled up his sleeves to pitch horseshoes.

And once, in the late afternoon of his public life, he descended from his judicial bench to the assembly floor. His native Virginia had called a convention to revise her local constitution. He was a very old man. But he stood beside the youngest delegates—"tall, in a long surtout of blue, with a face of genius and an eye of fire."

But the fire was burning low. He had been stricken by an ailment in the kidney. His years made the prospect of a successful operation doubtful. At any rate, the doctor told him, it would be a painful procedure.

"I have no anxiety over the result. I have not the slightest desire to live, suffering as I do."

MARSHALL

He emerged successfully from the operation. But he could not escape his suffering. The death of his wife, followed by the passing of his oldest son—one of ten children—hastened his final journey.

At the age of seventy-two he was asked to write an autobiographical sketch. He commenced with an apology. "The events of my life are too unimportant, and have too little interest for any person not of my immediate family, to render them worth communicating or preserving."

He finished his last lines and was laid to rest amidst imposing ceremonies and weighty tributes.

"What was there about him that impressed you most?" a female relative was asked at the funeral.

"His great humility," she replied.

JEFFERSON

Important Dates in Life of Thomas Jefferson

1743—Born in Albemarle County, Virginia.

1760-62—Student at William and Mary College, Williamsburg, Virginia.

1762-67—Studied law.

1769-75—Member of the Virginia House of Burgesses.

1775-76—Delegate to the Second Continental Congress at Philadelphia.

1776—Wrote the Declaration of Independence.

1779-81—Governor of Virginia.

1785—Succeeded Benjamin Franklin as Minister to France.

1790—Appointed Secretary of State in the first administration of President Washington.

1793—Resigned from Cabinet in protest against Hamilton's financial policy. Founded party of "Democratic Republicans."

1796—Elected Vice-President in administration of John Adams.

1800—Elected third President of the United States.

1801-02—Successful war against Barbary Pirates.

1803—Purchased Louisiana Territory from France.

1807—Declared embargo against French and British to retaliate against their impressment of American sailors.

1809—Retired to private life after two terms in the White House.

1819—Established the University of Virginia.

1826—Died at Monticello on the Fourth of July, same day as John Adams.

Thomas Jefferson

Thomas Jefferson
1743–1826

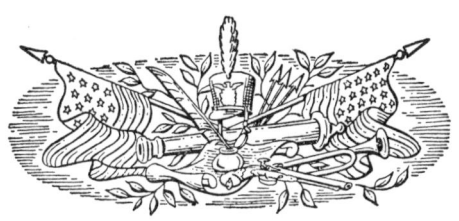

W<small>HEN</small> Jefferson ran for the Presidency (1800), the following "intimate portrait of his character" came from the lips of an opposition stump orator:

"Tom Jefferson . . . is nothing but a mean-spirited, low-lived fellow, the son of a half-breed Indian squaw, sired by a Virginia mulatto father, as is well known in the neighbourhood where he has been raised wholly on hoe-cake . . . bacon and hominy, with an occasional change of fricasseed bullfrog, for which abominable reptiles he has acquired a taste during his residence among the French at Paris, to whom there can be no question he will sell his country at the first offer made to him cash down, should he be elected to fill the Presidency . . ."

Jefferson, continued his opponents, was not only a half-breed but a scoundrel. "He has defrauded the widows and the fatherless children!" And—they added—he was not only a scoundrel but an atheist. "If Jefferson is elected, the ties of marriage will be dissolved, our wives and daughters will be thrown into the stews, our children will be cast into the world and forgotten. Can the imagination paint anything more dreadful this side of hell?" The women of America were warned, in the event of his election, to bury their Bibles in their gardens, or he would confiscate and burn them "in a general holocaust of infidelity."

And what was Jefferson doing all this time? Quietly sitting at home and compiling the *Morals of Jesus*. He made no effort to reply to the avalanche of accusations that had been let loose against him. "While I should be answering one, twenty new ones would be invented." It is a common human failing, he observed, "to transfer to the person the hatred they bear to his political opinions."

And they hated his political opinions for but a single reason. He believed in the protection of the weak against the strong.

II

ON HIS mother's side he was descended from the aristocracy; on his father's, from farmer and pioneer stock. His heritage therefore was twofold. He possessed a genteel love for beauty and a rugged respect for work. His father, a giant of a man morally as well as physically, had expressed three wishes for his son. He wanted Tom to have a strong body, a classical education and a gentle heart. Although he died when Tom was only fourteen, his three wishes were granted. For he had taken care to give the boy a proper start in life. He had taught him to ride hard, to study diligently and to put himself whenever possible "in the other fellow's place."

At seventeen he entered William and Mary College at Williamsburg—Jefferson referred to it as *Devilsburg*. Here, at the "headquarters of the aristocracy," he lived a studious, observant and somewhat aloof life. He took frequent rides into the countryside, in order to escape from the "drinking and the gambling and the fox-hunting gentry" into the homes of the farmers and the trappers dressed in their coonskin caps, moccasins and buckskin breeches. Much of his time he whiled away playing on his fiddle. He was very fond of his music. In one of his early

JEFFERSON

letters he complained that while he slept at a friend's house during the Christmas holidays, "the cursed rats" had eaten up his pocketbook, his "jemmy-worked silk garters and half-a-dozen new minuets I had just got." But then he added good-naturedly, "Oh, well, rats will be rats."

Good-natured, tall, rangy, soft-spoken, shy, freckled and blue-eyed and red-headed, young Tom Jefferson made a favorable impression on Dr. William Small, professor of mathematics at William and Mary. And Dr. Small, in turn, made a favorable impression on Tom Jefferson. "From his conversation," wrote Jefferson many years later, "I got my first views . . . of the system of things in which we are placed." Thanks to Dr. Small, Jefferson became acquainted with a "young lawyer named George Wythe" (who was later to be one of the signers of the Declaration of Independence). This man of inflexible integrity, wrote Jefferson, inspired within him a feeling of "warm patriotism" and a respect for "the natural and equal rights of man."

Such were some of the influences that went into the growth of the character that was Thomas Jefferson. Yet when he left college, his character was still in the formative stage. He couldn't make up his mind as to his future career—whether to become "a lawyer, a farmer or a lover." He settled his perplexity by becoming all three—he passed the bar, he enlarged his inherited farm, and he began to pay court to Rebecca Burwell. In the first two ventures he was fairly successful, but in the third he failed. Rebecca married his rival and for a time he plunged into the "dissipation of dancing and flirting" with the pretty girls at "Devilsburg." Jefferson, however, was not cast in the character of a devil's disciple. He enjoyed neither smoking nor drinking nor gambling. Before long he found himself out of step with the lightfooted denizens of the primrose path. He returned to his studies and his hard work. "His working day," we are told, "averaged fifteen hours." Although he had a great many servants, as became a landed aristocrat at that period, he always rose early to build his own fire in his bedroom. "For what purpose have our hands been given us if not for labor?"

Man is made for labor—and for love. At thirty Jefferson once more began to pay court to a young woman. And this time he was successful. On New Year's Day, 1772, he married the twenty-three-year-old Martha Skelton, and carried his "personable little bride" over the threshold of his newly-built home on the hilltop of Monticello.

It was a journey of a hundred frosty miles from her home in Charles City to Monticello. They had started in a phaeton but they had been obliged to abandon it and to go forward on horseback. The last stage of the journey was over a footpath two feet deep in snow. When they arrived at Monticello late at night, there were no servants, no fire, no food to greet them. But the bride and the bridegroom were happy in the warmth of a mutual affection.

This wedding journey to Monticello was symbolical of their wedding journey through life—sad and bleak and affectionate. And tragically short. Within ten years they lost three of their children. And then the mother followed them. Jefferson never married again.

III

SHORTLY after his marriage Jefferson gave up his law and went into politics. "The lawyer tries to take advantage of *bad* laws. The politician—or rather the statesman—tries to bring about the adoption of *good* laws." He regarded his politics as an adjunct to his farming. It is the business of the farmer to produce the proper food for the nation. It is the business of the politician to see that the nation is properly fed. The immortal *Declaration of Independence,* which Jefferson wrote, was but a step in this direction. This Gospel of Justice, based upon the philosophy of Plato, Locke, Montesquieu, Rousseau and Voltaire, "will enable the citizenry . . . to understand their rights, to maintain them, and to exercise with intelligence their parts in self-government." And in self-sustenance. His objective was not only

JEFFERSON

political and social independence, but economic independence as well. He was anxious to "prevent the accumulation and perpetuation of wealth in select families."

It was this spirit that animated his entire political life. He endeavored to transform America from an *aristocracy* to a *democracy*—from the arbitrary rule of *private wealth* to the equitable rule of the *commonwealth*.

Jefferson entered upon his political career with no personal hope of gain. Statesmanship in those days was not an attractive profession. It meant hard work, inadequate pay and neglect of one's private affairs at a time when such neglect might prove very costly. Many a well-to-do statesman found himself, at the end of his official career, financially ruined. This was to prove true in the case of Jefferson, and he probably knew it from the very start. It was with reluctance, therefore, that he accepted his political jobs. He would have preferred the uninterrupted enjoyment of "my family, my friends, my farm and my books." Nature, he observed in one of his letters, had intended him "for the tranquil pursuits of science." But the nation demanded his services, and Jefferson accepted his job as a public duty.

He first served his nation as the Governor of Virginia (1779). Plunged into his gubernatorial duties in the middle of the Revolution, he had little opportunity to display his constructive statesmanship. But even at this early period of his career he distinctly showed the democratic trend of his philosophy. He stood for free education, free libraries, religious tolerance, the emancipation of the Negroes, and the abolition of primogeniture —that is, the custom of handing down the entire inheritance of an estate to the first born. Through the abolition of primogeniture he hoped to keep the land of the nation divided into small parcels among a large number of people, instead of allowing it to pass into the hands of a few owners of enormous estates. "Ill fares the land, to hastening ills a prey, where wealth accumulates and men decay." Like the English poet, Jefferson wanted to see a land of distributed blessings rather than one of concentrated glory. And that was why the Tories—the men who held the reins of concentration in their hands—so heartily detested Jefferson. "He was the first American," as Claude G. Bowers points out in his *Jefferson and Hamilton,* "to invite the hate of a class."

It was as an enemy of the exploiting class that he was hailed in Paris when he arrived there as ambassador in 1784. He came there both as a student, and as a teacher, of revolution. He traveled over the countryside, observed the life of the peasants, sat with them at table to see what they ate, rested on their beds to note whether they were comfortable, and inquired into their ideas and their hopes and their fears. As a result of his study he came to the conclusion that "every man here is either the hammer or the anvil." And he threw himself heartily into the cause of the "ever beaten, ever resisting" anvils. The government of France, the governments of all the other European countries, he observed, are "mere devices for taking money out of one man's pocket and putting it into another's." They are "governments of wolves over sheep." He returned from France more firmly convinced than ever that "the republican is the only form of government which is not eternally at open or secret war with the rights of mankind."

IV

ON HIS return to America he was invited to enter George Washington's Cabinet as Secretary of State. He arrived in New York, the temporary capital, in the winter of 1790. And immediately he found himself with a first class fight on his hands. America had won the war, but it had not attained its independence. The country was now threatened by a new tyranny—the absolute power of wealth. The people who had shed their blood in the Revolution now discovered, to their dismay, that they had exchanged an English *autocracy* for an American *aurocracy*—a government of gold. There was an open struggle between the

JEFFERSON

producers of wealth on the one hand, and the *exploiters* of wealth on the other. Jefferson aligned himself on the side of the producers—the manufacturers, the farmers and the laborers—all those who used either their money or their hands to make goods. The other side had found their leader in Alexander Hamilton, who represented the interests of the exploiters—the monopolists, the bankers and the speculators—all those who used either their capital or their ingenuity to make money. Jefferson was an idealist, a dreamer ahead of his day. Hamilton was a realist, a perfect product of his day.

And, strangely enough, the idealist was triumphant over the realist. When the smoke of the battle had lifted, America was seen heading diffidently but definitely in the direction of democracy. And out of the fight emerged two opponents worthy of one another's respect. For both of them were sincere, and each of them respected the sincerity of the other. "Alexander Hamilton," wrote Jefferson of him some years later, "was disinterested, honest and honorable in all private transactions." As for his public acts, "Mr. Hamilton formed his conclusions after the most mature consideration . . . His principles were conscientiously adopted." And Hamilton, though given to invective in the heat of battle, retired after his defeat with the acknowledgment that America might have been put into less trustworthy hands than Jefferson's. "After all, Jefferson has . . . character."

V

JEFFERSON had character. This was clearly shown in his relations toward his servants. And in the relations of his servants toward their master. He is on his way to Monticello, returning home for a spell after a term of public service. The slaves, "all adorned in their Sunday splendor," are waiting for him at the foot of the hill. The carriage appears around a bend in the road. The slaves, singing, laughing, shouting, weeping for joy, rush forward to greet "Marse Jeff'son." Unhitching the horses, they pull and push the carriage up the hill. "Glory be you'se back home safe!" They kiss his hands, his feet, the hem of his cloak. And now they have arrived at the summit. Lifting their beloved master on their shoulders, they carry him in to a banquet fit for a king. "Only you'se no king, praise de Lawd, you'se a republican."

And it was as a republican—a believer in the public administration of the public affairs—that Jefferson was elected to the Presidency. Almost the entire press had fought against him. "With Jefferson holding the reins our civilization will be wrecked . . . It is dreadful to contemplate the results of his election."

But there was nothing dreadful either in the ideas or in the acts of President Jefferson. His first inaugural may be not inaccurately described as a political *Sermon on the Mount*. In this inaugural he outlines his policy as the servant of a free and democratic country. "I approach my task," he begins, "with those anxious and awful presentiments which the greatness of the charge and the weakness of my powers so justly inspire." For he realizes that his country, young and inexperienced and none too vigorous, is entering upon a career among nations "who feel power and forget right." Yet this country, he goes on, "is the world's best hope." The republican government is "the strongest government on earth."

And what is this republican government that he envisions in this inaugural? It is a government in which the will of the majority shall rule, the rights of the minority shall be protected, religious intolerance shall be abolished, labor shall not be exploited, justice shall be dispensed equally to all men, peace and honest friendship shall be maintained with all nations, and entangling alliances shall be made with none. And then he ends his inaugural with a simple and sincere prayer to the Infinite Power "to lead our councils to what is best, and to give them a favorable issue for our peace and prosperity."

In Washington—which had now become the seat of the government—Jefferson lived as peacefully and as simply as he had

JEFFERSON

lived at Monticello. The British minister to the United States, a sullen individual by the name of Merry, was scandalized one day when, calling on business at the White House, he was received by Mr. Jefferson in slippers and a dressing gown.

"I want to be known as plain Mr. Jefferson . . . I hope that the terms of Excellency, Worship and Esquire have disappeared from among us forever." He disliked official kowtowing and ceremonial formality. "We have suppressed," he wrote to Kosciusko, "those public forms and ceremonies which tended to familiarize the public eye to the . . . less democratic forms of government."

He was a plain man administering justice from a plain city. "Washington," wrote Gouverneur Morris sarcastically, "is the best city in the world to live in—in the future." One could travel through the city for miles, remarked Abigail Adams, without seeing a human being. Washington was indeed a capital of "magnificent distances." The streets were "unlighted swamps and forests." A party of Federalist leaders, returning home from a friend who lived only two miles away, lost their bearings in the "impenetrable blackness" and wandered all night over the wastelands. The inhabitants of the city were few and widely scattered. "From the steps of the Capitol one could count seven or eight boarding-houses, one tailor's shop, one shoemaker's, one printing establishment, the home of a washerwoman, a grocery shop, a stationery store, a drygoods house, and an oyster market." A symbol of American democracy at that period. And of Jefferson's character. Wide horizons, and an all-inclusive sympathy from printer to President.

Jefferson's two terms in Washington were on the whole uneventful. His great liberalizing work had been completed before his election to the Presidency. One of the events of his administration, however, was of the greatest importance. This was the Louisiana Purchase (1803) from Napoleon, who had previously acquired it from the Spanish king. The territory which now became a part of the United States is not to be confused with the present State of Louisiana. The land which Jefferson's envoys purchased from Napoleon, and which at that period went under the name of Louisiana, comprised an enormous territory reaching all the way from the Mississippi to the Rockies, and from Canada to the Gulf of Mexico. It more than doubled the size of the United States and it opened up the West to the flood of pioneers who poured in from the East. And all this territory Jefferson was able to get for only fifteen million dollars. It was "the most stupendous bargain in history."

VI

Jefferson retired from political life "with hands as clean as they are empty." He had always as a public servant refused presents, however small. For he was anxious, as he wrote to Samuel Hawkins, "to retain that consciousness of a disinterested administration of the public trusts which is essential to perfect tranquillity of mind."

And so it was with perfect tranquillity of mind that he departed from his public duties. "Nothing is more incumbent on the old," he observed, "than to know when they should get out of the way, and relinquish to younger successors . . . the duties they can no longer perform."

He returned to Monticello—and to financial ruin. Far from enriching himself at the expense of the government, he had paid out of his own pocket for the many social functions necessitated by his official duties. And his plantation, under the inefficient management of his overseers during his absence, had sunk into a deep morass of red ink. He now found himself burdened with a debt from which he was unable to emerge to the end of his days. In order to pay off a part of this debt, he was obliged to sell his entire library—a collection of books he had accumulated during a lifetime of diversified interests.

Yet in spite of his poverty he retained the catholic scope of his interests. Echoing the ancient Latin poet he said, "I am

JEFFERSON

a man, and therefore everything human is within my horizon." He devoted his declining years to farming, philosophy, science, art, music, literature, religion—and above all, education. For "education, the ploughing and the planting of human thought, produces the universal food of human progress."

With this object in mind he not only conceived the idea, but drew up the architectural plans, for the University of Virginia. His chief interests, he said, were intellectual and ethical rather than political. He requested that his tombstone should proclaim nothing of his career as Governor and ambassador and President. He wanted the inscription to mention only three things by which he hoped to be remembered: his writing of the *Declaration of Independence,* his fighting for Religious Freedom, and his founding of the University of Virginia.

And now, in his eighty-fourth year, he found himself face to face with the prospect of being turned out of doors. He was obliged to sell his estate in a lottery in order to save his "home in Monticello to lay my head in, and a plot of land for my burial."

Assured at last of his home and his grave, he was ready for the end—"that great adventure, untried by the living, unreported by the dead." He was tired, he said, of "pulling off my shoes and stockings at night, and putting them on again in the morning." He prayed for only one thing—that "the Benevolent Being who presides over the world" might spare his life until the next Independence Day.

And God heard his prayer. Thomas Jefferson died on the Fourth of July, 1826.

MADISON

Important Dates in Life of James Madison

1751—Born in King George County, Virginia.
1769—Entered the College of New Jersey (now Princeton University).
1777—Chosen member of the Virginia Privy Council.
1778—Delegate to the Continental Congress.
1783—Helped to put through bill for separation of Church and State.
1786-87—Drew up outline of the Constitution.
1787-88—As "Father of Constitution" helped to interpret it, along with Hamilton, in *Federalist Papers*.
1789—Entered House of Representatives. Introduced nine amendments to the Constitution—these amendments forming the basis for the Bill of Rights.
1790—Joined Jefferson in the formation of the "Democratic Republican" party.
1794—Married "Dolly" Todd.
1798—Became Secretary of State under President Jefferson.
1808—Elected fourth President of the United States.
1812—Led nation in war to protect American right to travel on the high seas.
1817—Retired from the Presidency.
1836—Died at Montpelier, Virginia.

James Madison

James Madison
1751–1836

H<small>E CAME</small> of the seed of planters and carpenters, men who cultivated the earth and carved its trees. His was the blood of the builders—the genuine aristocracy of brawn and toil. But when "Jemmy" was born, his family had risen from the *takers* to the *givers* of orders. Slaves now worked on the Madison plantation in Virginia. The minds and the bodies of the clan had undergone a mighty evolution. Jemmy was born with the flower of a great mind growing out of the soil of a little body. The old Madison planters had at last performed their greatest miracle.

He grew to manhood in Montpelier, at the gateway to the mountains. Here he spent the years of his maturity, and here he died. Throughout his life he carried within him the vision of Parnassus and the challenge to climb to the peak. At the summit he was certain he would find, side by side with the other nine Muses, a tenth Muse. In his early classical studies, he had received his first intimations of her. She had been frequently on the lips of Cicero and of Demosthenes. And soon he learned that she had stamped her golden fire on many ages and a thousand tongues. He felt her warming the heart of Plato, the mind of

Euclid, the political vision of John Locke. He found that she was the sun around which the world of Copernicus moved, the flame that animated Shakespeare's plays, the light that illumined the lovable soul of Donald Robertson, the eccentric tutor of King and Queen County who taught Jemmy his French "with a broad Scotch accent."

"My son," said Robertson, "she is an inspiration and a challenge. I call her *Free Conscience*." Madison named her—*Liberty*.

II

JEMMY grew up sallow and bashful and undersized, with a thin hesitant voice and the reddened eyes of a scholar. When he had finished his preliminary schooling, he saddled his horse and rode with his books to the College of New Jersey. Here he joined the debating society and wrote, in Latin, an argument to prove that "all men are created equal and are endowed with natural rights."

But while he wrote and studied and gathered more knowledge, the light of the candle revealed a complexion even more sallow. At his elbow rested the latest newspaper from Boston telling of a massacre. This was an age when all scholarship would be tested on the battlefield. Shedding of blood . . . He winced. He had so little blood to spare.

He listened to the outraged words of his companions—echoes that had reached the students of New Jersey from Harvard College which was at the seat of the trouble. "Dirty cringing ministers, pimps and puppies, Oxonian bigots." And other cries. "Throw down your books and fight!" Four years of education—and all for this! "A classical academy has been transformed into a wrangling marketplace." But he was a scholar meant for the age of the monasteries. Born too late! He must take sides with a musket for Locke or for Bossuet, for Colbert or for Adam Smith. This was a strange epoch for a man with a philosophical mind and with a distaste for fighting.

MADISON

At Commencement, along with the rest of the seniors, he wore a robe of American cloth—no true liberal dared to dress himself in goods imported from Britain—and he applauded loudly at the Latin salutatory on human society and at the moving hymn to America.

But when he returned home, a deep melancholy possessed him. Now—where to go, what to do? He had the mournful features of a good pulpit orator. But his voice would never carry God's messages to the back benches of the Church. He had no promising appearance for the courthouse. He mourned and moped and wrote letters to his college friends complaining of aches and pains. "I am too dull and infirm to look out for any extraordinary things in this world," he declared at twenty-one. But one of his friends pointed out to him the case of Pope who was as fragile as a spider and who yet outlived many of his strong contemporaries.

And, in the meantime, stirring things were afoot. A group of intrepid farmers had driven the King's Redcoats back from Lexington. All through the country rang the call to arms . . .

Jemmy sighed. *He* would never be fit for military service. He buried his head in his books. An attack of dysentery descended upon the plantation and carried off his brother and his sister and a company of husky blacks. All around him Virginians were dying from swamp diseases. And Madison showed surprising resistance.

The books piled high on his desk. Studying, theorizing, dreaming. He read political science, he learned Hebrew and Sanskrit. And he taught his younger brother and sister the beginnings of literature. It was glorious to settle down on the plantation. The air was bracing and quiet for his nerves . . .

And then one day he discovered new springs of vitality within him. He rose restlessly from his study. Oppression was at high tide around the world. Of what use was philosophy if it refused to march forward on two good legs? James Madison marched forward.

III

HE WAS elected, together with his father, to one of the committees organized throughout the land for the raising and the arming of the militia. And when Virginia had declared her existence as an independent state, he was appointed to the Governor's Council. Finally he was sent as a delegate to the Continental Congress at Philadelphia. Here he took a prominent part in the discussions. By virtue of his untiring perseverance and superior scholarship, he soon acquired a reputation as "the little machine of the intellect." He served on dozens of committees and had practically no time left for a personal life.

However, he did find the time to fall in love. He courted the young lady by proxy—sitting in the parlor and discussing political science and economic theory with her father. And then, when he ventured to speak to the lady herself, he found that she had spent the time on the porch giving her heart to a handsome young pastor. "I sincerely lament the misadventure that has happened to you," wrote his friend, Tom Jefferson. He, too, had been paying court to a young lady, and with equally disappointing results. But when Madison received the letter he had already forgotten the incident. He was deep in the study of the ancient Greek historian, Thucydides.

And now, in addition to his historical and his philosophical studies, he acquired a new interest—a passion for science. On his return to Virginia from the Continental Congress, he undertook the examination of an animal called the *Monax*. He measured its teeth and took its temperature, he gathered statistics on weasels, tested and criticized the prevailing theories about the central heat of the earth, kept a meteorological diary with the aid of a thermometer and a barometer, and studied the French physiocrats. On the battlefield men's emotions were running high. Yet the future of American society, he believed, would be decided by the reason of the few as well as by the emotions of

MADISON

the many. Once there had been an age of prophets. "But today the philosophers and the scientists will write the gospel for the brotherhood of man."

The war was now over. And Madison, bending over his portfolio like a little judge in his black coat, composed letters to people of influence the country over. A nation must be made. A government must be constructed on a basis no less philosophical than that of the Republic of Plato. "The purpose of all government is simple—to administer justice." Madison ran his pale fingers over the worn pages. A great and eternal idea—this Platonic translation of political theory into ethical truth.

But the eternal idea is only faintly and inadequately reflected in the fragments of antagonistic interests known as human society. The American government, Madison realized, would be appraised not for its philosophy but for its ability to protect American property. "If men were angels, no government would be necessary at all."

Madison had been born for this moment in the destiny of America. All his genius, all the experiences of his years of seclusion, all his researches into the complexities of history and of political science, were now summoned to the unique task. Almost single-handed in the spring of 1787 he evolved the essential scheme of our Republican government. A new thing under the sun. "The novelty of this undertaking," he wrote in one of his letters, "will immediately strike you."

Expressing the characteristically American distrust of a too powerful central government, he planned a Bill of Rights to check the abuses of excessive power. As a further check, he incorporated the basic policy of Montesquieu and of other liberal writers on political constitutions—he separated the executive and the legislative branches of the government. The "purse" and the "sword" must not be put into the same pair of hands. But the ultimate source of all power must spring from the consent of the people.

When the delegates of the people met in Philadelphia for the purpose of shaping the Constitution into a workable unit, James Madison, with characteristic conscientiousness, selected a seat in front of the President of the Assembly and took detailed notes of the proceedings. And in this way he left behind him a golden record of evidence for future historians. He watched the bickerings of the various interests—those of the small states demanding an equal representation with the larger, those of the greater states insisting upon a representation determined by the population; he jotted down the pleadings of the slave interests, of the manufacturers, of the ship builders, of the "bigwigs" of the various sections who felt that a strong central government would rob them of their own local prestige; and he concluded with an observation that might have come from the philosopher Locke: "The diversity of opinion among men of equal integrity and discernment is . . . a melancholy proof of the fallibility of the human judgment."

The final compromise which emerged from the session—the document known as the United States Constitution—was somewhat different from his recommendation, but it preserved the essentials of his philosophy. At any rate he was determined to defend it as his "own child." He argued eloquently against the combined opposition of Henry, Mason, Lee and Monroe in his native state, and he bombarded Governor Randolph with his pleadings to "join the Federalists for ratification." Together with Hamilton he wrote scores of papers discussing the new Constitution and the nature of the Federal government. And when the Federalists had won their fight, he prepared to stand for a seat in the legislature.

His friends urged him to run for the Senate, but he modestly chose the House of Representatives. For "this office would less require a style of life with which my finances do not square." Moreover, like most of the founders of the Republic he was convinced that the House would be the stronger political body. The Senate had determined to hold its discussions in secret, "and for many years it was not heard from."

MADISON

He campaigned in the snow and ice and spoke until "his tongue clove to his palate" and his nose grew numb with frostbite. And when the election was over, he mounted his horse and rode reflectively through the mud and the trackless forests to New York. A knight of the new crusade.

IV

DURING the first years of the Republic the scholar yielded grudgingly to the politician. His Utopia had been built to work with the impartiality and the precision of a machine. But soon he realized that this Utopia would be ruled, administered, and opposed by the prejudices and the passions of men. He thoroughly understood the principles of political science, but he had failed to grasp the perversities of the human mind.

He had deplored the factional spirit in England which divided the people into parties, "inflamed them with mutual animosity, and rendered them much more disposed to vex and oppress each other than to coöperate for their common good." But barely had he entered Congress when he saw the emergence of partisan interests within his own government. He had been shocked at Alexander Hamilton's partiality for "high finance." He himself was a country gentleman. His interests were not with the bankers and the manufacturers but with the planters, the farmers. These men needed a party of their own to protect them. And so he lent a hand in the formation of the "Party of the Republicans"—men who "were conscious that their power lay in the masses of the people."

This new party was organized for the express purpose of fighting against Alexander Hamilton's plan for a "financial monopoly." But it gained strength and color not through its domestic fight but through its involvement in the foreign crisis. The American Revolution had been the first wave in the upheaval of the common people throughout the world. The French Revolution, rolling ominously behind, was breaking into the second wave of this worldwide tide. Everywhere the forces of opposition were gathering to stem the rising waters. In America, as elsewhere, the people were divided into two camps—the revolutionists and the anti-revolutionists. Madison the scholar and Jefferson the dreamer, Republicans both, had taken their stand at the side of the French insurgents. When they learned that England had joined the continental European monarchies in an effort "to crush the newly-won liberties of France," they became inflexibly anti-British. And anti-monarchist. "All those throughout the world who fight for the same ideals are faced with the selfsame fate." They realized that the loss of a battle for Republicanism in the valley of the Rhine was a repulse for Republicanism in America.

Yet Madison had not lost his senses. He was ready to admit that the conduct of the French revolutionists was "rabid and distorted." But their cause, he insisted, was just. For it was the cause of liberty. He was amazed—he said—to see the Federalists aligned on the side of the British king, "on the side of might against right." When the Federalist administration had sent John Jay to negotiate a "profitable" treaty of commerce with the British, and Jay had returned "like a whipped errand-boy" to report the failure of his mission, the remark of a fellow Republican shocked Madison's fastidiousness but sweetened his ear. "Damn John Jay! Damn everyone who won't damn John Jay! Damn everyone who won't put his lights in his windows and sit up all night damning John Jay!"

The Federalists, alarmed at the military successes of the French armies in Europe and fearing an invasion of ideas if not of soldiers, had passed a law permitting the President "to deport any aliens considered hostile to the safety of the country and to imprison anyone spreading false or malicious statements about the American government." Madison, who felt convinced that the safety of the country was not at stake, construed the law as an attempt to destroy the Republican Party. He therefore introduced into the Virginia legislature a resolution declaring that

MADISON

any state acting on its constitutional right might refuse to obey such a law. In this championship of the right of nullification, Madison showed more eagerness than wisdom. For he thus inadvertently set in motion an idea which was later to develop into the vicious doctrine of "the right of secession." Madison was a good theoretical scholar, but a poor practical statesman.

A presidential election. The "little scholar" watched his friend, Thomas Jefferson, ride to victory at the polls. And when Jefferson had taken his oath, he appointed Madison his Secretary of State. Madison accepted the office, as he had accepted all his other public duties, in the selfsame spirit of theoretical idealism. "The destiny of a nation, like that of an individual, must be fulfilled by a strict adherence to virtue." Virtue, he should have added, backed up by the defense of an iron fist.

V

HE WAS past middle age now—bald and wizened and famous. And he still had left a little enthusiasm for private matters. Several years earlier his eye had been attracted to a charming young widow who ran a boarding house for Congressmen. Dressing himself one day in his most immaculate black suit—he never varied the color of his garb—he went to Dolly Todd and asked for her hand. She readily accepted the "great little Madison." He wrote to Jefferson briefly about his conquest. "I have had the happiness to accomplish the alliance which I intimated to you I had been sometime soliciting." Not a word about the charms of his partner. And they were manifold.

Dolly Madison supplied the color to the drabness of his personality, the fragrance of the rose to the odor of old parchment. Jefferson, who was now a widower, invited her to preside over the social functions at the White House. She acted the Queen, and she played her part in making her husband King.

For, as Jefferson's administration wore on, it became apparent that Madison was to be the heir. And he owed this "inheritance" not so much to his own politics as to his wife's popularity. Dolly

Madison was already the first lady of the land. It needed but little persuasion on the part of the people to make her "silent, scholarly husband" the first man.

It was in 1808 that James Madison was elected to this honor. The Inauguration Ball that followed his induction into the Presidency was a pageant of unequaled splendor. The President alone seemed to be out of place. He stood "lonesomely and lugubriously" in a corner amidst the music and the excitement, mopped the sweat from his brow for a few embarrassing minutes, and then stole silently upstairs to bed.

VI

MADISON had come into the Presidency at a critical hour. Throughout his life the world had been fighting. And he had tried hard to come to "philosophical grips" with the grim reality of force. He was fifty-seven now, and no longer a student entrenched in the ivory tower of his philosophy. He was the leader of a people actively seeking for the light. And he must show them the way.

Yet he still recoiled. In his scholastic years the black night of revolution had challenged him as he sat in the candle-gleam of his studies. And now again the night! England was fighting Napoleon's new order. The winds of strife were threatening once more to snuff out the light of his candle. President Jefferson had tried to keep the flame alive. But Jefferson was a dreamer in its fantastic shadows. "We are a peaceful and neutral nation," he declared, "and we must keep out of the European trouble."

But how to keep the British sea raiders from preying upon American ships engaged in their lawful trade? "By negotiation," said Jefferson. "We must plead with the belligerent countries to cease violating the rights of neutrals on the high seas. To respect neutral rights . . ."

President Madison looked gloomily ahead. All the negotiations of his predecessor had failed. And now, at such a moment, it was *he* who had been elected to assume the leadership. What could his nation do? Accept the verdict of the belligerents? Keep her ships off the ocean out of harm's way? Lower the American flag? Get out of the world for the comfort of other nations? Or sail the ships and fight!

His pacifism struggled with his reason. The Muse of Liberty lived high and lonely on the summit of Parnassus. The way to reach her had never seemed so dangerous as now. It lay through snow and ice and treacherous winds . . .

He asked Congress for a declaration of war against England. He had never worn a uniform, never led an army. Well, what did it matter? There must always be a first good fight to make the fighter. He put on a round military hat with a huge cockade —America's first Philosopher-Commander-in-Chief.

It was a long, hard task for an unwarlike nation to turn itself into a military machine. Except for a few fanatics from the West, the American people had no zest for the shedding of other people's blood. The Secretary of War was a "respectable physician from New England." Many of the senior officers of the army had never led a regiment against the enemy in action. Patiently the President sifted his personnel and, after many defeats, he found the men who led the army to victory. The people of the nation put their shoulders to the task, learned the business with American thoroughness—all but a handful of Eastern merchants who put their self-interest above their patriotism and who were to confess their shame before the war was over.

The British forces invaded the Atlantic coast, and set fire to the city of Washington. The President escaped to the woods and spent the night in a hut. But in the morning he returned and together with his people built a new city from the burning embers.

VII

Peace came to America. And once more there was a place for scholars. Madison retired to the tranquil routine of his plantation and his books. He received a letter from Noah Webster requesting his endorsement for a "new dictionary"; a paper from a scientist setting forth the new researches in phrenology; a pamphlet from a theologian "proving definitely the existence of God." Madison was once more in his element.

And as the years went on, he studied the Malthusian theory on population and the socialism of Robert Owen. He wrote letters to Jefferson with rheumatic and emaciated fingers and dreamed away his time in the fairy-world of old age. And yet his pen was ever ready for the service of his country. The American Credo must be brought home to the younger generations of soldiers and scholars and dreamers. The burden of his living and his thinking. This United Country! "Let the open enemy to our country be regarded as a Pandora with her box (of plagues) opened, and the disguised one as the serpent creeping with his deadly wiles into Paradise." But whether open or disguised, let no enemy of America ever be allowed to prevail!

MONROE

Important Dates in Life of James Monroe

1758—Born in Westmoreland County, Virginia.

1776—Left the College of William and Mary to fight in the Revolutionary War.

1780—Studied law under Thomas Jefferson.

1783-86—Served in Congress of the Confederation.

1790—Elected to the United States Senate.

1794—Appointed Minister to France.

1799-1802—Served three terms as Governor of Virginia.

1803—Went to France as envoy, together with Livingston, to negotiate the purchase of the Louisiana Territory. Then went as American Ambassador to London.

1811—Appointed President Madison's Secretary of State.

1812—Served for a time as President Madison's Secretary of War.

1816—Elected the fifth President of the United States.

1820—Re-elected during an "era of good feeling."

1823—Promulgated the Monroe Doctrine.

1824—Retired from the Presidency.

1831—Died in New York City.

James Monroe

James Monroe
1758–1831

James Monroe came from "plain" people. He had the Scotch and Welsh sincerity in his blood, but no "quality." There were grander lineages in Virginia than the parentage of James Monroe, of John Marshall, of Tom Jefferson, of James Madison—and even of George Washington who on one occasion, when he asked for the hand of the distinguished daughter of Wilson Cary, was met with the frosty rejoinder that "the young lady, if you please, is accustomed to ride in her coach." Generally speaking, the families with the greatest traditions in the past had little to do with the future of America.

Young Jim Monroe was lean and lanky. He rode expertly to the hunt. When the time arrived for his "learning," he joined the pupils at Parson Campbell's school and reluctantly came forward to receive his "lashes and his Latin." At sixteen he left Westmoreland County for Williamsburg and the College of William and Mary. Here he tried hard to stick to his books.

But it was no use trying. How could a young man read the history footnotes at a time when the main text was being written on the Williamsburg Green, at the Raleigh Tavern and in the

Boston Harbor? Old men were huddling together with frightened eyes; soldiers were marching through the streets; rebellion was stirring in youthful hearts; and over in St. John's Church a fiery Scotch-American, Patrick Henry, had thundered to an eager crowd, "Gentlemen may cry, Peace, Peace—but there is no peace!" In this year of 1775 a young man just couldn't concentrate on Caesar's *Gallic Wars*.

"We've got to learn to handle muskets. There'll be real fighting." In Boston, it was rumored, the students had thrown away their books and left off wrestling with their verbs. "This thing has gone too far to stop." Yet, strangely enough, some of the better dressed people here in Williamsburg still went to the theater and the races and the cockfights and refused to see the gathering storm. "Boston's war isn't our war," they said.

One afternoon young Monroe was startled to see a band of fellows from the swamps and the forests of the frontier parading with their muddy boots over the Williamsburg Green. On their chests they wore a legend in large white letters—"Liberty or Death." Everywhere the word went round, "Minute Men!"

Day after day they drilled quietly without causing any trouble. People were generally agreed that these Minute Men would never have to be employed in defense of the city. They would be sent to a few skirmishes in Boston hundreds of miles away. The war would never reach Virginia.

But news from the front became ever more disturbing. The citizens of Williamsburg—carpenters and blacksmiths, butchers and tanners and tavernkeepers—had begun to join the ranks of the Minute Men. They enlisted under the banner of the snake and the scroll: "Don't tread on me!" Even the Williamsburg gentry were recruited. And Monroe, along with the other university students, was enrolled as a "gentleman cadet."

He trained on the campus and listened to the stories of officers who had seen real action at the front, in Charlestown and on Dorchester Heights. Jim hadn't any illusions. He knew he would be in the thick of the fighting. Virginia had just declared, together with the other colonies, that her peace aims were nothing short of complete independence.

And it was not long before Monroe was "in the middle of it." He received a captain's commission in one of the ten companies under the command of William Washington, a relative of George Washington. He was in the party of scouts who fought in the Battle of Trenton, an aide-de-camp to General Stirling at Brandywine, Germantown and Valley Forge. Then he decided that he had had enough of it. He received his discharge from the army and took a trip to the South to collect military information for the Governor of Virginia. Finally he returned to Williamsburg and began to prepare himself for a role in the most novel experiment of government since the days of the ancient Greeks.

II

MONROE entered the Virginia Assembly and served as one of the delegates to the Continental Congress at Philadelphia. He took part in the debates on the adoption of the proposed United States Constitution—whose success he was at first inclined to doubt. A centralized government, he feared, would deprive the individual states of their independence. Together with Patrick Henry, he believed that such a government "squints toward monarchy." Might not a President once elected secure his reelection for life?

As the Virginia Assembly voted on the question of joining the Union, young Monroe was filled with misgiving. But when the vote was counted and the state had decided to join, he was ready like a good patriot to abide by the decision of the majority. "Young Monroe," observed his friend and counselor, Thomas Jefferson, "is a man to be trusted in the public service . . . He may lack the shrewdness of the politician, but he possesses the honesty of the statesman."

And Washington agreed with Jefferson. Jim Monroe was not a man of the world. Though married to the daughter of a well-to-do merchant, he was downright simple in taste and dress. He felt always a little embarrassed in the drawing room. He was too forthright to be regarded as witty. Yet in spite of these social defects—or rather *because* of them—President Washington selected him as a worthy representative of the republic of the New World to the republicans of the Old World.

Monroe was rather proud of his appointment as the American Minister to the People's Convention of Paris. It pleased him to note that the slogans of the French Revolution had been borrowed from the American Declaration of Independence. He set sail for Paris on May 28, 1794, and arrived there with the highest expectations. What an opportunity for a young man! He was the custodian of a New Testament of Freedom. The Secretary of State had given him a heartening message to the French. "Our President has been an early and decided friend of the Revolution." He would never, went on the message reassuringly, extend any sympathy to the British or to the other monarchies in their efforts to put this revolution down.

Citizen Monroe averted his eyes from the guillotine and presented his credentials. He received a ceremonious kiss from the French presiding officer—and a slap in the face from his home government.

For Washington had sent to France's mortal enemy, England, the Anglophile minister John Jay to negotiate a treaty of friendship and commerce. And while Monroe was reporting to the French about America's gratitude for the services of Lafayette, he was presented with the news of an Anglo-American treaty which apparently violated the spirit of the Franco-American alliance of 1778.

James Monroe, along with the French people, was amazed at this first display of large scale diplomacy upon the part of his republic. Then the amazement of a "sincere and artless soul" gave way to the blinded rage of a partisan enthusiast. He had been betrayed by the Federalists! He had been crucified by the Machiavellian politicians! And now Randolph, the Secretary of State, was ordering him to defend the treaty to the French people. Was this the sort of "idealistic" foreign policy evolved by the fathers of the American Revolution? Was it for this he had taken a Hessian bullet at Trenton?

He retired to his country residence in Virginia and sulked like Achilles in his tent away from the scene of the political battles. But gradually he began to perceive that the President had been in the right. Now that the harangues of the politicians had died away, the words of Washington stood out in all their noble strength. No permanent commitments to any single foreign interest. Absolute neutrality toward all. And the nation must assume the mastery of her own destiny, to decide "when we may choose peace or war, as our interest guided by our justice shall counsel." James Monroe, like a youngster reprimanded, was slowly feeling his way.

III

WHEN Jefferson became President (in 1800), he introduced an important modification to Washington's policy of neutrality. And he selected Monroe to serve as one of the agents in this historic step. Monroe, approaching middle age, had just completed a term as Governor of Virginia. It was a delicate mission on which he now found himself aboard a vessel—headed once more for France. He must negotiate, if possible, the purchase of Louisiana from Napoleon, who had "induced" Spain to give him this territory with the port of New Orleans. It was rumored that Napoleon was planning to bottle up the prosperity of the West by closing this port at the mouth of the Mississippi.

In view of this danger, Jefferson had taken a drastic step. His idea—and Monroe thoroughly agreed with him—was that no European nation with possessions on the North American continent must be permitted to transfer them to any other European nation and thus to change the balance of power within our shores. France must never be allowed to take Louisiana. The United States would buy the territory for herself. Jefferson was prepared to dig deep down into his treasury for the necessary funds—his strongest weapon of national defense.

The irony of the situation did not escape even the humorless Monroe. He was traveling to join Livingston in order that they might transact a business negotiation with Bonaparte, "the greatest highwayman in history." And what fuel for the fire-eaters back home! "What, put money into the treasury of Napoleon?" shouted Fisher Ames, the Federalist. "He will utilize this very money in the conquest of America after he has completed the conquest of Europe!" To which criticism Jefferson retorted: "Our interests demand the possession of America by Americans."

Napoleon met Monroe cordially enough. "You Americans did brilliant things in your war with England," he remarked. "You'll do the same again." He was willing to sell; for he was ready to invade England and he needed the money. Whoever held the Mississippi Valley, he had observed shrewdly, would some day become the most powerful nation on earth. The United States was a friendly nation. It would be good business to preserve this friendship.

And so the United States bought the Louisiana territory and thus doubled her national boundaries "without firing a shot." She had demonstrated to the startled nations of Europe a new formula for conquest—through business instead of bloodshed. In 1776 the Old World governors had been amazed by a New World experiment in government. And now the Old World diplomats were equally amazed at the New World experiment in diplomacy.

IV

MONROE's diplomatic duties had now extended to other parts of Europe. Carefully dressed in his "dark blue coat, buff vest, small clothes and top boots," he came to be regarded as the "popular Yankee trader" in several of the European courts.

But not at the Court of St. James. The hatred of England for its "truant child," the United States, had grown by leaps and bounds. The independence of America had seriously damaged the British commercial system which had hitherto monopolized the trade of her colonies and maintained her mastery over the seas. Now, at the turn of the century, the "miserable" little country in America "whose merchants had started the revolution for pieces of silver" were daring to send their merchant marine into all the ports of the world. British tonnage was steadily being decreased by the competition. The puny republic, "which didn't even have a respectable navy to back up her demands," was mouthing phrases about the "rights of neutrals" and the "freedom of the seas."

Monroe arrived in England, together with his wife and his two daughters, in the midsummer of 1803. He was greeted with a salvo of insults. On the occasion of his first state dinner he found himself seated at the foot of the table next to two ministers from petty German provinces. He was beside himself with rage. "James Monroe doesn't care where he eats his dinner," he wrote home, "but to find the American Minister put at the bottom of the table between two little principalities no bigger than my farm in Albermarle made me mad."

When a toast to the King was proposed, his blind fury had not subsided. Upon resuming his seat he accidentally thrust his wineglass into the fingerbowl and deluged the tablecloth with water. But then the Russian Minister rose and offered a toast. "A health and welcome to our latest comer, the President of the United States." Monroe acknowledged with a smile the compliment to his Chief Executive. He would carry on for Jefferson's sake!

Among his instructions was the order to negotiate a treaty with Britain concerning two sore points: America must be allowed to reopen her trade with the West Indies—a trade which had been closed by the British as a result of the Revolutionary War; and England must put an end to her practice of seizing American trading vessels and kidnaping American sailors.

England felt her high-handed rule of the seas justified. She was fighting a life and death struggle with the dictator Napoleon who had already made himself master of the continent and who was now preparing to invade the "tight little isle." England's chief weapon of defense was her powerful navy; and her chief technique of warfare against Napoleon's armies was the blockade of the continent. It irked her that America, a land with the same basic ideals and culture and blood as her own, should attempt to do "business as usual" with Napoleon by sending her ships to his ports of trade.

It was a ticklish situation, and it came to a head in June, 1807, when the British frigate *Leopard* overhauled and fired upon our frigate *Chesapeake* and took away four of her sailors. Had Jefferson declared war as a result of this incident, he would have had a united country behind him. But Jefferson abhorred war. He was a man who all his life had been consumed with a passion for peace. In the Cabinet of Washington, and now as President, he had studiously opposed all suggestions from the Federalists to build up an American navy and a standing army. These warlike steps, he had believed, would lead to imperialism abroad and to dictatorship at home. He wanted no conquests, no military establishment in a Republic.

Yet under the circumstances he felt constrained to enforce the rights and the dignity of the American nation against the insults of the British. He must insist upon the freedom of the seas. To do this he adopted economic rather than military measures. He imposed an embargo on all American ships—an act which resulted in biting the nose to spite the face. The merchants along the Atlantic seaboard protested bitterly against the ruin of their trade by their own government. "God help us," said John Randolph. "I do not wish another philosopher for President."

MONROE

Such was the state of affairs when Monroe tried to negotiate a favorable treaty with England. The treaty failed, the embargo failed, and Monroe returned to America a sadder and wiser man. England had refused to concede to Jefferson's request that she stop seizing our ships and our sailors. "If America wants concessions," declared Monroe, "she must fight for them." Just as the other nations had fought for them. "We must purchase our power with our blood." Jefferson, he felt, had merely postponed an inevitable war. And subsequent events proved that he was right.

V

MONROE returned to the governorship of Virginia—an unprepossessing little fellow, "owlish and ordinary, without dignity either of form or feature." His dress always gave people the impression of being "somewhat rusty." His neck-cloth was small, ropy, and carelessly tied. His face, weatherbeaten with age and care, was scarcely enlivened by his small, gray, glimmering eyes set deeply back in their sockets.

But there was a great deal of political wisdom behind those eyes. When Madison was elected to the Presidency, he appointed him as his Secretary of War. Monroe entered upon his duties in Washington firm in the conviction that the United States would never be respected by the Great Powers until she was prepared to enforce her principles by the use of arms.

And the time came, in spite of the unwarlike character of Madison, when America was compelled to go to war. When the British army invaded the Atlantic seaboard, Monroe set out on a personal scouting tour. Day after day he rode in the saddle, observing the movements of the enemy as they advanced toward Washington. And the resolve grew in his heart that no foreign nation must ever invade America again.

The British entered Washington and set fire to the White House and to several of the other public buildings. "I never saw a scene more terrible," wrote the French Minister to his foreign office. The following day the wind rose and spread the flames into a gale.

Madison never got over the shock of that August day. From then on he walked through the remainder of his life with a look of horror in his eyes—the look of a man who had prepared his nation only for peace—peace at any price.

VI

IN 1817 Monroe became the fifth President of the United States. In his inaugural address he reversed the pacifist policy of his predecessors. To those who objected that a program of national armaments would put too heavy a tax upon the public, he replied: "A single campaign of invasion by a naval force superior to our own, aided by a few thousand land troops, would expose us to a greater expense."

America had entered upon a period of peace and national unity. The Federalist Party had so discredited itself by its unpatriotic threats to secede from the Union that it had died a political death with the coming of the peace. The ringing words of Jefferson were now more true than ever. There were no longer any Federalists, any Republicans, only Americans.

America, secure within her own borders, was ready to turn her back upon the nations of Europe. But the nations of Europe were not ready to turn their backs upon America. The New World was too lucrative a prize for the predatory nations of the Old World. At the conclusion of the Napoleonic Wars the reactionary powers of Europe had banded themselves (1817) into what they called a "Holy Alliance." In reality it was an unholy conspiracy to stifle the independence of the small nations of Europe. And of America. A rash of revolutions had broken out over the brooding face of monarchy. The Greeks had risen in revolt, and the Italians and the Spaniards. And then the colonies of Central and South America, inspired by the example of free nations everywhere, had thrown off the yoke of the Spanish king.

And the Holy Alliance, alarmed over this universal trend toward democracy, tried to stifle it by tightening around it a noose of absolute dictatorship. So long as the aggressiveness of the Holy Alliance was confined to Europe, Monroe made no move to check it. But the European aggressors were beginning to throw greedy eyes upon the Republics of the Western Hemisphere. This sort of interference with the freedom of America, declared Monroe, must never be allowed.

As Monroe sat over his papers debating the course to take, his mind ran back over half a century of public service. What an evolution of foreign policy had taken place since the colonists had decided to be free! He had lived through it all—enlisted in the struggle for political independence, served as Secretary of War during America's struggle for the freedom of the seas. And now as President, he was ready to defy the threats of the military aggressors against the freedom of the South American colonies.

For Monroe realized that the American ideal and the American destiny were inextricably bound up with the ideals and the destinies of the rest of the world. The dream of isolationism had turned to ashes. Politically as well as morally the United States was part of the world scheme of progress. Through a foreign alliance with France the Republic had first won its independence. Morally the American Revolution had struck fire in the hearts of the French people and had swept them on to freedom, was sweeping the oppressed peoples everywhere into the ranks of the crusaders for freedom. And wherever there was a defeat for these freedom-loving nations in any part of the world, the United States as the source and inspiration of this freedom was bound to suffer. America as the leader of the New Order was destined to be the chief target of attack by the aggressors who from time to time would arise to reimpose the Old Order.

In addition to the independent spirit of the United States, there was one other obstacle that stood between the Holy Alliance and America. And this obstacle was the British fleet. England alone of the great European powers had refused to join the

Holy Alliance. And without the help of the British fleet, as Jefferson wrote to Monroe in 1822, all Europe combined would not dare to undertake a war against America.

President Monroe had grown wise with experience. Life, he realized, is a play of paradoxes. Though formerly a bitter enemy of Great Britain, he had come to understand that in spite of two wars there was a definite community of interests between the two countries. He was fully aware of the strategic power that would result from an American-British understanding. It would take courage to shake the hand of a former foe. Well, Jim Monroe had the courage.

It was therefore with faith in the British fleet that Monroe issued "the most important American document since the *Declaration of Independence*"—the world-famous *Monroe Doctrine:* "The American continents are henceforth not to be considered as subjects for future colonization by any European Power. We owe it therefore to candor . . . to declare that we would consider any attempt on their part to extend their system to any portion of this hemisphere as dangerous to our peace and safety." Furthermore, any effort on the part of the European Powers to oppress the South American States or to control their destiny would be viewed as the "manifestation of an unfriendly disposition toward the United States."

And thus there arose, as a challenge to the aggressive nations of Europe, a new Triple Alliance—the United States, South America, and Freedom.

VII

WHEN Monroe left office after two terms, America was definitely on the road to her destiny. The "lanky patriot in the cocked hat" retired to his shady country seat in Virginia. He paused a bit and fought a few delaying actions with time. A little more service before he was ready to be discharged—service as regent of the University of Virginia, local magistrate, member of the convention to revise the constitution of the state. And then, broken in health and funds, he began to write the story of his life. But he never finished the work. The living story was about over. Madison, Jefferson, Adams had all gone to their peace. And the bugle was calling to this new-old member of the "snuff-stained battalion," calling the hunter home from the hill.

JACKSON

Important Dates in Life of Andrew Jackson

1767—Born in Union County, North Carolina.
1780—Volunteered to serve in Revolutionary War.
1786—Admitted to the bar.
1788—Appointed Public Prosecutor in Tennessee "Bad Lands."
1791—Married Rachel Donelson.
1796—Elected first Representative from the newly admitted State of Tennessee.
1797—Appointed to the United States Senate.
1798—Elevated to the bench of the Supreme Court of Tennessee.
1801—Appointed Major General of the militia.
1815—Defeated the British at New Orleans.
1821—Governor of the territory of Florida.
1824—Received largest popular vote among four candidates for the Presidency. But failed to obtain a majority.
1828—Elected the seventh President of the United States.
1832—Frustrated plan of South Carolina to secede from the Union.
Re-elected President. Vetoed bill to renew charter of the Bank of the United States.
1837—Retired from public office.
1845—Died at the Hermitage, Tennessee.

Andrew Jackson

Andrew Jackson
1767–1845

He was Scotch and Irish, shrewd and fearless. His ancestors had migrated from Carrickfergus, North Ireland, to Twelve Mile Creek in the Carolinas. Here in the wilderness his father gave away his life clearing land and hauling trees and gathering food. Andrew was born a posthumous child in a neighbor's hut.

From the time he learned to walk he was a "nuisance and a trouble-maker"—the one disharmonious note among the children in his uncle's house. They sent him to a woodland shanty known as the Settlement School. They wanted him to be "a learner." But he enjoyed a fight better.

His fellow pupils knew him for a tough one. "I could throw him on the ground three times out of four," said a schoolmate, "but he never would stay throwed. Game, that's what he was." As iron-willed as anyone on the frontier. In his eyes there was a fire which turned the blue to steel at the slightest affront. And when he was angry he looked like "an avenging angel." His hair threw an ash-blond halo around his head. A fighting, two-fisted angel. He would thrash anyone and everybody for a principle. "He was the only bully ever seen who was not also a coward."

His folks decided they would make a Presbyterian minister out of him. They sent him to the "Academy"—a larger shanty than the primary school. Here taught the Reverend Dr. Humphrey who whitened at the words of his "swearing pupil." By heck, there was not another lad on the frontier who could string together so picturesque a combination of oaths as Sandy Andy!

Before he was fifteen, the Revolutionary War had reached the South. And some of the bloodiest skirmishes took place in Andy's neighborhood. His older brother, Hugh, gave his life in battle. Andy collected an arsenal of angry-looking weapons—long-bladed knives, tomahawks, stone clubs—and counted the months until he'd be old enough to join in the fighting. Especially he liked his scythe, with which he cut down the heads of the tall grasses near his home. He'd mow down the Redcoats this way, too, when he was a man!

One day a party of British dragoons had swept into his home town. A squadron rushed into Andy's dwelling, ransacked the furniture, crushed a baby's crib. An officer bawled to Andy an order to clean his boots.

The boy looked up calmly. "Sir, I'm a prisoner of war and claim to be treated as such." He'd black no man's boots.

The officer raised his sword and swung it down over Andy's head. But Andy deflected the blow and the sword slashed his cheek instead of his skull. Together with his brother Robert and with a number of other unfortunates he was thrown into prison. An epidemic of smallpox broke out among the prisoners. One of the victims who succumbed to it was Robert. Andy, too, had caught the disease. When he recovered, he received another shock—the news that his mother, his only friend in the world, had died while attending the sick and the wounded Americans aboard a British prison ship.

II

IT IS a tough and cruel world. But the lad is even tougher. Now at fifteen he is an orphan and destitute. None of his relatives

JACKSON

wants to take him in. He is growing too fast and developing too much muscle for a peaceful home life. He is a swaggerer and a fighter who expects no quarter from anyone. And no one may expect any quarter from him.

He got a job in a saddler's shop. But he left it for the "more exciting adventures of the big city"—Charleston. His relatives were only too glad to get him out of the way. They presented him with a horse for the trip. Now they were clear of all responsibility. He gambled and swigged and bet on the horses and the cockfights. And then he decided—of all things—to teach school.

He knew precious little about education. But the men and the boys around him knew even less. He cleared the backwoods and erected a schoolhouse. But after a spell he picked up his belongings and wandered on.

He couldn't stay put. Something was driving him forward. He set his horse toward Salisbury, Rowan County, seeking a teacher with whom to study the law. For out of the welter of his experiences and the turmoil of his feelings he had developed a legalistic mind. A lawyer can become quite a "big gun" in the settlements on the frontier. He can protect a squatter's land rights, and he can "spring a fellow free" from a murder charge.

He settled down with several other students in a "cross between a henhouse and a Negro cabin," littered with books, documents and pamphlets. But he didn't trouble the books much. In a society of rough-riders, horse sense alone would do well enough.

He paid his rent by winning large sums of money from his landlord at cards. The mere mention of his name brought a blush to the cheeks of the "respectable" ladies in Rowan County. At a Christmas ball sponsored by the social élite, Jackson appeared arm in arm with two women of the streets. "And why not?" he reasoned. "All women are created equal." The town bouncers showed the tall young "terror" to the door in an atmosphere of stunned silence.

Two years of this life, and Andy is ready for his license to practice law. He has left a bill of mounting debts in every tavern of the town and a record of exciting memories in every "disreputable" haunt.

Now he is ready for his first assignment in justice. He is offered a position as public prosecutor in the wildest section of the Union, five hundred miles from the nearest outposts of civilization—the Bad Lands of Tennessee.

III

MOST of the "legal" disputes in Tennessee were settled by an arbitration of the bullet. "The chief ambition of every man is to find a good pretext for the shooting of his neighbor." No respectable man's life was safe. This was an ideal country for Jackson. The majority of his clients were people to whom other people owed land or money. And Jackson rode out after the debtors and brought them into court at the point of the pistol. In addition there was the fashionable crime of mayhem—the biting of the nose and the ears of one's opponent. Jackson was magnificent in his duties as an officer of the law.

And while he thus earned his living, love came to him. He boarded at the home of an attractive young woman, Rachel Donelson, whose husband was insanely jealous of her and accused her of all sorts of intrigues. But for all that, Rachel was a "sweet and childlike girl who read her Bible regularly and smoked a long-stemmed clay pipe."

The chivalry of Jackson appealed strongly to Rachel. His sympathy for her unhappy married life overwhelmed her. Her husband had gone to Virginia to sue for a divorce. He was "raging mad" at the woman whom he accused of "communing with" the public prosecutor of Tennessee. But he preferred to defend his honor through the legal procedure of a divorce rather than to risk it in a duel.

Word reached Rachel from Virginia that she was a free

woman and when Jackson asked for her hand, she readily consented.

They were married in a simple ceremony at Natchez, Mississippi. Two years after their marriage they learned that Rachel's divorce from her former husband had only recently been legalized. Andrew Jackson bristled up and cleaned the barrels of his pistols. Would anybody make anything out of it? His friends advised him to get "married genuinely" now, to still the breath of scandal that was inevitable.

"By the Eternal, I've been married for two years and everyone around here knows it!" he shouted.

But wiser counsels prevailed. He underwent the ceremony a second time, and then threatened to shoot any "pickle-herring" who dared to capitalize on the humor of the situation.

In the meantime there were big political events in Tennessee. The population of the "Bad Lands" had grown materially and the settlers had begun to clamor for admission into the Union. Representatives from every county had assembled at Knoxville to draw up a constitution that would transform their territory into a state. Jackson was one of the delegates selected for the framing of the document.

Andrew is sitting by the fireplace, puffing at his pipe and poring over a sheaf of papers. Rachel's lips are puckered around the stem of her own clay pipe as she sits knitting a shawl.

"What are you reading, Mr. Jackson?" she asks him.

"Constitution, wife," he answers.

She looks up anxiously. "Ain't you well, Mr. Jackson?" In her cupboard she has several medicines for his constitution.

Tennessee was admitted into the Union and Jackson was chosen to represent it in the Congress of the United States. He bought himself a suit of broadcloth, plastered down his unruly hair, tied it into a queue with an eelskin ribbon and set out on horseback for Philadelphia, the "metropolis of urbane manners."

He created quite a sensation in the capital city. The polished Easterners stared with amazement at this "filthy democrat" from

Tennessee, with his pugnacious jaw and his arrogant stride. If this was a sample of the new West, they muttered, God help the future of the country!

Andrew Jackson had no greater admiration for the Easterners than the Easterners had for him. He longed to return to his cockfights and his two-fisted legal jousts. But his constituents wouldn't let him be. When his term as Representative was over, they elected him Senator. Rachel must continue to sit lonesomely by the fireside, waiting for her man to come back.

Finally he returned and was appointed judge of the State Supreme Court in recognition for his services "abroad." But he found the life on the bench too sluggish for his adventurous spirit. When he secured an offer to serve as major general of the state militia he fairly leaped at the chance. To be sure, his spirits were somewhat dampened at the fact that there was peace on Tennessee's borders at the time. But he hoped for the best. Sooner or later, war was bound to come. The quarrelsome human family would see to that.

And so he waited for his fighting chance. In the meantime he opened two retail stores—at Clover Bottom and at Gallatin. He sold hardware, gunpowder, whisky, salt and grindstones and received in exchange not money—for the Tennesseans distrusted the federal currency—but the more satisfactory currency of foods and goods, such as pork and wheat and potatoes, tobacco, cotton and skins. In addition to these activities, he built boats and he traded in horses and in Negro slaves. No matter what the polite society of Philadelphia might think of him, out here in Tennessee Andrew Jackson was regarded as a *gentleman* —an outstanding citizen of the frontier. Lord help anyone who questioned this!

And one man *did* question Jackson's claim to being called a gentleman. This skeptic, a handsome young devil of a rake named Charles Dickinson, was a political and business rival of Jackson's. Jealous of his success, he one day in his cups blurted out an innuendo about Jackson's irregular marriage to Rachel.

JACKSON

The idol of Tennessee challenged Dickinson to a duel. It was a rash thing to do, for Dickinson was known to be the best shot in the state. In the taverns the experts were laying heavy odds against Jackson's chances. Dickinson himself wagered five hundred dollars that he would kill his opponent at the first shot.

The day before the duel Andrew kissed his wife and told her he must leave on business. But he kept from her the nature of this business. All day long he rode with a party of friends to the meeting place in Logan County. He knew that Dickinson's aim would be true. "But by the Eternal, I too can aim." And then he added: "I'll get him even if he shoots me in the head!" At least there would be two graves instead of one.

He stops at the inn, eats a hearty supper, and enjoys a long smoke before he goes up to bed. In the dawn he throws a loose black cloak around him. Its folds, he trusts, will conceal the outlines of his long lank body from Dickinson, who will be aiming at his heart.

He meets his adversary. "Ready, aim, fire!" Dickinson's shot has been good. He smiles as he sees his opponent clutching at his breast. But then his face grows ghastly. His stricken adversary hasn't dropped to the ground. Instead, he takes deliberate aim and pulls the trigger of his gun.

There is no explosion, and Dickinson breathes more easily. Jackson's pistol has been half cocked.

There is a look of derision in Dickinson's eyes. He is about to say something, but his words remain unspoken. For Jackson has now fired his pistol. A spurt of blood from Dickinson's mouth, and his seconds carry away his dead body from the field.

Andrew Jackson walked to the inn with his friends. One of them noticed that a trickle of blood was dripping from his shoe. Jackson smiled. "Yes, he pinked me a little," he confessed.

They took him to his room and pulled off his clothes. Two of his ribs were shattered. The bullet had lodged near his heart. But not near enough to prove fatal. "He missed me," laughed Jackson, "by a fold of my loose black cloak."

To the end of his life Andrew kept a pistol over the mantelpiece in his parlor. And when any visitor looked at it, he took the pipe from his lips long enough to say casually, "That's the gun that stopped an evil tongue."

IV

THE Indian tribes in the West, goaded by the British in 1812, had broken out in mass hostility against the frontier settlements. Andrew Jackson, without waiting for the orders of the War Department, gathered the Tennessee militia around him and started on an expedition of vengeance. His pistols were his "passports." His arm was in a sling and he was weak from the loss of blood—which he had suffered in another of his interminable brawls. It had cost him physical agony to get out of his bed. The soldiers worshiped him for his courage. "Old Hickory" was their nickname for him from that day on.

These soldiers of Jackson's were reckless and ruthless fighters. They were bent upon exterminating the Creeks who had been massacring the Whites in Alabama. The battles of this Creek War were holocausts of murder. In village after village the "Tiger Men" left not a single warrior alive. As Jackson rode through one of these devastated villages he came upon a little papoose clutched tightly in the embrace of its dead mother.

He picks up the papoose and rides with it to his tent. He feeds him milk, wraps him in blankets, and watches over him like a father until the Indian wars are over. Then he takes him home to his wife, Rachel, and brings him up as a playmate to his son.

But Andrew is not often tender. Not when he faces an army of sullen snarling men who threaten to mutiny. Tired, disgusted and half starved on their rations of roasted acorns, they have started against his orders to march back home. Whirling around on his horse and pointing a gun at the rebels, Jackson shrivels them into submission with an outburst of invectives. "The first blackguard who stirs a foot marches straight into hell!"

The rebels cringe before his look. They growl and sulk but

dare not turn their steps homeward. For they know that he means what he says. What they do not know, however, is the fact that the gun which he has pointed at them was not loaded.

He marches them to New Orleans where he hears that the British will try to effect a landing for a drive up the Mississippi. His swashbuckling campaign in the West has gained him a sensational reputation, and when he enters New Orleans he is wined and dined by the fashionable society. "Huzzah for General Jackson!" The tables "groan under the weight" of the dishes prepared by the French cooks in his honor. But the General pushes aside the viands and calls for a bowl of hominy.

The British are now approaching the Queen City of the South. They are bent—so it is rumored—upon booty and beauty. But Old Hickory takes an oath that the Redcoats will never reach New Orleans except over his dead body. Up go the fortifications. Bales of cotton are rolled from the warehouses and piled into bastions. One of the owners rushes over to Jackson's quarters loudly complaining that the cotton which has been commandeered is his property. The General thrusts a gun into his hands. "Since this is your property, sir, it is your business to defend it. Get into the ranks!"

In the meanwhile the Federal Government had sent commissioners to meet the British at Ghent. Negotiations to end the war had been under way for some time. And finally they were concluded. Peace had come. But neither the commander of the British nor Andrew Jackson knew anything of this peace as they prepared for the battle. Such was the penalty of slow communication in the days before the Atlantic cable.

The British charged the American fortifications with drawn muskets and left over seven hundred killed and fourteen hundred wounded within a quarter of an hour. For them it was relatively the bloodiest battle of the century. The Americans suffered eight killed and thirteen wounded.

When the announcement of the armistice reached New Orleans, Andrew Jackson was furious. By the Eternal, he would like to hang all those meddling politicians who made peace just when he was getting into his stride!

Crestfallen, he disbanded his army; cheerlessly he received the plaudits of the multitude. There were no more Creeks to kill. The British were departing. He had nothing left to do. If only the Government gave the word, he'd march into Florida, and take it from the Spaniards. "By the Eternal, that's an idea!"

V

OLD HICKORY had now become the Hero of New Orleans. The entire country gave him a roaring welcome. He sent a letter to Rachel enclosing a piece of chipped bone to remind her of his wounded arm which was now rapidly healing. And then he set out for Washington. In Virginia old Tom Jefferson invited him to a banquet. In the White House Dolly Madison presided over a celebration in his honor. But for all his prestige he still hadn't learnt to spell, or to speak grammatically. He wrote a letter of advice to his nephew, a young man who had just entered West Point. "You are now—amonsht Strangers, where it behoves you to be guarded at all points. Amonsht the vituous females, you ought to cultivate an aquaintance . . . and shun the intercourse of the others as you would the society . . . of a base charector. . . ."

But why worry about his illiteracy? The common man throughout the United States had learned to respect and love him. And he had become a powerful influence in federal politics. Ignoring the War Department and the State Department he marched his troops into Florida and drove the Spanish garrison out of St. Marks and the Spanish governor out of Pensacola. And then, just for good measure, he hanged two Englishmen whom he accused of being spies. And the government at Washington didn't dare to court-martial him, so great was his popularity with the people. A man on horseback!

In the meantime, Spain had resigned herself to the loss of the

JACKSON

Florida territory. She consented to sell it in good grace and collected indemnities. And Jackson was appointed Governor of this new acquisition. But he was definitely out of his element in civil office. He handed in his resignation.

It was the sixth administrative job from which he had resigned. President Monroe was at a loss as to what to do with this "trouble shooter." He considered giving him the portfolio as minister to Russia and asked Jefferson's opinion.

"My God," exclaimed the aged sage, "if you do this you will have a war on your hands inside of a month!"

But awaiting Old Hickory was another destiny far removed from the ambassadorship to Russia. The shrewd political friends of the homespun soldier had no less an aim for him than the Presidency of the United States. Was not Andrew the incarnation of the common man, the very image of the millions of uncouth and unlettered pioneers who dreamed of fighting their way to glory with their own right arm? The ideal candidate for the People's President!

As for his illiteracy, his managers observed, they would edit his speeches and his statements to the press. They would "polish his eccentricities, keep his mouth shut on every social occasion, restrain his impulses. . . ." There was a great deal of work to be done before they could succeed in hoisting Andrew Jackson from the people's shoulders into the White House.

And in their first attempt (in 1824) they failed. To be sure, Andrew Jackson had received a plurality of the popular vote over John Quincy Adams, Calhoun, Crawford and Clay. But he failed to get a majority of the electoral votes. The election was thus thrown into the House of Representatives. Henry Clay yielded in favor of Adams, the Eastern Conservative, and Jackson was thus "cheated"—as his friends alleged—out of the Presidency.

This "conspiracy against the will of the people" only served to enhance the popularity of Jackson. Over the country like wildfire swept the insinuation—"a corrupt bargain of politicians"—for Adams had appointed. Clay as his Secretary of State. The country was divided into "Adams men" and "Jackson men." When Adams was sworn into office, it was amidst a tempest of hisses and catcalls. Wherever Adams turned, whenever he laid his head upon a pillow, the jeers of the multitude thundered in his ears. The Forgotten Man had made a vow never to forget. In 1829 John Quincy Adams relinquished his office, a nervous and broken man, and Andrew Jackson rode triumphantly to the White House on the crest of a landslide vote.

But the victory was costly. The press of the East had poured forth a slanderous broadside in an effort to keep the "honest savage" from occupying the President's chair. The editors had revived the old whispering campaign about his peculiar marriage to Rachel. People had smacked their lips and whispered "adultery!" And Rachel's heart had been fatally wounded. Not long after the election she found a resting place in the family cemetery; and together with Rachel, all the gentleness of Andrew Jackson was laid to rest. He stood with wet eyes at the burial of his wife and of his heart. He was hungry to sit down with her once more in the long shadows by the fireside of heaven, but first he must attend to some unfinished business ... Grimly he looked toward Washington.

VI

WHEN President Jackson galloped into the White House, a whole tornado whirled in along with him. His inauguration was the most amazing in American history. The prim and stately minuets of the earlier inaugural balls were swept away in the hurricane of a frontier carnival. Jackson was the man of the people, and the people came to Washington to rejoice. They pushed their way past the doorkeepers into the White House; they stormed the punch bowls and broke the glasses and spilled the contents on the floor; they shuffled over the carpets with

JACKSON

their muddy boots; they leaped on the damask chairs to have a look at their President; and they sang and shouted and rejoiced that a new day had dawned for the common folk.

And, indeed, a new day *had* dawned for them. One of Jackson's first official acts was to dismiss a whole cabinet because their wives had stuck up their noses at Peggy Eaton, the wife of the Secretary of War. Peggy was the daughter of a tavern keeper and therefore taboo in Washington society. But Jackson was more interested in humanity than he was in society. He remembered the injustice that had killed his own wife. He therefore took up the cudgels for Peggy Eaton, scandalized the higher social circles and won for himself the adoration of the scorned and the oppressed throughout the land.

He had struck a vigorous blow against snobbery. But now he found himself with another, and more serious, fight on his hands. A civil rebellion was brewing in America. The people of South Carolina were displeased with the federal tariff laws (1832) and they threatened to secede unless these laws were nullified. But Jackson, the queller of mutinies, would hear of no such thing. "The laws of the United States must be executed," he declared. For any state to disregard these laws, he went on, "is disunion; and disunion by armed force is treason." And, as a warning that he meant business, he dispatched seven revenue cutters and a ship of war to South Carolina with orders that if the gentlemen of that state persisted in their disobedience of the law, they were to be "hanged by their elegant necks."

This prompt and decisive action on the part of Old Hickory prevented a war of secession in 1833. South Carolina saw the light and returned to the fold.

Once more the strong man had won. But the malcontents continued to grumble against his "high handed actions." They called him "demagogue"—"dictator"—"czar." Very well, he retorted, the czar would fight against the emperor. Emperor Nicholas Biddle, head of the United States Bank, controller of the United States finances and manipulator of the invisible strings of the United States government. Under the influence of "Emperor Biddle" America had become a plutocracy—the very thing that Thomas Jefferson had feared and fought against. And now Jackson took up the fight and carried it to a finish. The old charter for the bank was to expire in 1836; and as early as 1832 the Board of Directors had applied for a recharter. They paved the way for favorable action by means of extensive loans—Jackson called them bribes—to fifty-nine members of Congress. They also made "good will loans" to the leading newspapers in order to insure a friendly press. The plan worked. Congress voted in favor of the recharter. But the Board of Directors had reckoned without Jackson, who promptly and emphatically vetoed the bill. In this veto he made it clear to the "farmers, mechanics and laborers" of America that he was "unalterably opposed" to any law which would "make the rich richer and the potent more powerful."

The veto created a sensation. An avalanche of editorials, full of fire and brimstone, descended upon his head. But Old Hickory stood firm. In 1832 he came up for re-election; and, in spite of a hostile press, he was swept into office by the overwhelming acclamation of the people.

But Jackson was not yet through with his fight. Immediately after his re-election he withdrew all the government deposits from the United States Bank. It was like withdrawing water from a fish. The bank gasped and floundered and expired.

The fight was over. The financial monopoly was smashed. But so was the strength of Andrew Jackson. He had spent too many months in the saddle sloshing through the malarial swamps at the head of his militia, he had suffered too many festering wounds in his duels and his battles, he had wasted too many sleepless nights in the taverns. And finally he had lost the residue of his vigor in the death of his wife. There was nothing but the backbone of an iron will that kept his head from drooping over his shoulders. During the last years of his office his lungs had been slowly bleeding to death. Tuberculosis.

JACKSON

Yet he remained active. He took trips through the country to contact the people, to learn how they felt about him, to discover whether their lives had been made in a little measure happier for his endeavors.

In due course he completed the "reign" which he had never wanted, which he had accepted only at the solicitations of his friends. He was happy now to retire to the affections of his constituents in the West—the untrained idol of an untrained folk.

VII

AGAIN and again Andrew Jackson had promised his wife that he would join the Church. But thus far his life had been too full of fights and exasperations for the fulfillment of such a promise. Now at last in the quiet of the hermitage he took long walks with the parson and discussed the plans for his religious conversion.

"General," remarked the parson on one of these walks, "there is a question which it is my duty to ask you. Can you forgive your enemies?"

Old Hickory bent his head in meditation, and then he looked up with his eyes flashing fire. "By the Eternal, I am not *that* old yet!"

Finally he softened. He was willing to compromise. "Well, I'm ready to forgive the whole crew of them collectively, but not as individuals. No, sir, not as *individuals.*"

The good parson smiled but accepted him nonetheless into the Presbyterian Church of his fathers.

And when the General was ready to depart for his final High Office in the West, there was an ardent prayer on his lips: "May I find that there, too, the Good Fight will go on!"

CLAY

Important Dates in Life of Henry Clay

1777—Born in Hanover County, Virginia.
1797—Admitted to the Virginia bar at Richmond.
1806—Appointed to the United States Senate.
1811—Chosen Speaker of the House of Representatives.
1815—Negotiated the Treaty of Ghent.
1824—Delivered oration on the "American system." Defeated in the election for the Presidency.
1825-29—Served as Secretary of State under John Quincy Adams.
1832—Defeated in the election for the Presidency.
1833—Introduced a compromise tariff bill checking the threatened secession of South Carolina.
1840—Defeated in the nomination for the Presidency.
1844—Defeated in the election for the Presidency.
1848—Defeated in the nomination for the Presidency.
1850—Introduced "Compromise" on the slavery question.
1852—Died at Washington.

Henry Clay

Henry Clay
1777–1852

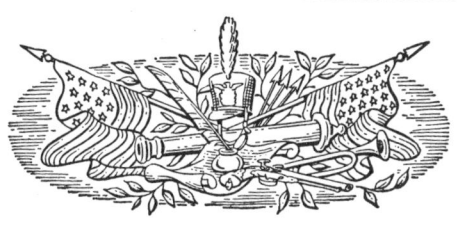

JUNE, 1781. Henry was four years old. His father had been buried the day before. At the Clay homestead in Hanover County, Virginia, there was madness added to mourning. For Tarleton's British raiders had just swept into the town. They were ransacking the Clay household, ripping the pillows, scattering the feathers, breaking the furniture, stealing Mrs. Clay's white satin wedding-gown. "You wicked men!" cried Henry, only to be stopped by the threats of one of Tarleton's drunken soldiers.

Disappointed in their fruitless quest for "treasure" within the household, they went outside and violated the newly-dug grave of Henry's father. In vain. No buried treasure was to be found. Tarleton turned to Mrs. Clay and with an awkward attempt at an apology emptied a purseful of coins upon the ground. She didn't refuse the "compensation" for the damage. But no sooner were the raiders out of sight than she scraped up the coins into her apron and threw them into the fire. "This, my children, is the way to treat the gifts of the enemy!"

II

He was born into a dramatic age, this seventh child of a fighting mother. His father, the Reverend John Clay, was a successful preacher. Henry inherited his mother's backbone and his father's tongue. "This youngster," said his stepfather, Henry Watkins, "should make a good lawyer."

And young Clay agreed with him. In the daytime he worked and perspired on the farm at Pamunkey Creek—Pamunkey is an Indian name meaning "the place where we take a sweat"—and at night he went into the cornfields and declaimed Patrick Henry's *Give Me Liberty* to an audience of crickets and stars.

At fourteen his stepfather placed him as a clerk in Dick Denny's retail store, near the Richmond Market. "Here you can earn money and meet people—two necessary preliminaries for a good legal training." And the following year, when Henry Watkins together with his wife and her fifteen children moved out to Kentucky, he placed his stepson Henry into the keeping of his friend Peter Tinsley, clerk of the Richmond High Court of Chancery. Mr. Tinsley not only hired young Clay as a deputy clerk but recommended him to the good graces of one of Virginia's leading lawyers, the seventy-year-old George Wythe.

It was an auspicious moment for Henry Clay. The aged lawyer's fingers were stiff with rheumatism, and he needed an amanuensis. He asked Henry for a specimen of his penmanship. "Good," he said, when he saw the clear and legible script. "Come into my office evenings and copy my briefs."

"Yes, sir. And may I ask, sir, if you will teach me the law in return?"

"Glad to!"

It was a mutually pleasant relationship. "Henry," remarked Mr. Wythe a few months after their first meeting, "you have given me a new hand."

CLAY

"And you, sir," replied young Clay, "have given me a new head."

III

WHEN Henry appeared among his fellow clerks at the High Court of Chancery, he created a mild sensation. Not because of his brilliant mind, but because of his bizarre appearance. Tall and lean and awkward, he was a caricature of a young man in his pepper-and-salt Figginy suit of silk and cotton, with a coat-tail standing out behind "at an angle of forty-five degrees," and a head protruding in front with amazingly small eyes and an amazingly large mouth. But Clay had no time to worry about the peculiarity of his appearance. He was too busy absorbing knowledge, attending to his business, watching the Richmond celebrities—Jefferson, Monroe, Marshall—as they pleaded their cases in the Court House.

And the celebrities, thanks to the kindly offices of George Wythe, watched Henry Clay. "This clumsy young farmer has the makings of a fine man." And so, encouraged by his "admired admirers," he continued his studies until he was ready (1797) to pass the bar. Accepted in the social circles of Richmond, he had lost something of his adolescent gaucherie. People no longer appraised him at his face value. They looked beyond his homely eyes and his "horsey" mouth—and they found underneath, a big and generous heart. He had developed into a political idealist and Jeffersonian Republican, a sympathizer of the French Revolution and a believer in the doctrine of popular rights.

And a superb speaker. His voice was like a musical instrument of many strings. He could attune it to all sorts of emotional chords—denunciation, scorn, anger, pity, persuasion, tenderness, mirth. This "old young man" of twenty-one—his hair had grown prematurely gray—looked about for a likely place to hang out his shingle. A place that would serve as a good theater for his impetuous, generous and ambitious histrionic talents. And he decided upon Kentucky, the wilderness on the frontier where men were pugnacious and lawsuits plentiful.

He became a favorite among the Kentucky settlers. For he loved his legal brawls and his brandy and his cards. And, above all, his fellow men. He was the life of the rough-and-tumble social gatherings of the frontier. At one of these social functions, when the dinner had ended and the bottle had circulated freely, he jumped upon the table and performed a dance along its entire stretch, a distance of sixty feet. The next morning he paid without a murmur the bill of $120 for the glass and china he had sent crashing to the floor.

And without a murmur, too, he paid his friends' debts and signed their bad notes whenever they came to him for his aid.

But he could afford these luxuries. He had married into a wealthy family, and he was being besieged with more cases than he could handle. Not only civil suits dealing with his father-in-law's business, but murder trials. He had acquired a reputation as one of the best criminal lawyers in the States. It was said that no frontiersman accused of murder and defended by Henry Clay was ever sentenced to death. "The justice of Kentucky may be sometimes blind, but it is never deaf to an eloquent plea." On one occasion, when he had brought about the discharge of a man accused of an unusually atrocious murder, he replied to the murderer's thanks with the remark: "Ah, Willis, poor fellow, I fear I have saved too many like you, who ought to be hanged."

As a general rule, however, Henry Clay refused to plead for a man unless he himself entertained a reasonable doubt as to the man's guilt. This was certainly the case when he undertook to defend Aaron Burr against the charge of conspiracy to overthrow the government. Before he assumed the burden of the defense, Clay had demanded from Burr a pledge to the effect that he "harbored no schemes hostile to the peace or union of the country." And Burr had unequivocally replied: "I have no design nor have I taken any measure to promote a dissolution of the Union, or a separation of any one or more states from the residue . . . I have no design to intermeddle with the Government or to disturb the tranquillity of the United States . . . I do not own a musket nor a bayonet, nor any single article of military stores, nor does any person for me, by my authority or with my knowledge . . . I have thought these explanations proper . . . to satisfy you that you have not espoused the cause of a man in any way unfriendly to the laws, the government, or the interests of his country."

Yet in spite of this conclusive evidence that he had undertaken Burr's defense in good faith, the gossip-mongers didn't fail to link Henry Clay's name with treason. This breath of scandal came near to ruining his legal career. And his political career, too. He had just been elected to the United States Senate, and his political opponents tried their best to "oust the young cockerel of an upstart from his high perch."

But he weathered the storm. Throughout his life he displayed a genius for provoking tempests and riding them out. He managed to sail safely into the harbor of his every ambition—save one, the Presidency of the United States. The tragedy of his life was his too great ambition. The gods, as the Greek dramatists have pointed out, are displeased with mortals who are overambitious. They compel them to blunder into their own defeat. In his effort to gain too many friends, he gained too many enemies. For nobody knew just where he stood. His social philosophy was like a feather in the crosscurrents of American politics. He allowed these currents to sweep him in every direction. But they never swept him into the one place where he was most anxious to go—the White House.

IV

It was a long and winding course that he entered in his quest for the White House. Again and again it turned back upon itself. His first public speech was in behalf of the Negro slaves. He advocated their emancipation. His next political gesture was to condemn the Sedition Act—a law passed at the instigation of the Federalists and designed to curtail the freedom of speech and of the press. He seemed to be headed definitely in the direction of American liberalism. "The Senator from Kentucky," observed John Quincy Adams, "is quite a young man—an orator—and a republican of the first fire."

But as Clay grew older, he became blinded with ambition and lost his republican way. He went from the Senate to the House of Representatives. For he regarded his new political job as a better jumping-off place for the Presidency. He had been promised the Speakership of the House—an eminence from which his voice would be heard throughout the land.

And when he became Speaker, he made his voice heard in a cause which to many seemed ignoble. Proclaiming himself as the "spirit of Young America," he drove his country, with the impetuosity of a thoughtless eloquence, into the whirlpool of war. "It may be said without exaggeration," writes Carl Schurz in his *Life of Henry Clay*, "that it was his leadership which hastened the War of 1812." Clay's motive for the war was a desire for aggressive expansion, the conquest and the annexation of Canada. "The conquest of Canada," he insisted, "is in your power. Is it nothing to acquire the entire fur-trade connected with that country?" He was an emotional youngster led astray by a reckless ambition. He was anxious to see himself and his country grow bigger. By instinct he was not so much a militarist as an opportunist. He generally advocated that cause which at the moment seemed to promise him the greatest chance for personal glory.

Yet he was not dishonest. On the contrary, he honestly and sincerely believed that his own destiny was inseparably intertwined with the destiny of his nation. He felt himself divinely appointed to lead his country to greatness through his own greatness. "I love true glory," he exclaimed in one of his speeches before the House. "It is this sentiment which ought to be cherished; and in spite of cavils and sneers and attempts to put

CLAY

it down, it will finally conduct this nation to that height to which God and nature have destined it."

He felt that he, and he alone, would be able through his superior wisdom to bring his nation to the desired height. He was a politician with a Messianic complex. Unfortunately he possessed the one weakness that was to prove fatal to his Messianic hope. He had a positive genius for choosing the unpopular side on almost every question.

He had chosen the unpopular side in his advocacy of the War of 1812. His annexationist policy in that war was a failure; and Henry Clay, instead of raising *himself* to the Presidency, succeeded only in raising a rival *against* himself—the hero of the Battle of New Orleans, Andrew Jackson.

He first ran against Jackson in 1824. It was a three-cornered fight—Clay, Jackson and Adams. And none of them received a majority of the electoral vote. The choice for the Presidency was thus thrown into the House of Representatives; and Clay, as the Speaker of the House, engineered the election of Adams.

It was then that Jackson conceived his lifelong hatred against Clay. For Adams had appointed Clay as his Secretary of State—a clear case, contended Jackson, of political bargaining and corruption. Clay retorted, and truthfully, that he had made no bargain, that he had never sought the office, and that he didn't much care for it anyhow. All that he cared for was the Presidency; and to get that, he must now *fight* and *defeat* his new rival. Accordingly he set himself against Jackson and against every political and social doctrine for which Old Hickory stood. It was an unequal match—a feather against a hurricane. But Clay failed to see the impossibility of his position. Every defeat made him eager for a new attack, which in turn led to an even more disastrous defeat. It was one of the most pathetically courageous fights in American history.

For a time he was a man without a party. The old Federalist Party of Hamilton was extinct; and the Democrats, with Jackson at their head, were in virtual control of the government. In order to overthrow Jackson, Clay decided to create a new party. And a new cause.

He called his new party the *National Whig Party;* and he named his new cause the *American System*. This "American System" was in reality a European chaos. It was based upon the commercial greed and the national ambitions that had retarded the social progress of the Old World. It advocated a threefold policy: the protection of monopoly, the exploitation of labor, and the distribution of public funds for private enterprise—and private graft. It was a reactionary policy that went against the very current of progressive Americanism. Once more Henry Clay had set himself a hopeless task. He was asking his future-minded countrymen to return to the past. It was as if he were saying to an advancing army, "About face—forward march!" His policy was doomed to failure from the start.

Yet even this policy might have succeeded, temporarily at least, to the extent of putting him into the White House. But Clay never gave it a fair trial. In his effort—always unsuccessful—to keep his finger on the political pulse of the people, he kept constantly changing his course. From a bristling fighter he had become a "great pacificator"; from a fiery radical, a determined reactionary. Nobody, not even his most ardent adherents, could ever tell just where he was going next. He was a whirling dervish, turning furiously around and around, yet never getting anywhere for all his breathless activity.

And whenever he adopted a new course, he felt firmly convinced that this was the one final course toward which his whole past career, the whole past career of his country, had been pointing the way. He was, above all, anxious to do the fair thing. Though he admitted his ambition for the Presidency, he solemnly insisted, "I had rather be right than be President." It was his misfortune that he was never President and hardly ever right.

CLAY

V

HE FOUGHT a couple of duels, bought his acres at Ashland, entertained his guests,—"he never dines alone but always has a social company at dinner,"—educated his children and lavished upon his wife a wealth of bracelets and velvets and marabou feathers that would "wash like silk," and then went forth to his second "Presidential Crusade" against Jackson, in 1832. Since Jackson had proclaimed himself as the enemy of the United States Bank, Clay felt "in duty bound" to proclaim himself as its champion. It was another political somersault, for Clay had been an opponent of the Bank in 1811.

And it was another political blunder, for the trend of the times and the temper of the public were decidedly opposed to a financial monopoly. "Here's to Henry Clay," ran a sarcastic toast drunk in South Carolina during the campaign. "Would to God he were like Jonah in the whale's belly; the whale to the devil; the devil in hell; the door locked, key lost, and not a sun of Vulcan within a million miles to make another key."

Clay was overwhelmingly defeated at the polls.

His next political blunder was a blow which he aimed at Jackson through Van Buren—a blow which turned out to be a boomerang. Clay had reason to dislike Van Buren. Once, on a memorable occasion during the Bank controversy, Clay had made a personal appeal to Van Buren to intercede with Jackson in behalf of the "threatened homes and hopes" of the American people. "Go to him," he cried to Van Buren, in the presence of the packed galleries in the Senate, "and tell him . . . the actual condition of his bleeding country . . . the heartrending wretchedness of the unemployed . . . the tears of the helpless widows . . . of the unclad and unfed orphans . . . Tell him that he has been abused, deceived, betrayed, by the wicked counsels of unprincipled men around him . . . Entreat him to pause and to reflect that there is a point beyond which human endurance cannot go, and let him not drive this brave, generous and patriotic people to madness and despair!"

When Clay had finished this emotional plea, the ladies in the galleries were dabbing with their handkerchiefs at their eyes. Here and there a stifled sob could be heard. Van Buren appeared to be visibly moved. Slowly the "Red Fox" walked down the aisle to Henry Clay's seat, asked for a pinch of snuff, inhaled it—and applauded the Kentuckian's eloquence with a resounding sneeze.

Clay never forgot this sneeze. When Jackson appointed Van Buren as Minister to England, "Old Eloquent" induced the Senate to reject the nomination. Whereupon Jackson decided to use Van Buren as the instrument of his vengeance against Henry Clay. He nominated the "Red Fox" as his successor to the Presidency. The people listened to Jackson, Van Buren was elected, and Clay was obliged to swallow another bitter cup of defeat.

His courage in the face of his defeats was something to marvel at. He arose with a new reservoir of strength after every political failure. And personal tragedy. Within a few years his daughter and his son's wife had died in childbirth. But he kept fighting resolutely on. And always with a face that displayed to the world a generous smile and an open heart. At the inauguration of Martin Van Buren (1837) he came face to face with Tom Ritchie, another of his old political enemies. Clay extended his hand, which Ritchie gladly accepted. "Time has dealt very gently with you, Henry."

"Yes, Tom," thrusting his two hands forward with vertical palms outstretched. "I mean to keep the Old Fellow off as long as I can."

A battered champion. Yet always eager for the next encounter. Still able, as of old, to electrify his audiences with his speeches. His phrases came like a constellation of glittering bubbles from his mouth. Having no substance, they burst into thin air. But what a spectacle they produced in the transitory moment of

CLAY

their glory! His enemies as well as his friends confessed to the enchantment of his voice. One of his bitterest political opponents, John Randolph—a man with whom he had fought a duel—was dying of tuberculosis. Having heard that Clay was about to make a speech, he begged to be taken into the Senate chamber. "I want to hear that voice again before I die."

VI

CLAY's golden voice proved to be his own undoing. It marked him as a superb actor but as a poor politician. It brought him applause but no votes. People listened to him to be entertained rather than to be convinced. For he himself had, it seemed to them, no firm convictions. When the question of slavery came up in the newly admitted states, Clay refused to take a definite stand one way or another. He decided, as usual, in favor of a compromise: to admit the states in pairs, one slave state and one free state at a time; to permit slavery in all the new states south of parallel 36°30'; and to prohibit it in all the new states north of that line. It was a beautifully balanced idea, as balanced as his rhetorical phrases. The only trouble with it was that it couldn't work. Clay failed to see what Lincoln saw so clearly a few years later—namely, that no country could endure half slave and half free.

The same tightrope balancing marked Clay's attitude on the question of the annexation of Texas. In 1820 he maintained that Texas had been included in the Louisiana Purchase, and that therefore it belonged to the United States. In 1827 he changed his mind, conceded that Texas belonged to Mexico and proposed that the United States should purchase it for five million dollars. Several years later (1836), when Texas declared its independence of Mexico, Clay was mildly in favor of a hands-off policy on the part of the United States. Still later (1844), he vigorously opposed the annexation of Texas. And then, in an evil hour, he decided to run once more for the Presidency (1848) and adopted a *blow-hot* and *blow-cold* policy on the Texas question. To the North, which had been opposed to the annexation of Texas and the war with Mexico, he proclaimed himself as a pacifist and anti-annexationist. And to the South, which had been in favor of the war, he declared himself as a militarist and annexationist.

The Mexican War was a personal tragedy to Clay. For in this war his favorite son and namesake, Henry, was killed. The loss of his son, he wrote to a friend, was "one of the greatest afflictions which has ever befallen me, in a life which has been full of domestic afflictions."

And then, to cap the climax of his sorrows, he suffered the greatest humiliation of his life. It was in the Presidential campaign of 1848—his fifth futile attempt to reach the White House. In this campaign he failed not only to get the nomination but to receive the endorsement from the delegates of his own state. Even his closest friends had grown tired of his everlasting political juggling.

And then, at the age of seventy-one, he gave up his Presidential ambition and took stock of his past life. A life of tangled threads, with no apparent purpose or meaning. And yet, was there not perhaps a definite pattern in all this meaningless jumble? Did not the personality that was Henry Clay stand for something clear and grand and purposeful in the welding of the American nation? Did not his very tendency to compromise indicate a blind but instinctive groping toward the light? In all his political blundering, in all his personal vacillation, there was a common denominator of undeviating sanity—a passionate love for a united America. "Sir," he exclaimed in one of his speeches, "I have heard something said about allegiance to the South. I know no South, no North, no East, no West, to which I owe any allegiance." These words, expressing as they did the very gist of the American Ideal, produced one of the most spontaneous demonstrations in the history of the Senate. Clay waited until the cheering had subsided; and then, raising his proud old head and throwing back his bent and tired shoulders, he went on: "If Kentucky tomorrow unfurls the banner of resistance unjustly, I never will fight under that banner. I owe a paramount allegiance to the whole Union—a subordinate one to my own state. When my state is right . . . I will then share her fortunes. But if she summons me . . . to support her in any cause which is unjust, against the Union, never, *never* will I engage with her in such a cause!"

A united and unmolested America. This was his ethical, political, religious creed. "If anyone desire to know the leading and paramount object of my life," he wrote in one of his characteristic letters, *"the preservation of this Union will furnish him the key."*

WEBSTER

Important Dates in Life of Daniel Webster

1782—Born in Salisbury, New Hampshire.
1797—Entered Dartmouth College.
1805—Admitted to the Massachusetts bar.
1813—Elected to Congress.
1818—Argued the "Dartmouth College" case.
1820—Delivered his oration on the Pilgrim Fathers.
1825—Delivered his Bunker Hill address.
1830—Made his famous "Reply to Hayne"—an interpretation and defense of the American Constitution.
1840—Appointed Secretary of State in Harrison's cabinet.
1842—Made treaty with Ashburton about the northeastern boundary of the United States.
1850—Delivered speech in favor of Clay's "Compromise" on slavery.
1852—Died at Marshfield, Massachusetts.

Daniel Webster

Daniel Webster
1782–1852

"THAT large, dark forehead may not be a sign of greatness in your son, but of rickets." His head grows ever larger and his skin darker. Can it be Negro blood somewhere in Ebenezer's lineage that has come out in his son Dan'l? "Surely there's something of the dark South in this New Hampshire Yankee lad." Doesn't act as though he were baptized in the bracing East Wind. Looks as if the lazy South Wind had cradled him in his infancy.

But laziness doesn't thrive well in the loam of a New Hampshire farm. It just won't grow in the salty air. There are no lotus islands in the dreams of the New England farmer when he puts his muddy shoes by the bed. Come on, Daniel, you weren't meant to dream, but to pitch hay!

"He's so damn lazy, I'll send him off to school," decided old Ebenezer. "Ain't got enough brains to be of much use around here, anyhow."

"The child is so weak in body," supplemented his mother. "He'll be much better off larnin' than pickin' whortleberries with his sisters."

Come to think of it, education isn't such a bad thing after all. Take Ebenezer Webster, for example. See what it might have done for him. An old veteran of the Revolution, he had been selected in a guard of honor to keep post near Washington's tent. But did it get him to Congress when the whole business was over? Not at all! "I sweat and toil tryin' to grow vegetables out of the sand, while Old Abiel Foster from Canterbury gets six dollars a day in Washington." All because Abiel had gone to school.

So Daniel went to school with his father's blessing. And how Eben could bless—and curse! Daniel sat at the foot of the freshman class at Phillips Academy. And it was an expensive seat. It took all his father's savings to keep him there. Cheaper by far to sit on a haystack and dream. But out on the haystack you dreamed away your life saying never a word. And here at Phillips Daniel sat among a crowd of people. He made friends and talked. Here a fellow was compelled to use words in order to get along. And Daniel discovered he had a voice. So did all the masters and boys around him. Lord, he could talk people into a hypnotic spell with that musical voice of his. And what did he talk about? Why, nothing at all! Just words. Glittering golden words.

When he plodded toward the hills of Hanover to take his entrance examinations for Dartmouth College, he remembered the advice of his schoolmaster at Phillips Academy. "Bear a bold front, boy, bear a bold front. Your Latin is no great thing. Your Greek is worse. And your geography? Oh, fie! But you have the gift of the gab. You'll make a glib tongue carry a lame mind . . ." Such was the rough psychology handed down by a New England school teacher in the land of the cold East Wind.

II

"The less he knows, the more he crows," the other students in their bowlers said of Dan'l. Jealousy! Their hats weren't nearly as large as his. They envied his gigantic cranium. By this time everybody knew it wasn't a case of rickets. They regarded him with envy mingled with contempt.

And they had reason for their envy. What a way he had with the ladies! How he could "catch" a pretty ankle!

Yet he was "thin as a weasel and swarthy as a crow." What was it, then, that so captivated the maidens of New Hampshire? It must have been his eyes. Those eyes of Dan'l Webster were "black as death." They seemed to penetrate every secret. They were the eyes of the devil. That's what fascinated the women. The irresistible devil in Dan'l Webster.

Yes, he was quite a character. They used to say in those days that Dartmouth had "four professors, three chapels, a college bell, a deficit—and Black Dan'l."

And now he was out of college and nothing to do. For a while he tried teaching school at Freyburg. And then he entered the office of the great Boston lawyer, Christopher Gore, in order to learn the "mysteries of legal procedure." Not that Daniel cared one grain of alfalfa for the law. It bored him. His head was too large and labyrinthine for the straight and precise technicalities of the courtroom; it ached for the surges of the wind, for the sweeping of a tropical tempest to stir up the great frozen chambers of his New England imagination.

He loved to talk, to sway a jury with a torrent of words. It was the hours of research, the painful agony of forming the legal brief, all the hateful contents of the green bag, that annoyed him. Well, Lawyer Gore knew that a strong haul of wine would help young Dan'l to forget his annoyance.

Finally the patient Mr. Gore made Daniel learned in the law and felt like an enchanter who had given away the gravest secrets of his magic. Now with his new found power the fledgling lawyer could become a ruthless tyrant. Or a glowing prophet. "Make yourself useful to your friends, Daniel," was Gore's final injunction. "And a little formidable to your enemies. And whatever bread you eat, let it be the bread of independence."

III

Daniel put on his finest pearl-buttoned broadcloth from the lapels of which you could see the fringes of his sarsenet shirt. He put aside the brightly colored whip which he had carried to fairs in his student days and replaced it with a malacca cane. And he strode like a cavalier into the grim Puritan dinginess of the New England courtroom to commence his pleadings. The judges and the juries who heard him were men from the surrounding farm lands, neighbors who had known him and his father for many years. Ebenezer himself had been appointed lay judge for one of the county courts, and the old farmer sat proudly listening to his son's plea in a minor case. He looked around the courtroom, and his eyes grew dim as he saw the open-mouthed astonishment of the spectators. Is this young Dan Webster, the little fellow with the big head who used to sit dreaming lazily by the roadside?

Numbers of people flocked to the new lawyer. He had such an uncanny power to sway juries. "It ain't what he says. But you can't keep from weepin' out loud when he says it."

"Yes, an' when he puts his mind to it, he can frighten you, too. Sometimes it seems as if the Lord is shinin' in his eyes, an' sometimes the devil."

And Daniel threw back his shaggy head and laughed.

IV

Like the Pied Piper of Hamelin who had cast a spell over the burghers' children, Dan Webster was able to charm the moneybags away from the merchants of Boston. The coins like the children followed the piper wherever he went. As his legend grew, he felt it increasingly necessary to clothe himself in a vision of gold. A man who is thought to be godlike must be a god with a golden halo. "I never heard," observed Daniel, "what particular substance Archimedes wished his world-moving fulcrum to be . . . But if his design had been to move everything in the world, he would have wished it to be a fulcrum of hard cash . . ."

Cash! Money! Without it he was a New Hampshire peasant. With it he could be king.

To make money became the master-motive of his life. He had entered the Temple of Justice as a humble suppliant. Soon he was established as a money changer within its precincts. Here he did his business, boosted his stock for more clients and higher fees. Every thundering sentence was a price quotation, every forensic gesture an invitation to haggle.

A lawyer could get a good price for trying to outsmart the law, and a still better price for making a new and more suitable law. A lawyer who is ambitious should become a legislator. To the Congress, then, said Daniel Webster!

He went to Congress as the representative of the solid businessmen of New England. Their interests spoke through the massive sounding-board of his oratory. He had become the voice of the Federalists. A young Demosthenes, fired with the ambition of Croesus. There was a war going on with England (1812) over the impressment of American seamen—"Mr. Madison's War." The merchants of New England wanted nothing to do with it. They were losing too much profitable business with the Empire on account of a "silly squabble over principles." They sent this young man to Washington as an obstructionist—a deep-browed, golden-voiced advocate of peace. Here comes Dan Webster—devilishly handsome, incredibly ambitious. "Warn the ladies, and tell that Southerner, Henry Clay, that a rival has entered the field."

He did a great deal of talking at Washington, and a great deal of drinking. That famous "Daniel Webster punch." The strong stimulants gave him moments of exaltation even though they slowly undermined his health. He lived in a world of enchantment and temptation and ever accumulating riches. He owned a house in Boston, an estate at Marshfield, horses, yachts, hunting dogs, champagne-filled cellars. Was not the possession of things the very essence of the happy life?

He returned from Washington and strode again into the chambers of the law and pleaded his cases until even his enemies became his clients. His voice rose to pitches of agony and his face assumed a mask of suffering and he drew tears, this modern Orpheus, from the iron countenances of the learned justices of the Supreme Court.

And then, when Andrew Jackson became President, Webster was returned to the Senate and commenced his pleadings in behalf of the most powerful client in the United States. The Bank of Nicholas Biddle had "engaged" Webster, along with Henry Clay and a "select" group of other Senators, to jockey through the Senate the bill for its recharter. Webster was high on the list of the men who received regular fees for his endeavors. And when the Bank was slow in its "retainers," Webster did not hesitate to demand his usual "refreshments." Such were the legislative ethics of those days.

But it was exciting. You never knew who your next client would be. Daniel was intoxicated with his power. And he would accept all newcomers—those with a price to pay and those without a price provided the case fascinated him.

And then, in the midst of all this aimless splendor, a new client began to appear in the company of Daniel Webster. As he sat over his punch bowl and surveyed the glory and the vanity of his brilliant career, his mind reverted to some of the speeches he had read in his student days—the patriotic appeals of Pericles, of Cicero, of Edmund Burke. It was at such moments that this new client made his most insistent demands. And little by little he won Daniel Webster over to his cause. "The mere reading of the Constitution of the United States brings tears to my eyes." This overwhelmingly persuasive client refused to be denied. His country!

WEBSTER

V

DAN WEBSTER made his first conspicuous appeal in behalf of his country on a cold January day in 1830, when the Senate gallery was aglow with the finery of the Washington aristocracy and the floor was jammed with angry, bickering legislators. General Hayne of South Carolina had risen, on the occasion of an unimportant matter of legislation, to introduce into his argument a doctrine of political philosophy that had grown notorious among certain Southern gentlemen through the course of thirty years. He had declared that his state had the right to decide for herself as to whether any law passed by Congress was constitutional and that, moreover, his state had the right to disobey any law which she regarded as unconstitutional. Hayne's argument, the alleged right of a state to nullify a federal law, was the virus of anarchy. For it meant the breaking up of the United States into a disunited jumble of antagonistic governments.

But Hayne went even farther than that. If the federal government persisted in enforcing a law after the state legislature had nullified it, then the state had the right—declared Hayne—to secede from the Union. "For the Union is nothing but an agreement, a compact between the states from which any party may withdraw when dissatisfied."

Hayne's speech had struck Washington like a thunderbolt. Daniel Webster felt constrained to answer this speech—not only as an advocate of the North, but even more compellingly as a citizen of the United States. In the greatest defense of the Constitution ever heard in the Capitol the Senator from New Hampshire delivered an oration that was printed throughout the land and reached the heart of every patriot. Why, he asked, should any Southern state feel that the interests of the country as a whole are inimical to her? "Sir, we in New England do not reason thus. Our notion of things is entirely different. We do not impose geographical limits to our patriotic feeling or regard."

If—he declared—he were to vote narrow-mindedly against any legislation that was partial to the South, his constituents would feel betrayed. "These ... men would tell me that they had sent me to act for the whole country, and that anyone who possessed too little comprehension either of intellect or of feeling—one who was not large enough in mind and heart to embrace the whole—was not fit to be entrusted with the interest of any part."

The Constitution of the United States—he continued—was not a compact entered into by the states, but the law of the land as formulated and ratified by the American people. The law of the Constitution was superior to any legislation of the states. And any defiance of it was open rebellion, treason, "no matter what euphemistic name the Senator may choose to give it ... The people, sir, erected this government ... The people so willed it." Would the legislators of any one state presume to obstruct the will of the majority of the American people? It is folly to define liberty as the right to defy the sovereignty of the people. Such defiance is not liberty at all. There can be no such motto waving over America as "Liberty first and Union afterwards." There can only be "Liberty *and* Union, now and forever, one and inseparable."

When he had finished, a senator from the South who had supported Hayne walked over to him and declared: "Mr. Webster, I think you had better die now, and rest your fame on that speech."

But Webster was too busy to listen. He had already rushed off to other litigations. His interests were so manifold, always piling up. No wonder he drank so heavily ...

He needed money and more of it. He was adding acre upon acre to his dream farm at Marshfield. The upkeep of this farm was a constant drain upon his purse. Well, he could raise all the funds he needed now on the security of his reputation as the "Defender of the Constitution." He could get large loans from the most prominent men in the country. The finest investments were open to him. New England wasn't his only gold mine. He would travel West and speculate in land values out there. Throughout the country he was regarded as a "good risk." Every new honor that the press gave him was a gilt-edged security.

He took a trip to the West and mortgaged himself heavily and bowed to the thunderous applause. Why, he was popular enough to be President of the United States. He'd make a try for it. His sponsors would be the landowners of the West and the bankers of the East—an unbeatable combination. Could his rival Henry Clay, that insatiable aspirant for the Presidency, play a better hand than that?

Yet Webster had reckoned without his political hosts. The Whig convention turned a deaf ear to him in 1836, and again in 1840. The harmless old soldier, General Harrison, was selected as the standard-bearer of the Whig Party. He was guaranteed to be a faithful servant of Nicholas Biddle and his Bank. No fear of him. As a good party member, Webster was bound to support him. And the people accepted him as their President. What a relief to the Whigs after those "barbarian" Democrats, Jackson and Van Buren! To be sure, his running mate, John Tyler, was a dark horse. Nobody knew what his principles were. But why worry about the principles of a mere Vice-President?

President Harrison made Daniel Webster a handsome offer— the office of Secretary of State. His political friends urged him to accept, and Daniel did. Now he was in a real position to serve.

Then the blow fell. One month after his inauguration, old General Harrison passed away. And Mr. Tyler, the "Great Unknown," became President of the United States. When the Unknown made his principles known, the entire Whig Party was convulsed with fury. He had proved to be a traitor in their midst—a Jacksonian democrat opposed to sound money, big business, tariffs! When the Whigs had once again brought up the bill to recharter Biddle's Bank, Tyler had reacted exactly as Jackson and Van Buren had reacted before him. He had vetoed the bill. A horrible catastrophe had overtaken the Whig aspirations. There was nothing for the party to do now but to demand the resignation of all the Whig members of the Tyler Cabinet as a protest against his "treachery."

In the meantime Daniel Webster in his new office had been handling certain ticklish matters of foreign policy with the utmost skill. Trouble had been brewing between the United States and Great Britain over the Canadian boundaries. There had been border attacks, reprisals, arrests. The two nations were close to war. It would take the most delicate deliberation to keep the United States at peace.

It was in the midst of this deliberation that the crisis arose in the politics of the Whig Party. The leaders of this party, with Biddle pulling the purse strings, ordered Webster to leave the Tyler Cabinet. One by one the other members of the Cabinet had handed in their resignations.

Daniel felt strangely old of a sudden. He was the last Whig still remaining in the Cabinet. They would expect his resignation tomorrow. Yet he was in the midst of negotiations more important than party politics.

He sat in his office with his head heavy and a terrible odor of liquor on his breath. Couldn't he ever give up this confounded habit of drinking? Well, he drank because he was sick. That was it. He drank to forget the effects of the opium which he took to relieve the chronic ailment of his stomach. The famous "Daniel Webster punch." Really it deserved company along with him to taste it. This blend of Medford rum, brandy, champagne, arrack and maraschino. A base of strong tea laced with lemon . . . Really he should be drinking it along with some one.

He wasn't exactly sure but it *did* seem as though somebody had come in to help him drink his brew. He'd seen this company before.

"Mighty fine-tasting punch, Dan'l." And then, after a pause: "So you're going back to Boston tomorrow?"

"Yes, I'm through here."

"What about my business, Dan'l? Ain't you going to see my claim through? Have you forgotten me?"

WEBSTER

"I worked for you in 1830 and won you a decision against General Hayne. And what did it get me? The hatred of my Southern friends." Confound this fellow! Always turning up at the most embarrassing moments.

Daniel rose abruptly to go to bed. But the voice detained him. "Then I'll go to other lawyers, Dan'l. There are plenty of them in this country who will want my business. And they'll be remembered in after years for what they've done. Isn't it time you settled down again to a job that'll be worthy of Dan'l Webster? Well, go off to bed now . . . Ah, you hesitate . . . Can we talk business?"

VI

DANIEL WEBSTER remained in the Cabinet of President Tyler and continued to arbitrate the boundary dispute between the United States and Canada. He insisted on the rights of the Americans to the high seas and demanded that the British navy show respect for citizens sailing under the American flag.

But the entire Whig world was in a fury. When he returned to Boston and prepared to address her citizens in Faneuil Hall he faced a sullen and unfriendly crowd. Who was this inconsistent politician? Was he still a Whig? When England on the high seas had interfered with a cargo of runaway slaves from the Southern plantations he had demanded in the name of the Constitution that England return the slave property of the South. What was this Northerner, pro-slavery? Well, now, he would have to do some tall explaining.

"I give no pledges; I make no intimation one way or the other, and I will be as free when this day closes to act as duty calls as I was when the dawn of this day broke . . . Take it or leave it, Whigs of Massachusetts!"

They couldn't help cheering him. They admired his courage. Once more they knew him for their leader. But never again would he be, in the old sense, their idol as he once had been.

From now on they would keep a shrewd weather eye upon the "shifting currents" of his sympathies.

He settled a few more incidents that had created friction between England and the United States; and then, when his business was finished and his presence in the Cabinet could be no longer advantageous to the country, he resigned.

And now they began whispering strange stories about him. They said he was drinking harder than ever to keep going, that he made many of his speeches in a drunken stupor. "During his address to the farmers at the Rochester Fair he could hardly keep his feet." "In his speech at the banquet of the economists he dug into his wallet and offered to pay the national debt." Pay the national debt! Why he couldn't even pay his own debts. A curse had fastened itself upon his finances. He never had any cash. "His method of doing business is as impractical as that of a Hottentot." Always he was borrowing on notes to pay off other notes, always drafting on banks where he had friends but no funds. He was mortgaged to every money lender in Massachusetts. "The devil is snatching after him, determined to bring him to hell." He had sold his soul to old Beelzebub. Rich banquets and dazzling clothes and acres of estates—and hardly a penny of ready cash.

He went back to his law practice to recoup his finances. A case with the Goodrich Rubber Company and a claim for John Jacob Astor—and he paid off a good slice of his notes. And then again his notes began to pile higher and higher. It wasn't the devil; it was the men in State Street who had a mortgage on his very life.

But not on his tongue. Perhaps if they sent him again to Washington, they mused, he wouldn't be so free with his speech. He would realize where his soul belonged. They hadn't wished to punish such a tongue too severely! Yet they must try to restrain it somehow.

And so a group of businessmen met and collected a fund to send Daniel Webster back to Washington. To ward off the

WEBSTER

ugly charge of "vested interests," they called it a memorial fund —a sort of token of affection and esteem presented by his friends. With the "token" Webster ran a handsome campaign and was re-elected to the Senate.

Brave old fellow coming back to battle. And a battle royal it was! That same irresistible question that had split the Union for forty years had come up again in acute form. Should the South be allowed to extend her institution of slavery into any new territory incorporated into the Union? Would not this destroy the balance of political and financial power as between the North and the South, leaving the South finally in complete domination? But the Southerners, too, had their argument. When they moved into the new Western territory they insisted upon taking their slaves along with them. For a slave was property just as an article of household furniture or a covered van. The Constitution had declared this to be an established fact.

And thus the South was determined to force slavery upon the new land. The North, on the other hand, was equally determined that this new land be free. The South repeated the ominous arguments of General Hayne, justifying the right of secession from the Union whenever any state was dissatisfied with the federal laws as impinging upon its own sovereignty. And who was there to reply to this threat but Daniel Webster who had made a reply on that famous earlier occasion? Again he loomed as the foremost spokesman of the Northern Whigs—of the reactionary capitalists who were implacable foes of cheap plantation labor, as well as of the fanatical idealists who insisted upon nothing short of abolition throughout the United States.

In the Congress of the United States the situation (in 1850) seemed beyond the power of words. Two systems of economics and ideology were deadlocked. Senators concealed pistols in their pockets as they rose to speak. It was rumored that the Southern militia was ready to march upon Washington. In the North the Abolitionists invoked the lightning of heaven upon the heads of the transgressors.

And yet many men hoped that the words of one would win the day. Daniel Webster was a Northerner and a man of principle. And also a man of ambition. Didn't he have his eyes on the Presidency in 1852? He had been turned down four times by his party. But he still nursed his ambition, they said. Alexander the Great had conquered the world at thirty; and here was Daniel Webster, sixty-eight and the most brilliant speaker in the land, and not President yet? This time he would make the grade with the right speech. "Show the South your fist, Dan'l, and we Northerners will put you over."

And then in the cold of March he rose to his feet and trembled. If people only knew how he trembled inwardly when he spoke! He looked at the gentlemen on the floor and at the ladies in the gallery. Yes, he had made a very important speech here twenty years earlier, on another winter day, to another gallery. That would be when his beloved son Edward was eleven years old. His youngest son who was no more now than a picture on the bureau, a handful of dust in the soil of New England, a cypress tree above. Edward had died in the Mexican War—a war engineered by hotheads who were anxious to show their fists. And now once more there were hotheads in the North and the South who were eager to show their fists, to rush into another war, another killing of sons . . .

He spoke firmly and almost scornfully. He spoke in defense of the South's constitutional right to hold slaves. He hated slavery, but he was certain that it would die a natural death in the liberal progress of the world without fulmination from the North. It was ridiculous to assume in any controversy that all the goodness was on one side and all the wickedness on the other. He spoke for compromise and tolerance. And his eyes intermittently blackened with gloom and sparkled in exaltation. There could be only one alternative to a complete break—compromise, a gentle yielding of the extremists on both sides for the sake of the United Destiny of both, for the health and the liberty and the preservation of the Union. How could Daniel

WEBSTER

Webster be expected to make a stand on extreme Northern principles? Did they not remember the words he had once spoken? "One who is not large enough in mind and heart to embrace the whole . . . is not fit to be entrusted with the interest of any one part."

And when he had finished there was a chill silence—the first time that a speech of his had been received in chill silence. To keep the Union! For a moment he looked formidable and glowing—"like a transparent bronze statue brilliantly lighted from within."

Then he sat down cold and extinguished.

VII

THE North was stunned. And then it rose to a fury unequaled. There was a "traitor" in her midst!

Liberty! "This word in Webster's mouth is like the word *love* in the mouth of a courtesan . . . Every drop of blood in that man's veins has eyes that look downward."

Silently Webster accepted the portfolio of Secretary of State in the Cabinet of Fillmore, "in preparation for the Presidency which he expects to get through the support of the South in 1852." He came to Boston for an address. But the Board of Aldermen refused him Faneuil Hall. In his ears, wherever he went, rang the challenging words of Seward's reply to his speech: "There is a higher law than the Constitution!"

1852. The Whig Convention. The man "who sold out to the South" is waiting for the Southern Whigs to swing over to his support. He is waiting in vain. The South distrusts him. New England deserts him—first, his native state of New Hampshire; then, Vermont . . .

He waits. The lines of Whittier run through his mind like a sword:

> When faith is lost, when honor dies,
> The man is dead.

There was nothing left for him to do but to return to Marshfield. "Go back to your farm, Dan'l. You have done enough work here," counseled the client who of late had kept him faithful company. "Go back to the oxen and the Punch Brook pasture. Get away from all the yelping voices. Lie down and listen to the sea breaking her heart for you. Isn't it time you wrote your hired man a letter, Daniel, telling him you're coming home? . . . Maybe there will come wise men after you who will find a way to continue in peace. Maybe war is bound to come in any case. Never fear. You have kept your hands from brothers' blood."

He wrote a letter to his hired man. "John Taylor, I am coming home. You and I are farmers; we never talk politics—our talk is of oxen. But remember this: that any man who attempts to excite one part of this country against another is just as wicked as he who should attempt to get up a quarrel between John Taylor and his neighbor, old Mr. John Sanborn . . . I think I never wrote you a word upon politics. I shall not do it again. I only say, love your country and your whole country, and when men attempt to persuade you to get into a quarrel with the laws of other states, tell them that you mean to mind your own business and tell them to do the same . . . John Taylor, thank God morning and evening that you were born in such a country . . . John Taylor, never write to me another word upon politics."

SUMNER

Important Dates in Life of Charles Sumner

1811—Born in Boston, Massachusetts.
1830—Graduated from Harvard College.
1831–34—Studied law under Judge Story.
1849—Argued before the Supreme Court of Massachusetts against the constitutionality of separate schools for Negroes and whites.
1851—Appointed to the United States Senate.
1852—Argued for the repeal of the Fugitive Slave Law.
1856—Delivered speech on "The Crime against Kansas."
Attacked on Senate floor and beaten almost to death by advocates of slavery.
1857—Reappointed to the Senate, where he served during the last twenty-three years of his life.
1872–73—Introduced Bill of Civil Rights for the Negro.
1874—Died at Washington.

Charles Sumner

Charles Sumner
1811–1874

His fearless tongue almost cost him his life. Several of his Southern antagonists in the Senate—men who were aggressively fighting to retain slavery—had for some time been scheming to "get" him. They wouldn't challenge him to a duel; for duels are fought only between gentlemen, and Sumner—they said—was no gentleman. At last they hit upon a plan. He had just delivered his great speech, *The Crime Against Kansas,* in which he had castigated the bill to introduce slavery into that territory as "the rape of a virgin state . . . a hideous pollution and . . . in every respect a *swindle.*" The Senate had adjourned for the day, but Sumner remained in his seat, writing. He was a great bulk of a man—his more than two hundred pounds fixed firmly in his armchair, and his long legs sprawling under his desk. Now was the time for an attack; for, cramped as he was, he wouldn't be able to defend himself freely. Especially if they struck at him from the back. And so a group of Southern politicians, with Congressman Preston Brooks at their head, rushed upon him with a heavy gutta-percha cane and beat him again and again over the head. Sumner tried to tear himself free, but his legs were pinioned under the desk. He barely managed to wrench the desk loose from its iron fastenings before he fell, bleeding and senseless, to the floor.

When the doctor first examined him, he doubted whether the stricken Senator could survive. There were several deep and jagged cuts on the back of the head, one of the wounds having penetrated under the scalp to the very bone. For many weeks his ultimate recovery remained uncertain. And when finally he did recover, it was to a semi-invalid existence. He suffered from excruciating headaches for the rest of his days.

And yet, no sooner was he out of his sick bed than he continued his crusade from where he had left off. To his friends who urged him to stop fighting, he replied: "I *must* fight on, to liberate my soul. I expect again to be attacked, perhaps shot. Very well, I am content. The cause will live . . ."

"I don't believe," wrote Wendell Phillips, "that Charles Sumner knew what fear was."

II

HIS ancestors were farmers and fighters. His grandfather, Major Job Sumner, was the officer from whom George Washington received the last military salute at the conclusion of the Revolutionary War. It was only fitting that Charles Sumner should be the statesman from whom Abraham Lincoln was to receive the first clear bugle call for the declaration of the Civil War.

Yet Charles was not by nature a warrior. He preferred books to battles. Books of poetry, history, philosophy—anything that contained the stored-up wisdom of the human race. But not books of science. He cared next to nothing for science—or for mathematics. Once, when he flunked dismally at a recitation in the Boston Latin School, he remarked timidly: "I'm afraid, sir, I know very little about algebra."

"Algebra?" cried his teacher. "Why, we're not doing algebra now, we're doing physics!"

Specific gravity, square roots—they were all the same to him, equally distasteful and equally unknown. "Why should I dig for the roots of algebra?" he said. "I shall only find them bitter when I get them."

He was decidedly not a scholar. Yet the boys were fond of "gawky Charlie," as they called him. He had such an eloquent tongue in that great, big, shaggy head of his. And such a friendly personality. And his teachers, too, were fond of him—both at the Latin School and at Harvard. On only one point was there any friction between them. Sumner always insisted upon his individual tastes, not only in his speech but in his dress. He affected "a cloak of blue camlet lined with red" and "a buff-colored waistcoat." This sort of thing was taboo at Harvard, whose students were all required to dress in black. Again and again young Sumner was called before the "Parietal Board" to explain his "unorthodox investiture." But he insisted upon his right to "suit his clothing to his personality," and finally the Board dropped the matter.

At the end of his junior year he set out, together with four of his classmates, upon a tramping tour of some of the battle-fields of the Revolution. One by one his companions dropped out—at Bennington, at Saratoga, at West Point. But Sumner stuck it out to the end, all by himself. He had planned to go as far as Mt. Defiance, and as far as Mt. Defiance he would go. It was not in Sumner's nature to leave a job undone. "I was eager to visit the spot (of Burgoyne's surrender) . . . where the cause of the Colonies first began to brighten."

Yet in spite of his eagerness to visit the battlefields of the past, he had conceived a passionate hope that there would be no battlefields in the future. "I have found a new objective in life—to further the mild arts of peace."

But for the present he had a more immediate objective—to find a means of livelihood. For a man of his forensic ability there was but one logical profession—the law. He had heard Webster's pleas at several of the Boston trials. "Some day I hope to be a famous lawyer like him." And so—three years at the Harvard

Law School, and then the "great, tall, lank creature, quite heedless of the form and fashion of his garb," took his six-foot-four beanpole of a frame into the law office of Benjamin Rand. For all his towering height, he weighed as a young man only 120 pounds. His complexion was pale, his eyes were inflamed with too much reading, and his chest was hollow. Yet through that organ-barrel of a chest there vibrated a voice of tremendous persuasiveness and power.

And, in spite of his lankiness, he had a constitution that was as powerful as his voice. His friends were amazed at the strenuousness of his daily schedule. Six hours in the forenoon devoted to the law, afternoons given up to the Greek and the Latin poets, evenings to history and the modern poets, bedtime at two in the morning, and up again at sunrise.

He had very little time for social intercourse. And very little inclination. "Of all the men I ever knew at his age," wrote his friend, William Wetmore Story, "he was the least susceptible to the charms of women . . . This was a constant source of amusement to us, and we used to lay wagers with pretty girls that with all their art they could not keep him at their side a quarter of an hour . . . And the girls always lost their wagers."

He was interested mainly in his studies, in order to perfect himself "as a competent lawyer and useful citizen." As part of his legal education he took a trip to Washington, to attend the sessions of the Supreme Court. It was his first experience on the (newly invented) railway. And a thrilling experience it was. "There is something partaking of the sublime," he wrote to his sister, "in the feeling that you are going at the rate of fifteen miles an hour!"

On his return from Washington he borrowed several thousand dollars and started upon a much more extended educational journey—a trip to Europe. "This journey," he wrote to a friend, "will not be peculiarly legal. I shall try . . . to see men of all characters; to observe institutions and laws; to go circuits and attend terms and parliaments . . . In short, I shall aim to see society in all its forms which are accessible to me." For two and a half years he traveled over Europe, sat at the feet of Carlyle, Wordsworth, Landor, Humboldt, Macaulay, acquired wisdom and sympathy and a measure of cynicism from his educational contacts with the subjects of the Old World, and then he returned to the "grindstone of his legal contacts" with the citizens of the New.

He disliked his legal practice. "Though I earn my daily bread, I lay up none of the bread of life." He felt more at home in his literary than in his legal studies. "My real sigh will come for a canto of Dante, a rhapsody of Homer, a play of Schiller." Or a chapter of Isaiah. As a result of the crosscurrents of national interests which he had observed in Europe, he had become more than ever devoted to the cause of universal peace.

His "pacifistic proclivities" displeased the Brahmin circles of Beacon Hill. But Sumner didn't care to please them. He was merely anxious to make them think—to *shock* them into thinking, if possible. And in the summer of 1845 he gave them the shock of their lives. He had been invited to deliver the Fourth of July oration at Faneuil Hall. Among those present were many veterans of the old war (of 1812) and many advocates of the new war (against Mexico). All of them were resplendent in their military uniforms. They had expected him, on such an occasion, and before such an audience, to deliver a speech bristling with bayonets and rattling with drums. To their astonishment, however, he launched after a few preliminary remarks into the following audacious thesis: "In our age there can be no peace that is not honorable." And then he went on to expose the futility of war, its senselessness, its savagery, its "utter inadequacy to decide the question of right or wrong." Victory in war is merely a demonstration of the strength of your arms; it is never a proof of the justice of your cause. Indeed, "war crushes with bloody heel all justice, all happiness, all that is godlike in man." Sumner concluded his oration with an appeal for the peaceful emancipation of all slaves everywhere and for an American leadership in the disarmament of the world. "Then shall there be a victory, in comparison with which the victory of Bunker Hill shall be as a farthing candle held up to the sun . . . That victory shall need no monument of stone. It shall be written on the grateful hearts of uncounted multitudes . . . It shall be one of the greatest landmarks of civilization; nay, more, it shall be one of the links of the golden chain by which humanity shall connect itself with the throne of God."

And then in the peroration he summarized his argument as merely a modern rendering of the old Biblical *Law of Love*. His audience listened in anger and repaid him in hate. "This young man," remarked Mayor Eliot at the conclusion of the speech, "has cut his own throat." From that day on, Charles Sumner was "outside the pale of society." The doors of Beacon Hill were shut in his face, and the smiles of his aristocratic friends were turned into scowls. There had been talk of his appointment to the faculty of the Harvard Law School. But such an appointment was now out of the question. "I am too much of a reformer," he wrote to his brother, "to be trusted in a post of such commanding influence."

A social outcast, he decided to join the cause of the common folk. Indeed, this is where his heart had been dwelling throughout his groping years. "I belong to the seeking many, not to the satisfied few."

His decision to fight for the underdog resulted in a life of political success and of social loneliness. The common people elected him as their champion. But they did not accept him as their companion. He could think their thoughts, but he could not speak their language. Though in the eyes of the aristocrats he had descended to the level of the workingmen, yet in the eyes of the workingmen he remained always an aristocrat. As one of his biographers (Mrs. Anna L. Dawes) aptly observes, "he was the friend of the downtrodden, not their brother." Such was his anomalous position to the end of his days—rejected by the rich, respected by the poor, and the intimate of none.

SUMNER

He was lonely but far from unhappy. For he had become inspired with that "divine wrath" which, as Plato remarks, is at the root of all happiness. He had discovered the key to the meaning of his life. His job was in the legislature. He had been educated for a definite purpose—to teach the law not to the students of Harvard but to the statesmen of America. And so he went into politics.

Not that he liked politics. On the contrary, he positively disliked it. When he first learned of his election to the United States Senate, he was spending the evening at Longfellow's house. "The papers," wrote Longfellow in his Diary, "are all ringing with *Sumner, Sumner,* and the guns are thundering out their triumph. Meanwhile the hero of the strife is sitting quietly here, more saddened than exalted." But he had accepted the call as the ancient prophets had accepted theirs—a summons from heaven to the service of his fellowmen. "You told me once," wrote Theodore Parker on the occasion of Sumner's election, "that you were in morals, not in politics. And now I hope you will show that you are still in morals, although in politics."

This was the spirit in which Sumner accepted his senatorial office. Politics to him was not a career but a crusade. The event which had turned Sumner into a politician was the same one which had turned Mrs. Stowe into a novelist—the Fugitive Slave Act. The passage of this act had impelled many a lukewarm heart in Massachusetts to flame into sudden fury against the evil of slavery. An antislavery meeting had been organized in Boston, and Sumner had been invited to address it as the principal speaker. He appeared at this meeting, said one of his audience, "like an archangel with a sword." That speech against slavery, he wrote many years later, "was the event which changed the entire course of my life."

III

"You have come into the Senate too late," remarked one of his colleagues to Sumner. "All the great issues and all the great men are gone." All the great men were indeed gone. Clay had tottered out of the Senate chamber the very day on which Sumner had first entered it. Calhoun had died during the previous session. Webster had been appointed Secretary of State. The Senate had become "a dismal gathering of little men." As for the issues, however, they were greater than before—and more difficult of solution. The slavery question had come to the front. And the "obscure young Senator from Massachusetts" had set himself squarely to the task of solving it.

At the outset he found his task a lonely and hopeless struggle. His colleagues, in order to restrain his impetuous tongue, "shelved" him by assigning him to the "tail end" of two of the least important committees—on roads, and on revolutionary claims. "I feel heartsick here," he wrote to his friends in Boston.

But not for long. There was a job to be done, and he seized the first opportunity to do it. On August 26, 1852, he raised his voice in behalf of his "enslaved brothers." It was useless, he declared, to stem the current of pity for the black man that was sweeping over the heart of humanity. "As well attempt to check the tides of ocean, the currents of the Mississippi, or the rushing waters of Niagara . . . The movement against slavery is from the Everlasting Arm." He lashed out against those who maintained that the effort to curb slavery in the South was a sectional aggression on the part of the North. The love of liberty has no regional boundaries. "According to the spirit of the Constitution and the sentiments of the Fathers, slavery and not freedom is sectional, while freedom and not slavery is national." He expressed his determination to stand by his principles against every discouragement, every rebuff. "I will shrink from no responsibility even if I have to stand alone." He admitted the economic right of the slave owner to his property. "But, Sir, there is a greater right than that . . . *the right of a man to himself.*"

And now, having stated his position with regard to human rights, he defined his duty toward the Fugitive Slave Law—an enactment which in his opinion was illegal because it denied those rights. "The Slave Act . . . offends against the Divine Law . . . Hence my path of duty is clear. By the Supreme Law which commands me to do no injustice, by the comprehensive Christian Law of brotherhood, by the Constitution which I have sworn to support, *I am bound to disobey this Act.*"

A most daring stand for an officer of the United States Government. The Senators from the South, and not a few from the North, accused him of sedition. A handful of men, however, declared that a new era of greatness had arisen in the Senate. "Here at last," wrote Theodore Parker, "is a Senator with a conscience!"

IV

AGAIN and again his opponents threatened to expel him from the Senate. But he went fearlessly ahead, attacking not only the pro-slavery forces but all the backward-looking agencies in the United States. Referring to the Know-Nothing Party, the forerunner of the Ku Klux Klan, he wrote: "A party which, beginning in secret, interferes with religious beliefs, and founds a discrimination on the accident of birth, is out of harmony with the best American traditions." It was no wonder that he was so bitterly hated on so wide a front. And he did nothing ever to mitigate the hatred against him. He spoke with the zeal, and with the tactlessness, of the ancient prophets. He never argued with people; he scolded them. To Senator Butler, who on one occasion protested against his use of the term *slave-hunter,* he rejoined: "Sir, I choose to call things by their right names."

It was Senator Butler who, among others, induced Preston Brooks to waylay Sumner while he was sitting at his desk in the Senate chamber. And not satisfied with one victim, the associates of Senator Butler and of Congressman Brooks advocated "a caning or a cowhiding every day . . . for those other scullions who, like Sumner, ought to be taught to behave themselves like decent dogs."

Yet Sumner bore no grudge against Butler or Brooks or any other of his political opponents. His quarrel was with institutions, not with persons. Years later, when a friend asked him how he felt about Brooks, he replied: "Poor fellow, it was slavery, not *he,* that struck the blow . . . He was merely the unconscious agent of a malign power."

V

Sumner lived to see the passing of that malign power. But his work was done. The rest of his life was an anti-climax. Another trip to Europe, an ill-advised marriage which resulted in an early divorce, a number of additional stormy terms in the Senate, a feud with President Grant—there was bound to be a clash between two characters of such unyielding fiber, a long and painful siege of angina pectoris, and throughout it all the Messiah with a chip on the shoulder remained unbowed. As he grew older, his tone became a little too oracular. His private conversations took on the nature of lectures. He assumed too authoritative a tone on too many subjects. "Mr. Sumner doesn't believe in the Bible," a friend once remarked to Grant. "No, I suppose not," replied Grant. "He didn't write it."

Sumner was rather difficult now to get along with—a natural failing with aged prophets. The devoted young man had become an opinionated old man. His speeches had become longer than ever—and woe unto the unfortunate member of the audience who tried to steal out before the end. Sumner would stop short, glare at the retreating culprit, and keep on glaring until the door had shut behind the wretched fellow. "How dare you leave," once remarked a Senator to his neighbor, "while God speaks?"

He had come to believe that he could never be in the wrong. "One day," writes George William Curtis, "I was talking with him upon some public question; and as our conversation warmed, I said to him, 'Yes, but you forget the other side.' Whereupon

SUMNER

Sumner brought his clinched fist down upon the table till it rang, and his voice shook the room as he thundered in reply, 'There *is* no other side!' "

Stubborn, but kindly as ever. "He was domineering," wrote one of his private secretaries, "only to his equals. To his subordinates no one could be more considerate, more generous." Among his intimate friends was a Negro caterer. And to the end of his days he remained the advocate of the Negro's rights in accordance with the principles of the Constitution. "Anything for human rights," he declared, "is constitutional."

This, in a single sentence, summarizes the political philosophy of the "Black Man's Moses."

LINCOLN

Important Dates in Life of Abraham Lincoln

1809—Born in Kentucky.
1831—Employed as clerk in general store at New Salem, Illinois.
1834—Elected to the Illinois state legislature.
1835—Death of his betrothed, Ann Rutledge.
1837—Began practice of law.
1842—Married Mary Todd.
1847-49—Served in the House of Representatives.
1854—Delivered (in Peoria) speech against the extension of slavery.
1856—Joined the new Republican Party.
1858—Debated with Stephen A. Douglas on the question of slavery.
1860—Delivered address at Cooper Union.
Elected the sixteenth President of the United States.
1861—As Commander-in-Chief of the Union Army, assumed burden of Civil War.
1863—Issued Emancipation Proclamation.
Delivered Gettysburg Address.
1864—Re-elected President.
1865—Assassinated.

Abraham Lincoln

Abraham Lincoln
1809–1865

On the night of November 13, 1861, President Lincoln paid a visit to the home of George B. McClellan, General-in-Chief of the Union Army. The servant at the door said the General was out, but would soon return. "Very well," nodded Lincoln, "I will wait."

An hour later McClellan came in at the front door. "General," said the servant, "the President is waiting for you in the parlor."

"Is that so?" And without stopping to greet the President, McClellan walked upstairs.

Another half hour of waiting, and Lincoln became somewhat impatient. "Will you please inform the General," he said to the servant, "that I am still here?"

The servant went up to McClellan's room—and returned without his master. "Sorry, Mr. President, but the General asked me to tell you he's gone to bed."

McClellan was a strutting little cockerel of an officer whose bluster was far in excess of his ability. "What this fellow needs," observed Lincoln's friends, "is a good spanking with the flat of his own sword." But Lincoln only smiled. "I am ready to hold

McClellan's stirrup for him, if he will only win us victories."

Such was Abe Lincoln—a rare combination of humor and humility that made him the beloved of men.

II

No PLAYWRIGHT has ever created a more dramatic plot than the life of Lincoln. Like the hero in an ancient Greek tragedy, he failed in almost everything he undertook; and when he did succeed, he found success more bitter than failure. He lost the only woman he loved; and the woman he married was more anxious to see him famous than to see him happy. He entered business, and failed. He ran for the United States Senate, and was defeated. He applied for an appointment to the United States Land Office, and was rejected. He ran for the Vice-Presidency, and lost. When finally he was elected to the Presidency, it was in sorrow rather than in triumph that he rode into the White House. For, though passionately devoted to peace, he found himself compelled to plunge into war. Tenderest of fathers, he twice had to bow his head in mourning over the untimely graves of his children. Gentle toward every living thing, he was again and again called upon to sign the death warrants of runaway soldiers who were afraid to die. He was a soul attuned to the daylight yet forced to live in the night. And at last, when the dawn of victory arrived after the night of despair, Lincoln did not survive to see the day. His assassination came less than a week after the surrender of General Lee.

In the life of Lincoln the Great Dramatist of Heaven showed the little dramatists of the earth how to write a perfect tragedy.

III

THE day after Lincoln was born his nine-year-old cousin, Dennis Hanks, looked at him. "His skin makes me think of cherry pulp squeezed dry." The baby began to wail. "Aw, take him away!"

LINCOLN

exclaimed Dennis Hanks in disgust. "I guess he'll never come to much."

And indeed there was no reason for anyone to think otherwise. Lincoln's parents and three of his grandparents were uneducated and unambitious. But his fourth grandparent, the father of Nancy Hanks, was a "mysterious stranger from the South." Lincoln's mother, in other words, was a "natural" child. Lincoln thought that his poetical and political genius came from this unknown Southern grandfather. But his never-say-die spirit in the face of failure came to him from a whole line of pioneering ancestors. It took supreme courage to survive in the adventures of the American frontier. There was a concise and picturesque proverb that summarized the epic of America's migration to the Middle West: "The cowards never started and the weak ones died by the way."

Lincoln was descended from those who had the courage to start and the hardihood to survive. A poet born out of a race of pioneers. Lincoln's entire political career was a great epic poem in action.

As a young man he wanted to be a writer. He had drunk deep of the sap of the earth and the sweetness of the air. He had caught the rhythm of the swinging ax and the music of the growing grass. And he reproduced this rhythm and this music in a number of juvenile poems. He could work hard when he had to. But he preferred to *think* hard. "Abe Lincoln worked for me," remarked a neighbor, John Romine, "but he was always reading and thinking instead of attending to his job . . . He said to me one day that his father taught him to work, but he never taught him to love it."

When the day's work was over, he sat around swapping stories and "just learning to be friendly with people." One evening a farmer's wife upbraided him for his laziness. "What's going to become of you, Abe?"

"Me?" drawled Lincoln. "I'm going to be President of the United States."

Lincoln of course was spoofing when he said this. At the time he hadn't the slightest idea that he would attain to political distinction. But he had decided to go into politics. For he was not only a poetical pioneer but a practical Yankee as well. At an early age he had dedicated himself to a life of concrete usefulness. Instead of combining words into a great poem, he would help unite men into a great nation.

And so he announced himself as a candidate for public service. He canvassed his neighbors with humorous anecdotes and homely parables. These speeches were honest and unassuming prose poems. And his neighbors understood them just as readily as they understood the solid earth under their feet and the simple stars overhead. They trusted his uncouth ruggedness, his open smile and his generous heart. He was so much like them and yet so very much above them. Like an oak tree in a forest of saplings. "There's suthin' peculiarsome about Abe," they said, "yes, an' suthin' kindlike an' strong." He could split a rail and pull a boat faster than any other man in Sangamon County; he could floor the strongest "rassler" in the State of Illinois; he could lift an ax by the tip of the handle between the forefinger and the thumb; and he could talk like an apostle out of the Bible. He was quite the homeliest man in the state, and just as lovable as he was homely, was this awkward Honest Abe, with his big gnarled hands, and his ill-fitting clothes, and his furrowed face and sensitive mouth and gentle eyes. A first-rate man to look after their interests. "If elected, I shall consider the whole people of Sangamon my constituents, as well those that oppose as those that support me." They elected him to the state Assembly.

He was a young man of little learning and much wisdom. For he had touched life at many points. He had been field-hand and ferryman, woodchopper and butcher-boy, tanner and storekeeper and surveyor. And letter-writer for all the inarticulate folk of the neighborhood. He had learned to understand and to reproduce in his own simple honest phrases the innermost

LINCOLN

yearnings of his fellows—men who toiled and suffered and lost their loved ones and kept toiling on. He, too, had loved and suffered. He had lost his only sister, his mother, and the girl he was about to marry. For several weeks following the death of Ann Rutledge he was almost out of his mind with grief. One night in a thunderstorm he rushed to the door of his house and cried: "I can't bear to think of her lying out there alone, with the rain and the storm beating on her grave!"

But he pulled himself together and carried on.

IV

As A CHILD he had written in his notebook: "Abraham Lincoln his hand and pen he will be good but god knows when." And now he had made good much sooner than he, or anybody else, had expected. At a dinner given by his constituents in his honor the toastmaster referred to him as a young man "who has fulfilled the expectations of his friends and disappointed the hopes of his enemies."

Such was the verdict of the common people. But not of the expert politicians. When Lincoln took his seat in the Assembly, one of the other members gave him a quick and appraising glance. It was his custom to do this whenever a new member arrived. He wanted to size up the men who might become his possible rivals in the future. For, though short in stature, this young Assemblyman had a tall ambition. His brilliant mind was occupied with nothing less than senatorial and presidential dreams. His name was Stephen A. Douglas.

His quick appraisal of Lincoln apparently satisfied him that there was nothing to be feared from that quarter. Great statesmen, he concluded, were not hewn out of such unpromising timber. For a time he didn't even take the trouble to make Lincoln's acquaintance. And Lincoln, on his part, paid no attention to Douglas. Neither of them suspected how closely their lives were to be intertwined and how vital a role their own destiny was to play in the destiny of America. The clash in their characters, in their ambitions, in their very appearance was but another manifestation of the perfect drama woven around the life of Lincoln.

And now there appeared upon the scene a person who was to bring about the first complication in the plot. One evening the two Assemblymen met an aristocratic young lady from the South —a Becky Sharp type of character who was visiting her married sister in Springfield. Mary Todd was a buxom and beautiful and superficial little creature, whose mind was as bright as a bubble—and as empty. Puffed up with a superabundance of vanity, she was determined to become "the empress of all she surveyed." An exquisite dancer, she meant to dance her way into the heart of the most promising young man in America. When she met the suave Douglas and the uncouth Lincoln, she sized them up immediately. Crude power was nearer to the heart of America than cultivated splendor. Though Mary Todd's mind was shallow, her instinct was sound. She chose Lincoln as the more likely candidate for supreme honors. And so, much to the chagrin of Douglas—a feeling that was to play no little part in his future antagonism to the "homely interloper from the backwoods"—the elegant young lady gave her hand to Lincoln. Or, to be more exact, she took Lincoln's reluctant hand into her own and led him to the altar.

After his marriage, Lincoln settled down to the business of making a living. He entered into a law partnership with William A. Herndon, bought a rickety, leather-covered sofa on which he could stretch out his full length of six feet four and dream away his time, allowing the papers to pile up on the desk and the dust to accumulate on the floor until the grass began to sprout in the cracks. He was set down as the untidiest and most eccentric young man in Illinois. He steadfastly refused to represent unethical clients. "I shall not take your case," he said to a man who had pointed out how, by a legal technicality, he could win six hundred dollars. "You may be legally right, but you are morally wrong . . . And by the way," he added as the disgruntled client turned to leave, "you look like a pretty energetic fellow. Why not try an *honest* way of making six hundred dollars?"

As for Lincoln himself, he made a fairly satisfactory living in spite of his scruples. Perhaps *because* of his scruples. For his clients appreciated his candor, and the judges admired his common sense. What he lacked in good manners he made up in goodness. And *that,* to the simple folk of Illinois, was the yardstick by which they measured a man's character.

He was popular with everybody—except his own wife. Theirs was not a happy marriage. Lincoln's unrefined manners clashed all too frequently with Mary's ungovernable temper. She treated him like a precocious but ill-behaved schoolboy. She nagged him because he sat down to dinner in his shirt sleeves, and went out to milk the cow in his shuffling slippers, and held up his trousers with one suspender, and ran ahead of the maid to open the door when guests arrived, and spoke to his fashionable visitors about pigs and chickens and turnips and horses, "just like the vulgar yokels from whom he had sprung." She was ashamed of his kind, she reminded him, and she never invited any of his kinsfolk to her house. He was fit to associate only with workingmen and plowmen, she told him contemptuously. In short, he was merely one of the "common people."

Lincoln listened to these accusations and smiled—drat that irritating smile of his! she stormed—and he pleaded guilty. He loved the common people, he confessed. "God too must love them, I guess, or He wouldn't have made so many of them."

For Lincoln was not ashamed of his lowly origin. On the contrary, he wore it like a badge of pride. His heart went out to the underprivileged because he was one of them. Intent upon their investigation of Lincoln's attitude toward the black slaves, many students of history have overlooked his attitude toward the white toilers. Lincoln abhorred wage slavery as intensely as he abhorred black slavery. "Inasmuch as most good things are produced by labor," he said in one of his early campaign speeches, "it follows that all such things of right belong to those whose labor has produced them . . . To secure to each laborer the whole product of his labor . . . is a worthy object of any government."

Lincoln was a friend of labor and an apostle of liberty. But he took care to distinguish between two kinds of liberty—liberty from exploitation, and liberty to exploit. In one of his speeches he pointed out this distinction by means of a parable. "A shepherd drives the wolf from the throat of his sheep . . . and the sheep of course thanks the shepherd . . . but the wolf denounces him." To the sheep the shepherd has given liberty from exploitation; but from the wolf he has taken away the liberty to exploit. "Let not the wolves cry *liberty,* when the word that they really mean is *tyranny.*"

In every controversy between the so-called upper and lower classes, Lincoln was on the side of the underdog. He was not only the champion of the laborer but the friend of the immigrant as well. He laughed at the pretensions of those who referred to themselves as *Americans* and to their immigrant neighbors as *foreigners.* All of us, he said, are foreigners. The only native Americans are those who "wear the breechclout and carry the tomahawk." Our forefathers were immigrants when "they drove these Indians from their homes." How stupid therefore of us to look down upon "those not fortunate enough to come over so early as we or our forefathers."

Such was the ugly duckling with the strange figure and the unconventional ideas who walked through the streets of Springfield in the eighteen-fifties. So absorbed was he in his "peculiarsome" thoughts that he frequently passed by his friends without noticing them. One day he strolled along the sidewalk near his house, trundling behind him a cart in which his little son Willie was riding. The child fell out and lay crying on the street; but his father, unaware of what had happened, kept calmly pulling at the empty cart.

LINCOLN

Yet he loved his children with the tenderness of a man whose own childhood had had more than its share of suffering. He allowed them to make his office their playground. "The boys," writes Herndon, "were absolutely unrestrained . . . They pulled down the books from the shelves, bent the points of the pens, overturned the spittoon—but it never disturbed the serenity of their father's good nature." To all of Herndon's suggestions that Lincoln "wring their little necks" the father had but a single reply. "Let them play. Time enough for trouble when they grow up."

We see Lincoln in one of his most revealing moments on a midsummer afternoon when Willie is about four years old. His mother has been trying to give the child a bath. Willie has wriggled out of the tub and scampered naked into the street. His father, sitting on the porch, is holding his sides with laughter at the sight of his pink and white little "monkey" who has slipped under a fence and is scurrying across a field. His wife stalks angrily up to Lincoln. "Stop that stupid hilarity and go fetch your son!" Still laughing, Lincoln starts after Willie. He catches him half-way across the field, gathers him up in his long gentle arms, covers his wet little body with kisses and then mounts him on his shoulders to bring him back to his outraged mother.

Lincoln's tenderness toward his children extended to the entire human race. His was one of those rarely attuned organisms that rejoiced with the joys and suffered with the sufferings of his fellows. His universal sympathy included not only the whites but the blacks. From the very beginning he was interested in the emancipation of the slaves. As a young man he had taken a trip to New Orleans. There he saw the slave market where the Negroes were being auctioned off to the highest bidders. He saw a young girl driven like an animal up and down the platform in order that the prospective purchasers might look her over. "If ever I get a chance to hit that thing," he exclaimed,

"I'll hit it hard!" To this end he dedicated his entire life. When he was elected to Congress, he drafted a *Bill to Abolish Slavery in the District of Columbia.* The bill was defeated, but Lincoln refused to bow to his defeat. He returned to the fight again and again. During the Kansas controversy on slavery he raised his voice in behalf of the black men. When the Republican Party was formed (1854) on the Jeffersonian principle of democratic equality, Lincoln was one of its most active organizers. And when Douglas, in his ambition for the Presidency, was ready to encourage the extension of slavery in the South, Lincoln challenged him to a series of debates on the subject.

These debates between Lincoln and Douglas were something new in American politics. They were mental duels fought before a tribunal of the American people. And the weapons that the fighters used were the two sharpest tongues in the United States.

But in Lincoln's speeches there was something more than brilliance. To paraphrase his own words, it was out of the abundance of his heart that his mouth continued to speak.

It was during his debates with Douglas that his eyes began to fail him—the result of the continuous reading of historical and legal documents. To strengthen his physical vision he went into a jewelry store and bought a pair of eyeglasses—for thirty-eight cents. He fitted the glasses to his eyes by the then common method of trying on all kinds until he found the kind that enabled him to see well. And to strengthen his *mental* vision he used the selfsame method. He examined all kinds of human relationships until he found the kind that enabled men to get along well. And this relationship he summarized in the following words: "Stand with anybody that stands right."

As a result of this application of ethics to politics, Lincoln became a national figure. There had been talk of secession in the South, but Lincoln declared that America must remain united. "United and right." A house divided against itself cannot stand. And America must become not partially but completely free. "This government cannot endure permanently half slave and half free."

Douglas tried to belittle the significance of these words and the importance of Lincoln. "Mr. Lincoln," he said, "is a kind, amiable, intelligent gentleman, but not a national leader." But the common folk felt otherwise. He was just exactly the sort of leader they wanted in the national crisis of 1860. And so they rejected Douglas and elected Lincoln to the Presidency.

Between his election and his inauguration his friends came by the hundreds to wish him Godspeed. And in spite of his busy hours he found the time to exchange a kind word with every one of them. Among his visitors was an old lady he had known when he kept store in New Salem. Lincoln was talking to a group of distinguished politicians when she arrived. But as soon as he saw her he left the group and walked over to her with a cordial greeting. Timidly she opened a package wrapped in brown paper and handed him a pair of coarse woolen socks. "Take them socks to the White House, Abe. I spun the yarn an' did the knittin' all by myself." Lincoln thanked her warmly, took the socks and held them by the toes, one in each hand. "Gentlemen," he said to the astonished bigwigs, "the lady seems to have got my latitude and longitude just about right, don't you think?"

Yes, his friends had got his latitude and longitude—moral as well as physical—just about right.

V

LINCOLN'S election to the Presidency meant the fulfillment of Mary's ambition. But it also meant the end of Lincoln's peace of mind. The planters of the South had clamored for the election of Douglas. They had threatened to revolt in the event of a Republican victory. While still a candidate Lincoln had clearly understood the issue. His own election would result in a personal triumph and probably a national disaster. The election of

Douglas, on the other hand, would bring obscurity to Lincoln, but it might possibly avert the tragedy of a war. But would it? Could any power on earth at this stage divert the sweeping tide of hatred that had descended upon the country? And if war must come, would Douglas be the man to steer his nation safely through the storm? Wasn't he too self-centered, too devoid of moral backbone, to take a positive stand for freedom and unity? Was not his heart, as a matter of fact, on the side of the rebels, the seceders, the slaveholders? Would Lincoln be morally justified, therefore, in stepping out of the contest? Did not the Presidency need Lincoln more than Lincoln needed the Presidency?

Such were the thoughts that tormented him during his campaign and immediately after his election. Rarely in history did a man experience a more bitter triumph. He hated strife. When war had been declared against Mexico (1846), he had raised his voice in protest. It had sickened him to see his country embarked upon a course of military conquest—"that attractive rainbow that rises in showers of blood." And now here he was, the most peaceful of men, compelled to lead his people into another deluge of blood.

Yet even at this late date the war might have been avoided or at least postponed if Buchanan, the outgoing President, had possessed a character of greater firmness. Buchanan saw the gathering storm immediately after the election of Lincoln. But he did nothing to stop it. Let his successor worry about it—if indeed there would be any successor. Again and again he remarked lugubriously, "I am the last President of the United States."

And so he sat irresolutely in the White House while South Carolina seceded two and a half months before the inauguration of Lincoln. Had Buchanan taken a prompt and decided stand against the secession of this state in 1860, just as Jackson had done in 1833, the Civil War might have been nipped in the bud. But instead of discouraging South Carolina, Buchanan

LINCOLN

actually encouraged it. He not only retained in his Cabinet such men as Jacob Thompson, who had helped South Carolina to secede, but he permitted the transfer of arms from the North to the South. And he sat impassively by when six other states—Mississippi, Florida, Alabama, Georgia, Louisiana and Texas—seceded between the election and the inauguration of Lincoln. When Lincoln was sworn into office on March 4, 1861, Buchanan gave him the Civil War as an inauguration present.

VI

THROUGHOUT the war, Abraham Lincoln had a double danger to fight against—invasion from without, disloyalty from within. The Copperheads—a copperhead is a "venomous snake that strikes without warning"—were beclouding the issues of the war with the propaganda of racial hatred. But Lincoln faced the rebellion of the South and the obstructionism of the North with a single courageous purpose—to keep the states united. "My paramount object in this struggle," he said, "is to save the Union . . . If I could save the Union without freeing any slave, I would do it; and if I could do it by freeing all the slaves, I would do it; and if I could do it by freeing some and leaving others alone, I would do that. What I do about slavery and the colored race, I do because I believe it helps to save the Union."

Here we see Lincoln thinking aloud. And, as a result of his clear and logical thinking, he came to the conclusion that the only way in which he could save the Union was to free the slaves The Emancipation Proclamation was the inevitable final paragraph in the thesis of Lincoln's philosophy.

And Lincoln's entire philosophy may be summarized in a few simple words—impartial love for the united family of America. His attitude even toward the South was one of tenderness and pity. He always spoke of the rebels as "these Southern gentlemen." He had an intense hatred against slavery but no hatred against those who believed in it. "They are just what we would be in their situation." He regarded the slaveowners, no less than the slaves, as the victims of a diseased institution that must be purged out of society if the nation was to be healed. He wanted to bring about a twofold freedom—to free the black man from the slavery of his body and the white man from the slavery of his soul.

He was a man of infinite patience. He bore not only with the insults of McClellan, but with those of his official family as well. When Seward and Chase reviled him, and Stanton referred to him as "that damned, gawky, long-armed gorilla," he neither rebuked them nor dismissed them from the Cabinet. "It is a dangerous thing to swap horses in the middle of the stream." And when the swivel-chair patriots—the men who did all the inciting and none of the fighting—accused him of incompetence, he let them talk and went quietly on with his work.

The vituperations against Lincoln continued throughout his life. Everything he did, insisted his obstreperous opponents, was wrong. Even his Gettysburg Address was denounced in the hostile papers as "silly and sentimental and unworthy of the occasion." It was not until after his assassination that America awoke to his greatness. Destiny, it seemed, had deliberately injected a melodramatic climax in order to emphasize the beautiful drama of his life. For now, at last, Lincoln stood forth as a man among a nation of children. Father Abraham . . . with malice toward none, with charity for all.

JEFFERSON DAVIS

Important Dates in Life of Jefferson Davis

1808—Born in Todd County, Kentucky.

1821–24—Student at Transylvania College.

1828—Graduated from United States Military Academy.

1835—Married Sarah Knox Taylor, who died three months after their marriage.

1845—Elected to United States House of Representatives. Married Varina Howell.

1846—Appointed Colonel of First Mississippi Infantry in Mexican War.

1847—Appointed to United States Senate.

1853–57—Secretary of War under Franklin Pierce.

1857—Reappointed to the United States Senate.

1861—Bade farewell to Senate and joined secessionists.

Elected President of the Confederate States.

1865—Captured near Irwinville, Georgia, and taken to Fort Monroe, Virginia.

1867—Released on bail and allowed to go to Canada.

1881—Wrote *Rise and Fall of the Confederate Government*.

1889—Died at New Orleans.

Jefferson Davis

Jefferson Davis
1808–1889

H<small>E WAS</small> born on a cotton plantation. And his father baptized him *Jefferson* after the great "Southern" President. He grew up under the Kentucky moon, amidst the clear smells of the field and the humming of the Negroes as they plucked their white blossoms from the goodness of the earth.

But legions of black men had searched the soil until the yield of cotton had grown lean. And many of the planters, like their brother pioneers, had moved Westward and Southward to more fertile territory.

Jeff's father was one of these pioneers. He moved his family from Kentucky into the virgin cotton land of Mississippi. Here he gathered a few slaves, worked industriously by their side, and built a little empire of comfort for his declining years. He sent his youngest son, Jefferson, to study at the School of Saint Thomas Aquinas, back in his native state of Kentucky. Here the dark and slender and sensitive young student absorbed into his soul the fragrance of the incense and the beauty of the legends depicted in the stained glass windows. His character took on a tinge of religious mysticism—a vague yet none the less significant instinct for martyrdom.

He graduated from Saint Thomas and continued his education at the College of Transylvania. His interest in poetry had now developed into a passion for history. Especially *classical* history. He admired the devoted patriotism of the Romans. Rome, too, was a land of the South. It was under the Southern sun that Horatio had held his bridge against the enemy and Brutus had wielded his sword of justice. Brave crusaders these Romans, soldiers of the noble fight.

But here, too, there was fighting to be done, frontiers to be held, ideals to be defended. Jeff Davis had decided upon a military career. He turned to West Point.

II

Upon his graduation from the military academy he was assigned to duty on the frontier post of Wisconsin. "Here an Indian war is to be had for the asking." But the skirmishes with the now defeated Indians were not very exciting. "Much of the blood sacrificed for our country hereabouts is taken by the mosquitoes." The fevers of the swamps and the winter frosts produced more hardships than the flaming arrows. But the most deadly weapon at this post was boredom. After three years of this stultifying exile Jeff Davis was transferred to Fort Crawford, a post where for the first time in many months he was able to meet "women who were not married, or who were not Indian squaws."

And here he met love. His heart went out to a winsome young brunette whose father was the hardened old garrison commander himself. When Old Zach Taylor learned that his daughter was in love with one of his soldiers, he threatened to fight a duel to protect her honor. Jeff Davis was in a quandary. On the one hand, how could he fight his commanding officer? On the other hand, how could he win his beloved if he fought?

JEFFERSON DAVIS

Love demanded an unconditional surrender. He resigned from the army and married Zachary Taylor's daughter. But as they traveled across the plantations of Kentucky to their Mississippi home, an attack of the yellow fever—the scourge of the South—struck hard and laid them low. And one morning, when Jefferson Davis raised himself from his bed, he heard the voice of his bride from another room. She was singing in her delirium. When he reached her bedside, the last note had ended forever.

This was the first sharp wound for the soldier, the first lost battle. Bruised and heartstricken, he started on his retreat. Back to the plantation which his older brother had given him as a gift—*Brierfield*—with its thirty-six slaves and its melancholy loneliness. "My heart," he said, "is in the bridal sepulcher."

For ten years he passed through this Odyssey of dejection—and then one Christmas season a sprightly young girl of Northern ancestry stepped into his halls at Brierfield and under the mistletoe offered his heart a new resting place.

III

DURING the years of his self-imposed exile he had read and thought a great deal about the theory of government. This interest in government was an outgrowth of his former passion for history. And now that he had come once more into contact with life, his old crusading spirit returned to him. He had decided to enter the arena of national politics. He would take an active part in the shaping of his country's destiny.

And the road to his national prominence lay, as he himself would have wished it, through the hardships of the battlefield. When the Mexican War broke out, he organized a volunteer regiment of "Mississippi Rifles." He came home from Buena Vista on crutches—and touched the heart of Old Mississippi. He was elected to the Senate.

To Washington he came with his lovely wife. And when he rose to speak in the chamber, all men were instantly charmed by the music of his voice. But the words he spoke were no less modulated by the discipline of his thought. He had grown sensitive of the link of his own soul with the soul of the people —a great living soul that spread as far as the eye could travel over the cotton fields.

Invited to make a speech at a banquet in Washington, he was introduced as a "war hero—the brave commander of the Mississippi Rifles." His eyes grew soft with pity for them. Would they never understand? He was not a warrior but a worshiper, the poet of a religion, the dreamer of an idea. That was why he had been ready to don a uniform and to give his life. To keep these sounds and smells of his country, the feel of the Southern earth.

In a corner of the room sat a gawky Congressman from Illinois, listening with rapt attention. His hands, hardened on the ax, curled slightly. He, too, could feel an idea with his hands. And breathe it with his senses. And die for it. But Jefferson Davis's eye never met the eye of Abraham Lincoln . . .

More of his enchanting speeches in the Senate. An unsuccessful campaign for the governorship of Mississippi. An appointment to the Cabinet. And then, when Franklin Pierce was elected President, Davis became his Secretary of War. And a right good Secretary, people said.

He loved his soil. It must grow into a vast empire. And it must have a huge army to defend every acre of it. Why not annex Cuba, that Pearl of the Antilles, and Mexico, and Central America? Manifest destiny! Send the Negroes, black waves upon waves of them, to unroll that magic carpet of white cotton . . .

He increased the size of the army, he advocated the purchase of African camels for the transportation of the Southern cotton, he engineered a new system of waterworks for Washington and dreamed ever greater dreams for the expansion of his country. And then he went back to the Senate and joined in the general restlessness.

JEFFERSON DAVIS

For America *was* restless. Again and again the same accusations and counter accusations were being hurled across the Senate floor. "Down with that Southern madness of slavery!" "No, down with the madness of those Northerners who would interfere with our Southern rights!" These contradictory challenges were gradually being fused into a single sentence of doom with a black and tragic exclamation point, bayonet shaped. "And some foolish men are still talking of compromise. As if we would give up our slaves without a fight!"

Slaves? He had a number of them. Thirty-six happy souls, to be exact. And he never had laid a hand of punishment on a single one of them. They were not his slaves, but his helpers —members of his plantation family. James Pemberton from Africa was their overseer in the field—as black as any one of them—"and as white." When he came to see Mr. Davis in his office, it was always, "Pull up a chair and sit down, James." And he gave him a cigar. Why this formal *James?* Why didn't he call him *Jim?* Because Pemberton might take it as a sign of contemptuous familiarity, and it wouldn't do to hurt an old and trusted friend . . .

Slavery? That man from Illinois, his hands gnarled on the ax, was elected President by a small, a very small section of the people. Well, maybe they were right in liking him. That was their business. But there were other people who thought differently; they didn't feel bound by his determination to "dictate" to them about their way of life, to compel them to remain in the Union against their will. They decided to go about their own business in peace, with their own elections and their own solutions to their Southern problems.

As Jefferson Davis sat in the Senate of the United States in 1861, word came to him that Mississippi had voted to leave the Union. His face turned instinctively to the Union flag. "I love this old Union. My father bled for it and I have fought for it." But Mississippi was his native *soil*. They had lowered his father in that Southern ground. The ground of the South was the grave of his beloved wife. Every part of his flesh, every particle of his memory, belonged to Mississippi.

It was not a philosophy of slavery, not an issue of politics that was calling him home. It was the cry of the father for the child.

He rose to the floor of the Senate chamber and made his farewell address. "Mr. President . . . I have served long; there have been points of collision; but whatever of offense there has been to me, I leave here; I carry with me no hostile remembrance . . . It remains only for me to bid you a final adieu."

As he walked from the halls of Congress his face was wet. Some miles to the South, Robert E. Lee was taking down the sword. Right or wrong, *his people*.

IV

JEFFERSON DAVIS went home. He believed his adventure was ended. Now he would return to his fields and his books. Pray Heaven that there would only be tears in the parting from Washington—not blood!

But one cloudless day as he tended his roses, a messenger boy sought him out. "Sir, we are directed to inform you that you are this day unanimously elected President of the Provisional Government of the Confederate States of America."

What an unexpected turn to his political career! The Presidency of *this* historic experiment. It was his duty to accept. His people had sent him to Congress at the time of their prosperity. Now they were calling him to lead the way for them in the day of their trial. There were other men in the South better qualified for statesmanship. "But you, Sir, are a soldier." There was soldiering to be done. He lingered for a moment among the roses. They were very red. Under the portrait of Thomas Jefferson he took the oath of office, as if in a dream.

He looked upon the people. Would there be war? "Moved by no interest or passion to invade the rights of others, anxious to cultivate peace and commerce with all nations, if we may not hope to avoid war, we may at least expect that posterity will acquit us of having needlessly engaged in it . . ."

The pangs of a chronic neuralgia had closed one eye. His continual headaches—a residue of the old-time fever that had taken off his bride—would not let him rest. But he kept his back erect. And he sat upon his horse with dignity as he rode into Richmond, the seat of the Confederate government. For he was conscious of something so *overwhelmingly* larger than himself; this something for which men lived with greater pain than his, in the single hope that for *this* they might be allowed to die.

Night after night he paced the floor of his White House in Richmond. It *was* war.

The generals came to him—Johnston, Beauregard, Cooper—and they told him to anticipate the slowly gathering strength of the North by marching on Washington immediately. But Jefferson Davis was shocked at the suggestion. "We shall never invade the North . . . We are fighting for the rights of a people to secede from an aggressive government. We can never use our army as an instrument of aggression."

The generals shook their realistic heads. "This man is an idealist. God help the South!" The people found him very prophetic and very sad. To the cheering aristocrats during the first mad summer months who passed around the champagne as though they were at the opera, he said sharply: "This will be a long war." There would be years—"champagneless years"—ahead. No golden goblets from which to drink, but the bitter cup of sacrifice for his people in the South. And the people stood awed.

Stephens of Georgia, the Vice-President under the new constitution, and Judah Benjamin, the Secretary of State of the Confederacy, were now beginning to glimpse the spirit of the sickly stately man who had been chosen as their President. Up to this time they had not really known him. In all great men there were hidden seeds of personality that required the roughest sort of nourishment before they could come to full bloom. And then they put forth startling and unexpected colors. "This man, Jefferson Davis, has entered the war less out of the sheer desire to win, than with the idea of vindicating a political principle."

Well, he was fighting his own way. You see, on the map, in the disposition of armies, in the fortunes of battle, you can fail of your objective. But never must you fail of the spirit. Whatever the outcome of the war, it simply never occurred to him that he would lose *his* fight.

He came before the people and told them that they were engaged in a total war for total freedom. And at first the members of his own Cabinet sat aghast. What did he propose to do? Tax the people directly? The people would never stand for taxes. Would he ask the plantation owners to give up planting cotton and to grow food instead? Why, not a single member of the Cabinet would listen to this "preposterous" idea!

He urged the passage of a military conscription bill to raise all the available manpower. Even at that, the South would be outnumbered by the North two to one. But the politicians advanced the curious age-old argument that such a measure would establish a military despotism at the very time when the people were fighting a war for freedom. Davis replied with determination. "A people must resolve to surrender its rights voluntarily in times of great struggle, or the fortunes of the battlefields will rob them in the end of all rights to surrender."

But gradually, as the great Confederate armies had begun to retreat, the great forces of the spirit had mobilized and had commenced to surge forward. Jefferson Davis felt he was no longer the leader of a lost cause. Ulysses Grant had cut the Confederacy in two as he struck a mighty blow at the fortress of Vicksburg on the Mississippi. "A whole generation of men in gray had bled to death" in a three days' fight at Gettysburg. General Sherman had marched with his devastating army like a scythe through the fields of Georgia. And the politicians in the

JEFFERSON DAVIS

Cabinet at Richmond looked with amazement at the exhilaration in their President's eye. There was no champagne now in the South. Not even coffee or sugar, vegetables or fruit. Not even meat. No bread. But in England Mr. Gladstone understood. In a burst of rhetoric he had declared that Jefferson Davis had built a *nation*.

Not a paper constitution, a senate or a flag. A nation built by suffering.

There was no champagne now. But at last there was a strong and sensitive link between a prophet and a people. They were partners in a great adventure of sorrow whose peace passed all understanding. Jefferson Davis rode to the camps and the hospitals to see the citizens of the new nation. Men from the front walked slowly and dazedly, blinded by the smoke of the guns. Men in the hospitals lay on bare boards in every state of mutilation, waiting for the surgeon who was far too busy to treat all of them. And young girls sat giving them water and fanning their faces as they died. And wagons piled with corpses rattled through the streets. Jefferson Davis saw one stiff dead arm raised to Heaven as if vowing vengeance.

Did he look at the map and grow pale at the prospect of his armies? He was dazed by his dream. He received a letter from Abraham Lincoln who expressed his desire to enter into negotiations of peace for "the people of our common country," and he replied in a kind of fascination—"Peace for the *two countries*." This was the climax of his life—the test of a great idea. A man must by right undergo the last extremity when he has given up the roses for an idea. What matter if the cause, like the flower, has died after a moment?

V

AND once on a spring day after five weary years of battles had brought nothing but further battles, he gave his wife a pistol, showed her how to load and fire it, informed her the enemies were approaching Richmond, warned her to escape. "If I live," he told her in the strange soft mystical way he had, "you can come to me when the struggle is ended. But I do not expect to survive the destruction of our constitutional liberty."

"The right of a people to abolish governments . . ." A phrase, a principle passing into the shadows, as Jefferson Davis fled from the armies of Lincoln into the lower South. Just before he reached the mountains he gave himself up to the Union troopers—a President without an army, without a government, without a people. But his head was high. As he marched with his jailers through the streets of Georgia on the way to Fortress Monroe, a little boy stared up at the great silent face in wonder. And the child who was one day to lead a *reunited* nation, slowly learned to understand.

The child was Woodrow Wilson.

CLEVELAND

Important Dates in Life of Grover Cleveland

1837—Born in Caldwell, New Jersey.
1855—Became clerk in Buffalo law office.
1859—Admitted to the bar.
1863—Appointed assistant district attorney of Erie County, New York.
1869—Elected sheriff of Erie County.
1881—Elected Mayor of Buffalo.
1882—Elected Governor of New York.
1884—Elected the twenty-second President of the United States.
1888—Unsuccessful candidate for re-election to the Presidency.
1892—Re-elected to the Presidency.
1893—Engineered repeal of the Sherman Silver Purchase Act.
1894—Sent militia to the Pullman strike at Chicago.
1895–96—Settled the Venezuela-British Guiana boundary dispute.
1897—Retired from politics.
1897–1908—Trustee of Princeton University.
1908—Died at Princeton, New Jersey.

Grover Cleveland

Grover Cleveland
1837–1908

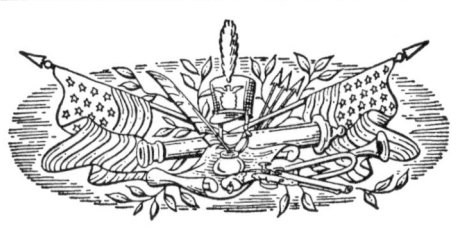

He had just sat down to one of his elaborate dinners at the White House. Suddenly he pricked up his nostrils. A familiar odor had come in through the open window.

"William," he said to the butler, "what is that smell?"

"I am sorry, Sir. It's the servants' dinner. Shall I close the window, Sir?"

"Certainly not!" And then, after a few more sniffs, "What is it, William—corned beef and cabbage?"

"Yes, Sir. Excuse me, Sir."

"I'll excuse you on only one condition. Take this dinner down to the servants, and bring their dinner up to me."

Grover Cleveland—the corned-beef-and-cabbage President.

II

He was a roughneck of a youngster. The roughest and the toughest of the nine children of the Reverend Richard Falley Cleveland. One night the inhabitants of Fayetteville (New York) were startled out of their sleep by the clanging of the academy bell. What was the meaning of that? A fire? An Indian attack? An earthquake? No, it was just Stevey Grover Cleveland snooping around in the belfry of the academy. He had climbed in through the window and up the narrow steps of the tower to see what would happen. And what happened was so terrifying to the little rascal that he scooted out of the nearest window and slid down the rain pipe to the ground.

It wasn't necessary for his father to punish Stevey. A piece of jagged metal in the rain pipe had done the job. For several days young Cleveland was laid up with a lacerated leg.

A mischievous cub. And untidy. Always came to school with grimy hands. Not that his mother didn't insist upon his scrubbing them clean before he started for school. But there were so many interesting things to be handled on the way. Finally his teacher warned him that she would give him a thrashing if he came to school again with such dirty hands. When he appeared the next day, it was evident that he had paid no attention to the warning. "Stephen," said the teacher, "hold out your hand!" Cleveland held it out. "Stephen," she said, "I will let you go unpunished if you can find me another hand in this room as dirty as this one." "Yes, ma'am," said Cleveland and promptly held out his other hand.

His teacher kept her word.

A rough, tough, untidy and clever little fellow with a generous heart. He had picked up a nondescript dog whom he had taught a number of tricks—such as standing on his hind legs, lying on his back and playing dead, and climbing a ladder. One day, while performing this last trick, the dog fell to the ground and broke his legs. Everybody advised Cleveland to have the dog shot. But Cleveland wouldn't hear of it. With the tears streaming down his face, he lifted the dog in his arms, carried him up to his room and with awkward tenderness set the broken legs in splints.

A zestful, fightful and thoughtful period—the boyhood of

CLEVELAND

Stephen Grover Cleveland. Whatever he did, whether he played or studied or worked, he did with his whole heart. "We must heartily and actively use every moment of our time," his teacher had told her pupils. She had asked them to write a composition on this topic. And here, in part, is what Cleveland wrote:

". . . If we expect to become great and good men . . . we must improve our time when we are young. George Washington improved his time when he was a boy and he was not sorry when he was at the head of a large army fighting for his country. A great many of our great men were poor . . . but by improving their time . . . they obtained their high standing. Jackson was a poor boy but he was placed in school and by improving his time he found himself a president of the United States . . . If we wish to become great and useful in the world we must improve our time . . ."

"We must improve our time." This thought ran like a refrain not only through his boyish composition but throughout his life.

III

HE HAD very little schooling. At sixteen he lost his father and found himself, together with his numerous company of brothers and sisters, heir to an empty purse. Fortunately for the family he got a job as "bookkeeper and general assistant" at the New York Institution for the Blind. A year of daily drudgery at his desk, interspersed with readings in Moore and Byron—his favorite poets—to the patients in the institution, a fistfight with a teacher who had given a thrashing to one of the blind little fellows, and then he started off to seek his fortune in the West.

He had expected to go as far as Cleveland, Ohio. "I was attracted by the name. It seemed that it was my town because it had my name." (Actually, though Cleveland didn't know it, the city had been named after one of his collateral ancestors.)

Young Grover—he preferred to be called by his middle name

—never reached his destination. He stopped over to see his uncle at Buffalo—and remained there for the greater part of his life. His uncle, Lewis F. Allen, owned a spacious estate in one of the Buffalo suburbs. He offered Grover a home and board in return for his services as one of the hands on his farm.

For a time young Cleveland worked diligently as a "hand," and then he told his uncle that he would prefer, if possible, to place the burden of his life's work upon his brain—and tongue.

"Not a bad idea," replied his uncle. "You've got a fairly good power of persuasion . . . At least, you've persuaded *me*."

And so his uncle secured him a job in one of the city's leading law firms—Rogers, Bowen and Rogers. Mr. Rogers Senior, a grumpy old fellow with an eye for ability, handed young Cleveland a volume of Blackstone, told him to "go to it, young fellow," and then left him to his own resources. Cleveland "went to it" with a will. One evening a junior member of the firm, surmising that he was the last to leave the office, locked the door. He had completely forgotten about that young apprentice who was sitting behind his desk in a corner, absorbed in his thoughts. It was some hours before Cleveland discovered that he was imprisoned for the night. "Good training for a lawyer," he chuckled as he turned on the lamp and opened his textbook. "Now I'll know what it feels like to be behind locked doors."

The next morning they found him in the office, a little the wearier and the wiser for his experience.

For three years he continued with his "law course self-taught," and then (in May, 1859) he was admitted to the bar.

And now began a routine of hard work and hard play. Attending to his clients—and he got not a few of them with his hearty handshake and his ready-for-a-fight spirit; stumping for the Democratic candidates and handing out the ballots at the polls; striking up friendships with the stablemen and the store keepers and the ditch diggers and the doctors and the financiers —his sympathies were as wide as the world; and visiting the taverns for a late evening snack of pretzels and beer. He was

CLEVELAND

regarded as one of the cleverest and chummiest young lawyers in Buffalo.

A little bit too chummy at times. That occasion, for example, when he met the young Englishman on the steamer *Clifton*. Grover Cleveland and several other lawyers were on their way to Fort Erie. They had been appointed on a committee of "good fellows" to entertain Prince Albert Edward of England on his visit to America.

They were having a merry time on shipboard. The cup had been passed around in a succession of international toasts. Suddenly a member of the British party bristled up. He had taken umbrage at the familiarity of the Americans and he was demanding an apology. Whereupon Cleveland looked upon him benignly and said, "Oh, rats!"

"I'll stand for no rats from anybody!" shouted the Englishman.

"Want to fight about it?" And Cleveland threw up his huge, capable fists.

It was then that the Englishman disclosed his identity. Grover Cleveland had come within an inch of exchanging blows with the Prince of Wales.

IV

HE SERVED as assistant district attorney of Erie County—"I hope I shall never descend from the virtues of a prosecutor to the vices of a persecutor"—slaked his thirst (but never beyond his mental poise) at the friendly tavern of Louis Goetz, accepted the office of sheriff and underwent the distasteful experience of presiding at the execution of two murderers, and finally accepted the nomination as the Democratic candidate for the mayoralty of Buffalo.

He won the election and proceeded to give his city an exciting spectacle—a bossless and graftless administration. He made a clean sweep of the "robbers" and the "wrongers" who had fastened themselves like barnacles upon the city. He discovered that his predecessors had been handing out inflated contracts for public printing, for street cleaning and for municipal building. He cut these contracts down to the actual cost and transferred the balance from the politicians' pockets into the city treasury. "The city," he said, "is my client, and it is my legal duty to protect my clients' interests."

He had served his city for only a few months when a grateful public elected him to the Governor's chair. Here he continued his courageous stewardship of the public funds. He paid out money only for good work and not for "good will." He had become known as the man of plain speech. He expressed his vetoes to various appropriation measures in clear and concise and cutting words. "I withhold my assent," he said in connection with one of the proposed contracts, "because I regard it as the culmination of a most barefaced, impudent, and shameless scheme to betray the interests of the people." On another bill which the legislature had passed with a view to defrauding the public he placed his veto with the following comment: "Of all the defective and shabby enactments which have come before me, this is the worst and most inexcusable."

Cleveland was an honest crusader. But he was also, as his opponents had discovered to their sorrow, a shrewd politician. Among those who tried to "knife" his political ambitions were the Tammany leaders, Tom Grady, "a man with a silver tongue and a scurvy mind," and "Honest John Kelly, so-called because he was crooked as a ram's horn." Cleveland not only accepted their challenge, but gloried in it. "A man," he said, "is known by the company he keeps, and also by the company from which he is kept out." As one of his followers, General Edward S. Bragg, so aptly phrased it, "men love Cleveland not only for himself . . . but they love him most for the enemies he has made."

This neat phrase did much to bring him the Presidential nomination on the Democratic ticket (1884) in spite of the strenuous opposition of Tammany Hall. The Republican nominee was James G. Blaine.

CLEVELAND

In the entire campaign that followed, Cleveland made only two speeches. He was well aware of his limitations. His corpulent body and his unimpressive face with his beady little eyes, his big fleshy nose and his walrus mustache made him look rather ridiculous in comparison with the dashing figure and the flashing smile of the "Plumed Knight" of the Republican Party. And Blaine made the best of his advantage. He stumped the country from end to end and "waved the bloody shirt." That is, he played upon the passions that were still smoldering as a result of the Civil War. He spread the rumor that Cleveland, in the event —"which Heaven forbid!"—of his election, would "put all the Negroes back into slavery." But that was not all. The campaign managers of Blaine—assisted by their "friendly enemies," the leaders of Tammany Hall—had descended from national issues to personal vilification. They accused Cleveland of being the father of an illegitimate child—an accusation which Cleveland promptly and frankly admitted. The election, with Tammany Hall lined up on the Republican side, and with Cleveland's personal character dragged through the mud of a public scandal, seemed to be "in the bag" for James G. Blaine. His managers were already sending him their congratulations. Blaine had nothing to fear from his enemies.

But he had everything to fear from his friends. One of them, the Reverend S. D. Burchard, inadvertently stabbed him with an intended caress. In a speech which Burchard delivered at the Fifth Avenue Hotel (New York) just a few days before the election, he referred to Blaine as the crusader against the "three evils sponsored by the Democratic candidate—Rum, Romanism, and Rebellion." This speech, as stupid as it was unfair, descended upon the country like a whirlwind and blew the entire Catholic vote into the Democratic camp. Cleveland was elected by a slender majority. It was the first Democratic victory in twenty-four years.

V

IN THE White House, Cleveland continued as the persistent No-man in American politics. He vetoed all sorts of unnecessary appropriations. "Public office is a public trust." He was the elected trustee of a going concern—the corporation of the United States. It was his business to keep this corporation upon a sound footing—not only by raising the numerator of its income but also by reducing the denominator of its expense. He weeded out all the fraudulent pensions that were being paid to Civil War veterans. One of these pensions, proposed by a Congressman from Ohio, was represented as "a just and necessary relief for the widow of a soldier who fell mortally wounded in the fight before Nashville . . . Two of her four sons were shot dead while fighting in the Union Army . . . a third returned home from the war with one eye shot out . . . the fourth had his arm shot off in the same battle in which his father fell . . . The poor widow, in the absence of the $8 a month voted by Congress and vetoed by Cleveland, has been compelled to take refuge in the county poor house."

At this revelation of the President's "cruelty," everybody cried "Shame!" The cry was changed to one of approval, however, when Cleveland made known the facts upon which he had based his veto. These facts, briefly, were as follows: The widow was not in the poor house. Instead, she was being supported by two of her sons—one of whom, incidentally, had received a postmastership from Cleveland at Bentonville, Ohio. This was the man who was represented as having had an "eye shot out" in battle. Actually, he lost the sight of one of his eyes long after the war, when a nail from a shoe he was repairing flew against his eyeball. The son with "his arm shot off" was even now in the possession and the full use of his two arms—he merely had a bullet scar on the fleshy part of one of them. The two sons pictured as having been "shot dead while fighting in the Union Army" had

CLEVELAND

never even been wounded in battle. Both of them had died years after the war: one, of yellow fever; the other, as the result of a fall from a cliff. As for the widow's husband "who fell mortally wounded . . . before Nashville," he had really died before that battle—"having choked on a piece of beef while gorging himself in a drunken spree."

Such were the spurious claims which Cleveland vetoed in his effort to save his country's treasury from being fleeced. By carefully investigating every case he was able to show that a great proportion of the claims were fraudulent. In some cases the men who were demanding pensions for their "patriotic services" had as a matter of fact served in jail for desertion instead of serving in the army at the battle front.

As for the *genuine* claims, however, Cleveland signed more pension bills than any of his predecessors. At no time did he refuse to be fair, but at all times he refused to be fooled.

His chief purpose as a public servant was to protect the individual against his unjust or greedy neighbors; to protect the weak against the strong—a reversal of the general practice among his contemporary politicians who protected the strong against the weak. He was a fighter for the underdog. He advocated a fair compensation for labor just as he advocated a fair profit for capital. He expressed his abhorrence for communism—whether in the ranks of labor or of capital. "Communism," he declared, "is a hateful thing, and a menace to peace and organized government. But the communism of combined wealth and capital, the outgrowth of overweening cupidity and selfishness, which insidiously undermines the justice and integrity of free institutions, is not less dangerous than the communism of poverty and toil, which, exasperated by injustice and discontent, attacks with wild disorder the citadel of rule."

He believed in the universal bill of rights—especially in the right of every individual the world over to consideration as a dignified human being regardless of his race, creed or color. When Emperor Francis Joseph refused to accept Anthony M.

Keiley as American Ambassador to Austria because Keiley had a Jewish wife, Cleveland as a rebuke left the Austrian post vacant. Nor was this a device at vote-fishing on Cleveland's part. At that period (1885) there were too few Jews in America to play any significant part in national elections.

Cleveland regarded himself as the attorney-general for the entire American people—the minority, the majority, the classes, the masses. He tried at all times to strike a just balance between the conflicting interests of the various groups in America. Having made a study of the question of international trade, he found that the high tariff, by raising the prices of goods, brought excessive profits to the rich and placed excessive burdens upon the poor. When the manufacturers, supported by college professors, undertook to explain the economic theory that "protection for the rich means prosperity for the poor," he retorted with the famous phrase that "it is a *condition* which confronts us, not a *theory*." He therefore sponsored a bill to bring about a drastic reduction in the tariff and thus gained the eternal enmity of the manufacturers.

And the hearty friendship of the common folk—a friendship which he heartily returned. People came from everywhere to have a look at that "friendly guy" who was their President. One day he went on a fishing trip to Lake Placid together with his physician, Dr. S. B. Ward. After a long tramp, the two tired "fishermen" sat down on a log to rest. They were soon joined by a third man. After an exchange of remarks about the weather, the newcomer volunteered the information that he was on his way to the Prospect House "to shake hands" with President Cleveland. "My name," said the stranger as he was getting ready to leave, "is Sam Perkins. And yours?"—turning to Cleveland's physician.

"Dr. Ward."

"And who," whispered the stranger, "is the good-natured fat guy sitting next to you?"

"Grover Cleveland."

CLEVELAND

VI

Grover cleveland, in spite of his friendly disposition, was gaining too many enemies through his political honesty. Referring to the leaders of his party just prior to his assumption of the Presidency he had declared: "They'll have to discover it sooner or later, and the sooner they'll discover it the better—that I'm not a figurehead to be put in front of a cigar store."

And the would-be manipulators of the invisible strings of the government discovered it soon enough. He put an end to the Spoils System. He dismissed the *old* scoundrels, but he refused to replace them with *new* scoundrels. He made civil service, rather than political bootlicking, the yardstick for the measurement of a man's right to a public job. The politicians who felt their friends thus "cheated out of a soft spot" were furious.

So, too, were the railroad speculators who, like the public job hunters, depended upon the "bounty" of the politicians. These railroad speculators had received, from a former administration, the "gift" of a hundred thousand acres of public land. Cleveland now restored this land to the public, for the use of individual homesteaders. Another hostile power arrayed against Cleveland's future ambition.

And in the presidential campaign of 1888, all the hostile powers had decided to pool their interests against Cleveland. In addition to their legitimate grievances they manufactured false charges. They called him "the Beast of Buffalo"—a drunkard, an adulterer, a wife-beater. (He had married during his first term in the White House, and even his enemies in their non-political moments admitted his gentleness and his generosity as a husband.) This time the smear campaign was successful. Cleveland was defeated for the Presidency.

He went back to the private practice of law. He had had enough—he believed—of public service and public abuse. Just before his retirement from the White House, a friend of his had come to see him. This friend was leading his five-year-old little boy by the hand. "Son," said Cleveland to the child, "I'll give you a wish to remember for the rest of your life. Pray to God that He never lets you become President of the United States!"

And then Cleveland turned to his friend. "What is the boy's name, by the way?"

"Franklin," piped up the child. "Franklin Delano Roosevelt."

VII

STRANGE how rarely people follow advice—even their own. In 1892 Cleveland ran once more for the Presidency, and this time he was re-elected.

It might have been better for his reputation as a statesman had he never been elected to a second term. For in this term he encountered two obstacles which he was not strong enough to overcome—the Panic of 1893 and the Pullman Strike of 1894.

The Panic of 1893, to be sure, was none of Cleveland's making. Like most other panics, it was due to a simple economic factor: overproduction on the one hand, and underconsumption on the other. The manufacturers had paid insufficient wages to the workers. Result—the workers had been unable to buy a sufficient quantity of the goods which they had produced. This meant the accumulation of an excessive inventory, the shutting down of factories, the unemployment of millions of workers, and that most shameful disease of our modern industrial system—starvation in the midst of plenty. Cleveland had nothing to do with this condition. But he received all the blame for it. From April 1 to October 1, there were more than eight thousand commercial failures, with the losses amounting to almost three hundred million dollars. And everybody pointed to Cleveland as the primary cause of the general distress.

In spite of the general criticism directed against him, Cleveland was not to blame for the hardships of the Panic. But he was to blame, at least in part, for the riots of the Pullman Strike.

CLEVELAND

For in this strike he did something very unusual for him—he lost his head. George Pullman, the inventor of the "palace cars" on the railroad trains, had built a "model village" for the employees of his company. He then raised their rents and reduced their wages to such a degree that it was impossible for them to get along. The workers, under the leadership of the then conservative Eugene V. Debs, complained that they were being squeezed at both ends. They requested George Pullman to submit the dispute to arbitration—a request that a good many businessmen as well as laborers, to say nothing of the general public, regarded as eminently fair. "It is the part of American sportsmanship," they said, "to leave it to the umpire."

But George Pullman wanted to play the game his own way. "We have nothing to arbitrate," he said. Whereupon Debs called out a general strike of the American Railway Union. It was a serious matter. The strike threatened to tie up the traffic of the entire country, including the United States Mail. Cleveland found himself faced with a vital decision—and his decision was vitally wrong. Instead of demanding an immediate arbitration between the *two* parties, he issued an immediate injunction against *one* of the parties—the workers. This injunction, the first of its kind in the history of labor, forbade the strikers "to interfere in any manner, direct or indirect," with the operations of the Pullman Company. A wave of resentment flared up in the ranks of the workingmen. They accused Cleveland of taking sides. Chicago, the headquarters of the Railway Union, had become a battlefield between the strikers and the strike-breakers. The Pullman Company asked Cleveland for the aid of federal troops. Governor John P. Altgeld of Illinois, on the other hand, insisted that the state militia was well able to take care of the situation. Cleveland listened to the Pullman Company. He sent two thousand federal soldiers to break the strike. Another flare of resentment on the part of the strikers. "He's sending us leaden bullets to feed our hungry bellies!" A clash between the strikers and the soldiers. Several of the strikers were killed, the strike collapsed, and Debs was sent to jail on the charge of "conspiracy to restrain legitimate business."

When the strike was over, Cleveland appointed a commission to investigate the merits of the case. It was like killing a man first and trying him afterward. The commission reported that the strikers had been in the right. But George Pullman, thanks to Cleveland's hotheaded decision, had been supplied with the might. And the might had conquered the right.

It is hard to understand how Cleveland, who all his life had been a friend of labor, could have so completely lost his head on this occasion. But perhaps we may find a clue to his hasty and inconsiderate action if we remember his physical condition at the time. In 1894 Cleveland was a sick man. Though the general public was unaware of the fact, he had just undergone a serious operation on a malignant tumor in his mouth. The greater part of his upper jaw had been replaced with a substitute of vulcanized rubber. "Even the gods err," Homer reminds us, "when they are in great distress."

VIII

IN SPITE of his occasional errors in judgment, he was asked to run for a third term. A shrewd and honest fighter was so rare a phenomenon in the political turmoil of that period. But he refused to run again. "I am not in politics. I am out for good."

He retired to a professorship in Princeton, where he became the idol of the students. And of the children of the town. It was at the urgent request of the children that he once more accepted a "public" office. He became "the Honorary President of the Boys' Nature Club."

A boyish heart to the very end. One evening he was entertaining a number of invited guests. But there was an uninvited guest, too—an Irish setter who followed one of the visitors into the library. The owner of the dog was about to drive him away. "No, no!" exclaimed Cleveland. "Don't let him stay out in the cold while we're enjoying the fire. There's room enough here for us all."

There's room enough for us all. And, he could have added, there's *kindness* enough for us all. As he lay on his death bed, too ill to see his friends, he was not too ill to speak to a nurse who was trying to make him comfortable. "Don't bother about me, please. Go out there into the garden instead, and save those birds from the cats." Glancing through the window, he had seen the cats lurking for their little feathered victims. And his last living thought—to protect the weak against the strong.

THEODORE ROOSEVELT

Important Dates in Life of Theodore Roosevelt

1858—Born in New York City.
1880—Graduated from Harvard College.
1881—Elected to the New York state legislature.
1889—Appointed by President Harrison to the United States Civil Service Commission.
1895—Appointed President of the New York City Board of Police Commissioners.
1897—Appointed by President McKinley as Assistant Secretary of the Navy.
1898—Led the Rough Riders in the Spanish-American War.
1899—Served as Governor of New York.
1900—Elected Vice-President of the United States.
1901—Became (upon the assassination of McKinley) the twenty-sixth President of the United States.
1902—Started "crusade of the people against the trusts."
Instituted policy of the "Square Deal."
1903—Sent a cruiser to Panama and secured the land for the Panama Canal.
1904—Re-elected to the Presidency.
1905—Negotiated the Peace of Portsmouth to end the Russo-Japanese War.
1907—Sent the United States battle fleet on a cruise around the world.
1908—Called a conference of State Governors for the conservation of the national soil and resources.
1912—Ran for the Presidency on the Progressive ticket. Defeated.
1919—Died in New York City.

Theodore Roosevelt

Theodore Roosevelt
1858–1919

THERE were rivulets of many diverse races that emptied into the blood stream of his nationality. Some of it flowed from the businesslike stubbornness of the Dutch mingled with the freedom-loving impetuosity of the French Huguenots and the fearless defiance of the Protestants in the Rhineland. And some of it was the blood of the fighting Scotch Highlanders and of the fierce Irishmen of Ulster who had resisted the British kings. Here, too, was the spirit of the Welsh Quakers who had died by the thousands for the cause of free worship, and of the Quakers of Pennsylvania who had given the American Indian a "square deal" among his fellow men. All of it was the blood of rebels, of the *protesters* of the human race.

In his immediate background there was a conflict in the fusion. His earliest years were passed in the turmoil of the Civil War. His father was a Northerner whose heart was in the Union; his mother came from a prominent social family in Georgia. And the child, who upon his father's lap had acquired an aversion against the South, received a scolding at his mother's knee when he asked in his prayers for a blessing upon the North.

His undersized body was in conflict with his rugged mind. His eyes were poor, his speech was defective, and his chest was racked with asthma. He was too sickly to go to school. And throughout his life, in memory of his own suffering and weakness, he sympathized with all human weakness and suffering.

But at the same time he had grown to possess an exaggerated and almost fanatical worship of physical strength. "Make your own body, Ted," his father had urged him. And from the first the child had determined to become a self-made man—a daring knight of the New World. He lifted weights and boxed and chinned the bar. He spent every clear day of his boyhood in the open air, toughening his muscles and strengthening his lungs and taking deep draughts of the energy of life. And as he grew older he traveled with his father over forest trails and mountain roads and sailed the oceans and fished and hunted and built up a powerful body to shelter a vigorous mind.

When he entered Harvard at eighteen he was physically well-equipped for life. "He was a little fellow five foot and a half high." But his small stature fooled none of his friends. A package of dynamite is also small.

II

AT HARVARD "Mr. Roosevelt of Oyster Bay" drove a team and dog cart—the only one of its kind in the college—spent his money freely and belonged to the most exclusive of the clubs. He had entered upon his education with the knowledge that he would never be forced to earn his living. In the gentleman's fashion of the day, he could choose the career that most interested him, or—if he preferred—no career at all. Too dynamic for a life of idleness, he thought for a time of becoming a naturalist adventurer like Humboldt or Darwin. In his senior year at Harvard he courted a young lady with such exuberant accounts of his "snakes and reptiles" which he kept in his college rooms that he "frightened her out of her wits."

But before long he turned his imagination from the jungles of the lions to the labyrinths of the law. Here, too, was ground for exciting adventure. Yet not exciting enough for his superabundant energy. What to do? For do something he *must*. This young man who had inherited a life of ease had developed a hunger for work—the hardest sort of work. The paradox could be resolved only through the choice of the right career.

He married his fiancée and traveled with her over the continent of Europe. And when he returned home, a new horizon had opened up in his reflections. The old childhood dream of knighthood in shining armor had taken on a sublimated form. There were intellectual as well as physical crusades to fight. Economic wrongs to be righted. Social injustices to be assailed. In this industrial struggle between the rich and the poor, each of the two sides blinded by a passionate self-interest to survive, was there not a crying need for a vigorous and cultured and disinterested Sir Galahad to insist upon a spirit of fair play? He, Theodore Roosevelt, would try to be this modern Sir Galahad. In the chaotic wilderness of politics he would search for the Holy Grail.

When he told his friends what he had in mind they were aghast. "Politics is a dirty business for ward-heelers and machine bosses. Gentlemen are not welcome." But Roosevelt persisted with a logical stubbornness. Why should a gentleman shrink from the responsibilities of government? "If we were at war with a foreign enemy, I wouldn't for a moment think of hiring somebody else to do the shooting for me. Well, I intend to do my own shooting in the dirty war of politics. In this way, perhaps, I may be able to clean up some of the dirt."

He decided to start the cleaning in the boss-ridden saloons of his own city. "I am going to try to help the cause of better government right here in New York."

III

THEODORE ROOSEVELT entered the twenty-first district Republican Club of New York. It was the New York of Tammany

Hall and of the Tweed Ring. The party bosses took one look at the "rich young man with an eye-glass, an evening dress and a Harvard accent" and were convulsed with laughter. "A dude, the way he combed his hair, the way he talked, the *whole thing!*"

But Roosevelt took his seat at their councils and immediately commanded their respect. He let it be known that he intended to judge them not as freaks but as human beings, and that he expected the same treatment from them.

Soon the party bosses were spellbound by his energy and his fight. They forgot his "r-a-w-t-h-e-r" and placed him in nomination for the New York Assembly. Canvassing for votes among the saloonkeepers he met one burly fellow who complained of the liquor taxes. "I hope you will do something for us when you get up to Albany, Mr. Roosevelt."

"Why should I?" replied the young candidate. "Your taxes aren't high enough by a long shot."

He won the election. The newsmen and the public were amused at the new legislator. "The exquisite Mr. Roosevelt of New York, a blond young man with English side-whiskers and a Dundreary drawl in his speech, made his maiden effort as an orator . . ."

Roosevelt was fast learning things. The world was his oyster. And when he opened it he found it rotten. The moral concepts on which he had been raised, he was now told, were unseasonable. The *seasoned* politicians advised him that "the whole duty of a man consists in making the best of himself . . . but it is not part of his business to join with others in trying to make things better for the many by curbing the abnormal and excessive development of the few."

And now the press and the public in Albany were little short of amazed to find that "the exquisite Mr. Roosevelt" had become a roaring lion. He inspected the slums and introduced a bill to improve the conditions of the sweatshop workers in the crowded tenement houses. He led an investigation into the corrupt activities of a high judiciary officer. He lunged out against the attempts of the New York Elevated Railway to bribe the legislature for a reduction of its taxes. He exposed the venality of the big business corporations in the state. He insisted upon carrying "private morality into public office"—a thing almost unheard-of in the political circles of the day.

And then suddenly a twofold blow in his domestic life halted him in his fight for "better government." Within twenty-four hours he lost his wife and his mother. The fighter was laid low. He bought a cattle ranch in the Dakotas as far from civilization as possible and left the city of New York for the wild lands in silence. His friends of the twenty-first political district understood and let him go. "You couldn't talk to him about it. You could see at once that it was a grief too deep . . . There was a sadness about his face that he never had before . . . He didn't want anybody to sympathize with him."

Here in the "bad lands" of Dakota, a country of elemental passions and elemental men, he began his emotional reconstruction. He drove his cattle and foregathered with sheriffs and helped keep the peace with his guns. Two years of hard adventure, and the realization that justice was only as strong as the weapons employed to enforce it. And then he turned East with the supreme conviction that the "guts" of the individual determined the goal of society.

He came back to the metropolis to carry on his fight. From now on there was no stopping him. The people knew him for a man of destiny.

IV

He had entered upon the political scene like a Don Quixote tilting at windmills. And he had changed the course of the wind. But the wishful politicians still persisted in the illusion that he was a knight in cardboard. They recommended him for an appointment to the civil service commission—and they were further relieved when the reform mayor of New York appointed him police commissioner of the city. Here, away from the turmoil of elective office—they believed—he would paddle in the duckpond of petty reform and sink finally into the obscurity of a contented life.

They didn't know their man. He plunged into his work with a crusading fervor. He revitalized the police force. He scraped it of corruption and scoured it as clean as the shiny brass buttons upon the policemen's uniforms. He walked along the streets with a broom to sweep the taverns of their gunmen. "Teddy the Scorcher" had become the hero of New York. Before his term was ended there was no crooked policeman in New York and no figure in America more colorful than Commissioner Roosevelt.

The Republicans applauded him for the prestige he gave them and fearfully watched for his next step.

This step was from the "duckpond" to the sea. President McKinley had appointed him Assistant Secretary of the Navy—and immediately his voice was heard above the broadside of the navy's guns. When asked what we should do if we were ever attacked, he shouted: "Build a battleship in every creek!" Now at last the young fighter had come into his own. His eye fairly glistened with the spray of the sea.

He asked Congress for an appropriation of five hundred thousand dollars for ammunition. And a few months later he asked for an additional eight hundred thousand dollars. Congress wanted to know what had happened to the first sum? "Spent it on target practice," he replied. He was asked what he would do with the second sum. "Spend it the same way." He got his money.

And then once more the pent-up current of his energy burst forth in all its momentum. He went out to challenge the fates. America had declared war on Spain. The place for a knight was on the battlefield, not in the armchair. Roosevelt tossed aside his maps and his conference notes, collected a volunteer company of "Rough Riders" and went on the hunt for Spaniards in the swamps and the hills of Cuba. Always he believed not only in *denouncing* evil but in personally *fighting* against it.

THEODORE ROOSEVELT

It was a regiment of tough soldiers that he collected for his fight. For he loved to tame the coarsest fiber with the steady hand of his discipline. Amidst a hailstorm of bullets he swung into the saddle—and the impetus of the charge carried him forward through the fighting and the peace and straight into the governorship of New York. His military exploits had been worth a hundred campaign speeches. With some of his shrewd good shooting he had set on fire the imagination of America.

And the bitter feelings of the politicians. They just couldn't cope with the unorthodox erratic who quoted Browning and busted broncos. An Andrew Jackson who wrote libraries of learned books. No such savage genius had ever joined Boss Platt's Republican Party in all the history of its stormy campaigns. They made one final effort to put this "strange animal with the mind of a scholar and the heart of a lion" back into his cage. When his term as governor had expired they solicitously prepared a burial for him in the graveyard of American politics. McKinley was up before the Republican Convention for renomination as the party standard-bearer for the new term. And the practical members of the party had hit upon the simple idea of nominating Theodore Roosevelt for the Vice-Presidency. "Four years of this honorable and dignified seclusion will deprive him of the public ear and enable us to shelve him forever."

Yet Marc Hanna, the manager of the Republican campaign, threw up his hands in a tremble when the big vote for Roosevelt was counted on the night of the election. "I wonder whether any of you realize that there's only one life between this madman and the White House?" And almost before he could bring his hands down again, the "one life" was removed by an anarchist's bullet, and the "madman" reigned.

V

THROUGH the labyrinthine course of illogic and a path bristling with excitement, Roosevelt had risen from a gentleman's sinecure at Harvard to the Presidency of the United States. Lady Luck had dealt him the ace cards in the deck of destiny. And now he was the ruler of all the people—those who had been consistently handed the joker and the deuce, as well as those who had been dishonestly shuffling the cards with the aces up their sleeves. Out in the "bad lands" of Dakota, Roosevelt had kept a gun by him to see that everybody got a square deal. And here in the White House he would use all the available machinery of the government to the same end. In the game of national industry as played between the businessman and the worker, the public and the private interests, the farmer, the banker and the middleman, and in the game of international trade as played between the various countries of the world, "there shall be no crookedness in the dealing."

That was his commandment. And he struck his vigorous hand upon his desk and the altar and the lectern in the classroom. And he showed his "toothful" smile of triumph wherever he went to hearten and to convince the people that his commandment would be obeyed.

He had become the gallant crusader for the Square Deal. "There can be no genuine feeling of patriotism of the kind that makes all men willing and eager to die for the land, unless there has been some measure of success in making the land worth living in for all alike." And the soldier of the Spanish War who himself had been ready to die, now turned his deadly fire upon all the combinations of the private monopolists who made it difficult for their fellow Americans to live. He was determined to "bust" the giant "business trusts" that were flourishing with fixed prices and fancy profits in the restraint of all competitive trade. He established an Interstate Commerce Commission which checked the "selfish concentration" of the great railroads. He broke strikes that threatened the health and the safety of the general public. He invited the leader of the Negro Race to dine with him in the White House. He laid plans to conserve the natural resources of the country—not only against the ravages

THEODORE ROOSEVELT

of the weather but also against the rapacity of the "despoilers of the earth for their private gain."

And he told his people that he was building a bigger and better and happier nation to the end that it might lead the way in the building of a bigger and better and happier world. "For such is the destiny of every great nation." He denounced the isolationists who were urging their countrymen to remain "cooped up" within their own little corner of the stage and to shut their eyes to the other actors and actions of the world's universal, interdependent drama. "We are not, and cannot, and never will be one of those nations that can progress from century to century doing little and suffering little, standing aside from the great world currents."

We must follow—he insisted—a vigorous and fearless foreign policy. No desire for peace should lower our sword when the stakes are decency and justice. He squared his shoulders to meet the taunts that the pacifists were hurling against him—"jingo, blusterer, warmonger." Even the Knights of the Holy Grail could never have kept the vows of Christ, save only by a handiness with the spear and a willingness to use the sword. He frankly confessed his "love for the blue steel unsheathed in the righteous cause." In 1902 the Monroe Doctrine had been put to the test. Kaiser Wilhelm had entered a financial claim against the government of Venezuela. And a German squadron had actually set sail to blockade the Venezuelan coast. Roosevelt's eyes narrowed. He was convinced that the German squadron was in American seas not merely to collect money. He believed that the Kaiser intended to take permanent possession of the seacoast of Venezuela and to make it a fortified jumping-off place for future aggression. And so Roosevelt requested the Reich to submit her financial claims to arbitration and to withdraw her battle fleet. With typical Prussian arrogance the Reich refused his request. Whereupon Roosevelt assembled the United States fleet under Admiral Dewey and gave him orders to be ready to shoot. Then he sent the Kaiser an ultimatum. "Either you withdraw from Venezuela, or we open fire." The Kaiser withdrew. But Roosevelt with a rare intuition into the Prussian mind had won the respect of Kaiser Wilhelm. The German aggressor had at last met a man who could outguess him and outforce him.

Roosevelt was unafraid. He collected his fleet and sent it on a tour of "friendship" around the world. And as the huge guns flashed at every port and the marines marched through the capitals of many nations, he grimly declared: "This, in my judgment, is the most important service that I have rendered to peace."

His was the "peace of action." The realization had come to him that a canal must be built across the narrow neck of land which joins the two Americas. For—he reasoned—if this country were to be faced with a two-ocean war, "Japan in the Pacific and Germany in the Atlantic, for example," our Pacific and Atlantic fleets would be separated by the entire stretch of the long voyage around South America. Roosevelt selected the Isthmus of Panama as the best site for the canal. When the government of Colombia refused to permit the building of this canal, he encouraged a revolution by the Department of Panama and sent warships to aid the revolutionists. The Republic of Panama was proclaimed and Roosevelt promptly recognized it.

The country was shocked at the "lack of nicety" in his procedure. But Roosevelt defended his action with honest bluntness. "I had two courses open. I might have taken the matter under advisement and put it before the Senate, in which case we would have had a number of most able speeches on the subject, and they would have been going on now, and the Panama Canal would be in the dim future yet. We would have had a half century of discussion, and then perhaps the Panama Canal," and his eyes flashed. "I preferred that we should have the Panama Canal first and the half century of discussion afterward."

The canal was built. But America felt at peace with the world. She had been lulled by sweet prosperity into an impractical dream, unaware of the importance of her role in the realistic struggle of the nations for existence. Roosevelt's warning was as welcome as a siren that blows in the middle of the night. The people dreamed on.

And when the two terms of his office were finished and he went off hunting in the jungles of Africa, a good many of his fellow Americans sighed with relief and declared, "That's where he belongs."

VI

INTO the jungles. And out again. Roosevelt was seeking to capture the biggest game of them all—an understanding of himself. To lay low his restlessness and to pluck out of his heart the meaning of the driving energy that would not give him peace.

But this prize eluded him. As he hunted the wild beasts in the African jungle, he knew that there were many wild dragons of political injustice still unslain at home. For him there was no peace. He must be President again. He returned home. The ghost of his ambition—ambition not so much for splendor as for service—refused to lie still. But the flesh and the blood of him had bequeathed this ambition to Taft four years ago. The Republican Party no longer wanted Roosevelt. Didn't this restless and erratic spirit who dared to gain entrance from another world realize that Theodore Roosevelt had died in March, 1909?

But Roosevelt would not stay politically dead. Repudiated by the Republican Convention, he formed his own party of "Progressives" and once more stalked the country making speeches, hunting votes. In vain. The people brushed him aside. Woodrow Wilson, the Democrat, was chosen chief of the nation. And Theodore Roosevelt once more took up his books and his guns and left America for another journey of exploration. To Brazil. As he paddled up the tropical rivers to their sources—always he was anxious to get at the *source* of things—an attack of jungle fever laid him low. His life of danger was finally threatening to take its toll. For many days he lay under the scorching skies in delirium. Slowly he fought his way back to his feet. Another victory for the happy warrior who refused to go down.

He came home again, and his eyes flashed as of old when he smiled. But he had left his strength behind him.

The old Rough Rider was hard upon his final journey. Suddenly across the seas a million-headed, steel-helmeted German monster swooped down upon Belgium on the way to Paris. The World War had begun!

Roosevelt rose from his bed and looked around for his armor. But the American Government refused to accept his services. There were millions of younger and sturdier crusaders eager to take his place. Among them was Roosevelt's own youngest son, Quentin. A gallant Rough Rider of the air. And one day they brought to the father the brief announcement about his son—"Died in the line of duty."

Good Lord, but this was *life*, this death of millions of Quentins. The father sat quietly on the porch of his home at Oyster Bay. He, too, was ready to be their soul's companion in the Great Adventure. "Only those are fit to live who do not fear to die."

WILSON

Important Dates in Life of Woodrow Wilson

1856—Born at Staunton, Virginia.
1879—Graduated from Princeton.
1886—Received degree of Doctor of Philosophy from Johns Hopkins University.
1888—Appointed Professor of History and Politics at Wesleyan University.
1890-1910—Served first as Professor of Political Jurisprudence and then as President of Princeton University.
1910—Elected Governor of New Jersey.
1912—Elected the twenty-eighth President of the United States.
1912-16—Engineered the Federal Reserve Act, the Federal Trade Commission, and the Clayton Act (against the abuses of large monopolies).
1916—Re-elected to the Presidency.
1917—Delivered message to Congress for declaration of war against Germany.
1918—Drew up the Fourteen Points and went to the Paris Peace Conference.
1919—Returned and laid before Congress the Versailles Treaty. Toured the country in behalf of the "League of Nations Covenant." Brokenhearted at the failure of his country to accept this covenant.
1924—Died at Washington.

Woodrow Wilson

Woodrow Wilson
1856–1924

ELECTION night, November 7, 1916. The tide had turned against Wilson, who was running for the second term. The East and the Middle West were rapidly drifting toward Charles Evans Hughes, the presidential candidate on the Republican ticket. At nine-thirty the *New York World,* Wilson's strongest newspaper supporter, conceded the election of Hughes. Wilson was resting in his New Jersey retreat at Shadow Lawn. At midnight his secretary, Joseph P. Tumulty, called him on the phone. "I'm sorry, Mr. President. It seems we're licked."

"Thank God!" was Wilson's reply.

The next morning, as he was shaving himself, his daughter Margaret tapped on the door of the bathroom. "Father, there's an extra edition of the *New York Times.* The West has swung in your favor. You've won the election!"

"Go tell it to the marines," retorted Wilson as he went on with his shaving.

Wilson dreaded the prospect of a second term in the White House. For it meant that he must lead his country into war. And he hated war with a hatred as intense as ever burned in the hearts of the ancient prophets. Both by training and temperament he was attuned to a life of constructive peace. He was a Celt, a visionary, a poet, a weaver of words, a dreamer of dreams. And a lover of his kind. He believed tenaciously in the might of right as against the right of might. As a child he had seen the devastation of the Civil War, and as a young man he had witnessed the degradation of its aftermath. He knew that when a country plunges into war it endangers the life not only of its body but of its soul. "Once lead the American people into war," he had remarked to Frank I. Cobb, editorial writer of the *New York World,* "and they will forget there was ever such a thing as tolerance. To fight, you must be brutal and ruthless. The spirit of ruthless brutality will enter into the very fiber of our national life . . ."

And so it was with a heavy heart that he allowed himself to be drafted into the campaign for the second term. "He kept us out of war" was the motto of his campaign managers. And, God willing, he *would* keep his country out of war. But he knew that he hoped against hope. In the avalanche of destruction let loose by the German military machine it was beyond the power of any man to keep America out of the war.

II

THOMAS WOODROW WILSON—he called himself "Tommy" until his senior year at Princeton—was a quiet little child who preferred fairy tales to fights. When the soldiers paraded through the streets, he sat alone and aloof. He had a frail body and a strong mind. And a temper. He bossed his parents, and they in turn babied him. "Poor little Tommy is so delicate, we mustn't hurt his feelings." Flaxen-haired, freckled, with a rebellious stomach and bespectacled eyes, he was "predestined" —as his father jestingly remarked—to mental rather than to physical gymnastics. In his barn loft he organized a juvenile baseball nine, "the Lightfoots." He was not, however, their captain or their manager, but their "parliamentary leader." He taught them how to conduct their meetings in accordance with Robert's *Rules of Order*. "Every one of the little chaps," Wilson recalled many years later, "knew perfectly well just what the previous question was, and that only two amendments to a resolution could be offered, which should be voted upon in the reverse order."

From earliest childhood he was a parliamentarian—and a disciplinarian. He was descended on both sides from a Scotch-Irish ancestry of printers and preachers. The love of, and the respect for, the Word was in his blood. It was not until his ninth year that he learned to read and to write—his parents wanted to shield him as long as possible from the hardships of a routine education. But he learned rapidly and he read voraciously. Night after night the light in his bedroom was on until long after nine, the prescribed bedtime hour for Tommy. But his parents never punished him. "Reading is the only dissipation I'm willing to allow him," said his father, the Reverend Doctor Joseph Wilson.

His father encouraged him in his reading—and in his writing. Both of them had a passion for the precise word. They delighted in verbal fencing. "You must wield the English language," Dr. Wilson advised him again and again, "into a flaming sword." Once, writes Newton D. Baker, Wilson took into his father's study an essay upon which he had spent much time and labor. "Dr. Wilson read the essay very slowly, and then turned to his son. 'Exactly what did you intend to say in this?' The boy explained. 'Then why not say it?' And without further words, Dr. Wilson tore up the manuscript and let it flutter into the wastebasket."

But if the father was critical of the son, the son was equally critical of the father. He listened to Dr. Wilson's sermons with a severe—though proud—attention. And often after the sermon was over he pointed out how his father might have improved a passage by the insertion of a different phrase, a more picturesque figure, a word with a more resonant sound.

Like his father, Tommy was eager to become an eloquent speaker. Often on week days he would go into the church and "deliver a sermon" to the empty walls. On a midsummer afternoon, as he walked home from one of these "sermons," he was surprised to see the Negroes on the streets bowing to him obsequiously as he passed by them. Finally, his curiosity getting the better of his shyness, he asked one of the Negroes to explain the reason for their sudden outburst of reverence toward him. "We bow to you, Marse Wilson," replied the awed Negro, "'cause you'se a great sup'rnatural preacher. We peeked in t'rough de window an' we seen you admonishin' de sperrits!"

III

BORN (December 28, 1856) in Virginia, Wilson was brought up in Georgia, whither his father had moved when Wilson was a year old. His training, therefore, was southern. He was able at first hand to witness the bitterness of a defeat in war. He saw the trail of ashes left by Sherman's march to the sea. He spoke to rebel veterans, sullen defiant men who, to use their own expression, were "conquered but unrepentant." He grew up with an overwhelming ambition—to help create a world without conquest or mastery or slavery or hate. And he trained his tongue and his pen to that end. His one hero was Lincoln. "When I remembered Lincoln and thought of all my greater material advantages . . . I believed I would be a poor creature indeed if, even without genius, I was not able to do some constructive work for the land that bore me and that I so loved."

"Even without genius." These words bothered him. Would he have the intellect necessary for the constructive work his country so desperately needed? In school he was mediocre—"neither good enough for distinction nor bad enough for censure." In September, 1873, he entered Davidson College and the following spring he returned home—a victim of physical and mental indigestion.

He retired to his room—his father was now pastor of the Presbyterian Church in Wilmington, North Carolina—and buried himself in his books. Especially books on history, philosophy, religion and the science of government. He was in search of the Golden Grail of intellectual conviction. And one morning he discovered it. He had been sitting up until the small hours, "his elbows on his knees and his nose in a book on Gladstone," when the certainty he had been seeking flashed suddenly upon him. "Father," he cried as he burst into Dr. Wilson's study, "I have found it!"

"Found what?"

"The fact that I have a mind. A mind that can think and create."

His father blew a cloud of smoke from his pipe. "In that case, son, you had better go to Princeton." His own alma mater, Princeton was to Dr. Wilson the one institution that could transform his son's intellectual yearning into practical achievement. His boy, he felt even at that time, was destined for something great.

And Wilson, too, shared this feeling. "Tommy," recalls a classmate, "seemed to have an uncanny sense that he was a man of destiny . . . He was always preparing himself, always looking forward to the time when he might be called to high service. When he walked alone it was, as he explained, to have opportunity for calm reflection." In the words of another classmate, "Tommy Wilson in his undergraduate days displayed a passion for three things—Gladstone, Government and God."

He loved society—especially the society of those who preferred mental to physical games. "The play of the mind was as exhilarating to him as the play of the body is to athletes." He joined the college debating club where he amazed the other students with the facile dexterity of his phrases. "He tossed them about like colored balls—and he never missed the mark."

True to his Calvinistic training, however, Wilson debated not to dazzle but to convince. On one occasion he was selected by lot to speak in favor of the protective tariff. He flatly refused to do this. "It is my principle to uphold only that which I believe."

His classmates derided and at the same time admired his stubborn honesty. "Tommy is different, but he is a jolly good mixer for all that." He took part in many of the leading college activities. He sang in the Glee Club, he edited the *Princetonian*, he joined the Athletic Association (as an advisor, not as a competitor), and he managed the varsity baseball team. And above all, he "practiced forever" at the most zestful game of them all —the exciting game of making friends. Princeton, as his father had anticipated, played no little part in completing Tommy Wilson's education.

IV

WOODROW WILSON—he had now dropped the "Tommy" from his name—was determined to be "someone" in the public life of the nation. At Princeton, whenever he met a tough opponent in an argument, he jestingly remarked: "I'll thresh it out with you when I meet you in the United States Senate." And now, as a preliminary step toward the Senate, he decided upon a legal career. A year's study at the University of Virginia Law School—and once more, as at Davidson College, he was obliged to leave his course uncompleted. An attack of the same old trouble, indigestion.

He returned home—and went on with his legal studies in private. Failure never bothered Wilson. He merely cast it off like an old garment. Within two years he passed the bar and opened a law office in Atlanta.

Business was slack, and one day Wilson went on a picnic. When the company arrived at the grounds, Wilson got lost— and with him, Ellie Lou, the pretty and piquant young daughter of the Reverend Samuel Edward Axson. Lunch time, and everybody "hungry as a bear." Where in the world is Woodrow?

"I know," piped one of the children. "He's over there cutting a heart on a beech tree."

Shortly after the picnic their engagement was announced. "Woodrow Wilson," confided Ellie Lou to her brother, "is the greatest man in the world—and the best."

But the "greatest man and the best" couldn't make a go of the law. He had a disconcerting way of preferring justice to legality—a fatal error for a lawyer whose business it was to win cases and not to reform the world. "Your talents," Ellie Lou advised him, "are meant for the classroom and not for the courts."

And so he decided to prepare himself for an academic life. "There are more roads than one to a career of public service." He entered the Graduate School at Johns Hopkins and won his doctorate with a thesis on Congressional Government.

He married Ellie Lou and accepted an offer to teach at Bryn Mawr—a newly opened college for "masculine women." Wilson was unhappy at Bryn Mawr. He preferred to associate with feminine women. And his students preferred to associate with masculine men. They showed little respect for their young professor who instead of an athletic body had developed an athletic mind. Wilson was glad to be relieved of his duties at Bryn Mawr when he received an offer to teach at Wesleyan University (in Middletown, Connecticut).

Wilson understood men, and men understood Wilson. They disregarded his awkwardness, his short body stilted upon his long legs, his big ears, his northern Irish "horse face," his jutting jaw and his large and sensuous mouth. They were interested mainly in the golden nuggets of wisdom that came tumbling out of that brave and homely mouth. And they forgave him for his inability to play football. For he had such an uncanny ability to devise winning formations for the players. Though never a member of a varsity team he was appointed assistant football coach—and directed the Wesleyan team to a championship.

He acquired a national reputation as a teacher. In the spring of 1890 Princeton invited him to return as Professor of Political Science. Wilson was elated. "If I cannot *lead* men, I can at least *teach* them to lead."

V

His career at Princeton is the story of an initial success and of a subsequent failure—a failure, however, which led to a greater success. Such was the destiny of Wilson. He was a man who never submitted to defeat. Even at the end of his life, as we shall see, it was not Wilson that failed. It was the world that failed Wilson.

But to return to Princeton. When Professor Wilson arrived at this "delightfully aristocratic" institution, he set out to transform it into a *devotedly democratic* institution. And the students, with the exception of a handful of silver-plated snobs, responded with the enthusiasm of youngsters invited to new intellectual adventures. For several years in succession the senior class voted him the most popular member of the faculty. They listened to him with something akin to adoration when, in October, 1896, Princeton College was formally reborn into Princeton University and "Godfather Wilson" was called upon to deliver the christening address. "The business of the world," he declared on that occasion, "is not individual success, but its own betterment, strengthening, and growth in spiritual insight." A new note in American education. A saner and humaner interpretation of the American credo. The Declaration of *Independence* means nothing less than the Declaration of *Interdependence*.

And this note he repeated six years later when he was elected president of Princeton. "We must deal with the spirits of men, not with their fortunes." No longer would Princeton be an adolescent "country club." From now on it would become an experimental laboratory in the fine art of democratic living. He raised and stiffened the academic requirements, with the result that over a hundred "gentlemen loafers" were expelled for failure in their studies.

WILSON

And then, while the fathers of these discredited youngsters were sharpening their axes, Wilson threw another bombshell into the academic sluggishness of the college campus. He proposed to abolish the aristocratic collegiate societies, with their exclusive eating halls and their luxurious clubhouses. In their place he outlined a group of democratic living quarters within a Gothic quadrangle—to be known as the "quad" system—eating-commons and sleeping-commons in which all the students were to be leveled up from social distinctions to simple devotions.

Wilson's bombshell exploded. The college world was in an uproar. "What—must a gentleman eat with a mucker?"

Wilson took up the fight for the muckers—and lost. The faculty refused to adopt his plan for the democratization of Princeton. But the loss of this battle led him to the winning of a far greater battle—the democratization of America. A number of political idealists had been following his fight. And as they watched this Scotch-Irish professor with the fearless heart and the peerless tongue, they saw in him the makings of a superior statesman. They offered him the candidacy for the governorship of New Jersey. He accepted the offer (1910) and won the election.

VI

THE political idealists of New Jersey had brought about his election. And now the political bosses of New Jersey hoped to bring about his submission. "Sure, he promised to fight political graft. But we know them teacher birds. Lots of gab and no go." What was their surprise to find that the academic Doctor Wilson possessed not only "go" but a vigorous boot! One of his first acts as governor-elect was to denounce Boss Jim Smith of New Jersey who was running for the United States Senate. "You can't do this to *me,* Mr. Wilson!" But Mr. Wilson went right ahead and kicked Jim Smith out of his senatorial dreams. The professional ward healers throughout the country rubbed their eyes in amazement. Here was a new phenomenon under the sun—a politician who kept his word! But the political idealists saw themselves a step nearer to the fulfillment of their vision. Here was a man to whom the word *Democracy* was not merely a campaign slogan but a religious creed. Presidential timber this—a leader who was upright, clean and unafraid.

And ambitious. Fortunately for the progress of America, Woodrow Wilson was selfish enough to crave for the glory as well as for the responsibility of leadership. His was not the humility of the saints, but the pride of the prophets. In order to be a great statesman, he knew that he must be a clever politician.

It was this double quality of adroit politics and solid statesmanship that won him the election to the Presidency in 1912. And it was this double quality that enabled him to sway the sentiment of the Congress into the enactment of several laws designed to help the weak against the strong. He carried on from where Jackson and Lincoln and Theodore Roosevelt had left off. He reduced the tariff, enacted a graduated income tax law based upon the principle "from each according to his ability to pay," dispersed the concentrated power of the banking interests into twelve federal units, imposed a legal curb upon the expansion of selfish corporations and unlawful monopolies, and strengthened the position of labor by legalizing trade unions and boycotts and picketing and by declaring that injunctions could not be issued against strikers except to prevent deliberate injury to property. Wilson was not a radical but a liberal. "We shall restore, not destroy," he had proclaimed in his inaugural. He was willing to leave the upperdog with his reasonable hunk of meat provided the underdog got his juicy bone. But it *must* be juicy, he insisted, and nourishing enough to sustain life and hope and the energy to emerge from the bottom of the heap. "Such is our national way of life."

His international, like his national, policy was based upon the principle of competitive fair play. In this principle of fair play he saw merely the modern application of the Golden Rule. He looked with approval upon every honest government that respected the rights and the opinions of the governed. He recognized the republic of Sun Yat-sen in China and he refused to recognize the dictatorship of Huerta in Mexico. The happiness of the people, he maintained, is of greater importance than the avarice of its rulers. Or of its investors. He put a drastic check upon the tendency to protect the foreign investments of American capitalists with the lives of American soldiers. It was his desire to abolish two false doctrines that stood in the way of human progress—the divine right of capital to rule the land, and the divine right of gunpowder to rule the world.

He was the happy leader of a peaceful nation. And then, in 1914, there came a double blow to him. His wife died, and Europe exploded into war. From that time on, there was no happiness or peace for Wilson.

From the firing of the first gun he knew that unless the war came to a speedy end, America would be dragged into it. The earth had grown too small for isolationism. The needs of humanity had become too complex, the exchange of world commerce too interdependent, the activity of every individual too closely related to the activity of every other individual, for any one country to remain unscathed when the other countries had been caught in a conflagration. When he accepted the burden of a second term, he did it as an unwilling soldier drafted into a hateful war. But the job had to be done. Perhaps, if he remained at the helm, he might make this a war to end war. A holy cause to die in—a noble vision for a man of peace.

When, on April 2, 1917, Wilson asked Congress to declare war, it was not Wilson nor the American government nor the American people that made the decision. It was the ruthlessness of the German military machine. Or, if you will, the inexorable course of human destiny.

Wilson was a tragic figure on that gray spring morning in

Washington. A prophet turned warrior. Like the prophets of old, he had prayed to God that the burden of the fatal message might never be his to proclaim. For a time he thought of resigning from the Presidency. But a soldier must never desert.

As he rode back to the White House on that tragic day, Pennsylvania Avenue was lined with cheering crowds. But there was no cheer in the President's heart. "How strange to applaud a message of war," he remarked. "A message of death for our young men."

VII

THE Allies won the war and Wilson launched his Fourteen Points—a brave argosy of peace in a tempest of vindictive and selfish hatreds. Open covenants openly arrived at . . . an end to secret diplomacy . . . absolute freedom of the seas . . . free trade among equal races . . . reduction of armaments . . . the right of all countries to govern themselves . . . a league of nations to make war forever a thing of the past. And the blind leaders of men, both here and abroad, took these Fourteen Points and tore them up and turned them into the confetti of a rancorous victory parade. They cheered Wilson to the echo and rejected his dream. They corrupted his peace without victory into victory without peace. The cynical politicians of the day made two fatal mistakes. They were too harsh and too lenient —too harsh to the German people, too lenient to their military machine. They shut Germany off from the means of making an honest living, and they allowed her to develop the means of subsisting through dishonest force. The treaty of Versailles was one of the most tragic paradoxes in history. It left the enemy both with the food for its venom and with the instrument for its sting.

Wilson foresaw this, and he knew that the scrapping of the Fourteen Points was but the prelude to another war. The world had failed him. The masters of the nations had betrayed his hopes—the hopes of their own people. His New Testament of international good will was too splendid for the spiritual astigmatism of 1919. "We are ruled," gibed Clemenceau with cynical candor, "by our dead."

But Wilson knew that his great vision would be judged by the living.

FRANKLIN DELANO ROOSEVELT

Important Dates in Life of Franklin Delano Roosevelt

1882—Born at Hyde Park, New York.
1904—Graduated from Harvard University.
1907—Admitted to the bar.
1911–12—Served in the New York state legislature.
1912—Appointed Assistant Secretary of the Navy under President Wilson.
1920—Defeated as the Democratic candidate for the Vice-Presidency.
1921—Stricken with infantile paralysis.
1924—Conquered the disease.
1928—Elected Governor of New York.
1930—Re-elected to the Governorship of New York.
1932—Elected the thirty-second President of the United States.
1933—Unsuccessful attempt to assassinate him at Miami, Florida.
1933–36—Inaugurated the "New Deal" in the economic and social life of America.
1936—Elected to a second term in the White House.
1940—Elected to a third term in the White House—an act without precedent in American history.
1941—Drew up, with Winston Churchill, the "Atlantic Charter."
Assumed duties as Commander-in-Chief of a united nation in the war against Germany, Italy and Japan.

Franklin Delano Roosevelt

Franklin Delano Roosevelt
1882–

FROM too close a view it is difficult to see a forest because of the trees. Similarly from too close a view it is difficult to see a man's character because of his characteristics. The perspective of time and space will be necessary for a final evaluation of Roosevelt's personality. Those of us among his contemporaries who try to appraise him are likely to slip into the dangerous pitfall of his too ardent admirers, who call him a St. Francis in politics, or into the equally dangerous pitfall of his too bitter opponents, who look upon him as a ravenous wolf in sheep's clothing. To an impartial observer—and at such a stormy period no observer can be altogether impartial—Roosevelt seems to be a dynamo of energy dominated by an instinct for justice. His energy often drives him into error, but his justice generally brings him back to the right course. Roosevelt is a man who loves to fight—and who fights to love.

II

HE CAME by his love for fighting and his instinct for affection through the Roosevelt ancestral strain. The Roosevelts are a peculiar tribe—a family of strong rich adventurers who possess a friendly sympathy for those that are not strong enough to adventure for riches. Born on the banks of the Hudson, he grew up to look upon humanity as a stream of travelers going up and down the river—an endless and living unit of interdependent motion. His father, like many of the other Roosevelts a combination of the successful businessman and the practical philosopher, explained and strengthened in his growing boy this American sense of active interdependence. Not only this, but the constitutional and the ethical right of every human creature to his life, his liberty and his pursuit of happiness. On Sundays he pointed out the pleasure yachts that took the wealthy upon their cruises, and the passenger boats that carried the workers upon their excursions. "God has made the same river and the same sky for us all. And He wants all of us alike to share in their bounty."

The only child of his father's second marriage—he had a grown-up half-brother by his father's first marriage—young Franklin developed a great hunger for companionship. And his father encouraged, rather than hindered, this wholesome hunger. Although he educated him at home, he allowed him to make the acquaintance of the village youngsters—the children of the farmers and the butchers and the coachmen and the grocers and the gardeners of Hyde Park. These children, Franklin was surprised to learn, were—save for their clothes and other such unimportant externals—just as human and just as likable as the wealthier children who came to visit them at their Hyde Park estate. This so-called *estate,* his father maintained, was in reality just a mere *farm.* There was nothing pretentious about James Roosevelt. A simple, companionable, democratic, human father who possessed a rare gift—he knew how to train a sensitive child into a sensible man.

From his father and from his companions young Roosevelt got his love for human beings. And from his mother he derived his love for the sea. She told him how her father had captained

FRANKLIN DELANO ROOSEVELT

his own sailing ship and had brought his cargoes of tea from China. As a child she had sailed on her father's ship and once in a storm she had come dangerously close to losing her life. But, added his mother, she was never afraid.

Excellent environment for the unfolding of an impressionable character. In his father he found a superior teacher, in his mother a superb playmate. She was so very much nearer to Franklin's own age—there was a difference of thirty years between his father and his mother. The Roosevelt family represented *three* rather than *two* generations—a long stretch of years and experiences for young Franklin to absorb.

Such was the heritage of Franklin Roosevelt: an eagerness to see humanity on the go, a passion for universal companionship, a longing for adventure and a laughing fearlessness in the face of danger. He was growing up into fit timber either for the captain of a ship or the leader of a state. Whatever might be his future career, he was pretty certain to show the necessary spunk.

And the proper kind of education. His father saw to that. As a supplement to his book study, James Roosevelt enabled him to travel and to study places and men. For eight successive years, between the ages of seven and fourteen, young Roosevelt spent his vacations abroad in the company of his parents. And thus he learned to know the peoples of Europe and their languages and their ways. And, too, he got to know the difference between free nations and those that were led by the leash. In London he and his tutor were once stopped at the door of the Kensington Museum. "Sorry," said the attendant, "but you can't go in. The Prince of Wales is inside." Whereupon Roosevelt showed his membership card in a nature club to which his father had once in a playful moment elected him. "Oh, well," remarked the attendant, "in that case you can go right in." And within a few moments, Roosevelt found himself face to face with the future king of England.

Quite different, however, was his experience in Germany

where he once spent a cycling holiday with his tutor. As they were passing through the countryside near Strasbourg, they were arrested four times within a single day—once for picking cherries, once for taking their bicycles into a railroad station, and twice for other inadvertent infringements of the universal German *Verboten*. "The German credo," laughed Roosevelt, "is—*Forbidden to live!*"

III

His frequent vacations on shipboard had aroused in him a desire to go to sea like his grandfather. But his parents advised him that he must first round out his education. They must send him to a good preparatory school and to a good college. Groton and Harvard.

He entered Groton, where his hearty voice and his handsome features stamped him at once as a "regular guy." He displayed not the slightest arrogance toward anybody—except the arrogant. For these "blustering cymbals of gilded brass" he had little sympathy. He criticized them for their boastfulness about their fathers' income. "How much does that income add to the value of your character?"

Yet Roosevelt was no prig. Even when he criticized, he did so with a good-natured smile. If some of his classmates acted foolishly at times—"well, we are all of us fools, most of the time." He held out the hand of unaffected friendship to all those who were unaffectedly willing to meet him half way. "There goes a real thoroughbred!" said the boys at Groton.

And at Harvard. They elected him to their clubs, they took him into their confidence, and they appointed him to the editorial board of the *Crimson*. Here, too, as at Groton, he insisted upon taking a fellow for what he *was* rather than for what he *had*. In an editorial which he wrote just prior to the election of the Class Day officers he insisted that these officers be elected on the basis of fitness rather than on the basis of friendship. "There is a higher duty than to vote for one's personal friend, and

FRANKLIN DELANO ROOSEVELT

that is to secure for the whole class leaders who really deserve the position." Let the class poet and the class orator, for example, be selected from among those who were most highly gifted rather than from among those who were most highly pedigreed.

Already he was feeling his way toward a new kind of politics —democracy based upon honest common sense.

And it was about this time that he became definitely interested in a political rather than in a naval career. His fifth cousin, Theodore Roosevelt, had just been elevated to the Presidency of the United States. It was like a bugle call to Franklin. Cousin Theodore was a fighter for justice. Had been so all his life. A fine man to emulate. A fine career to follow—this setting to right the wrongs of his fellow men.

Yet the call at the start was none too insistent. He was a young man just out of college, with a personal income of $5000 a year—his father had recently died and left him a substantial fortune—with a healthy appetite for living and a resplendent and congenial world in which to live. A carefree and pursefree Prince Charming, adored by the ladies, admired by the men. A favorite of fortune, destined for an early marriage and a life of contented ease.

He married. But he did not settle down to an easy life. For his young wife was like himself a Roosevelt. A fighter of the good fight and a righter of wrong. Eleanor Roosevelt, a niece of Theodore Roosevelt, was as sensitive as Franklin. But her sensitiveness was translated into thought rather than into action. She represented the poetry, as he represented the prose, of the human quest for justice. Like Franklin, she was an ardent observer of life; but unlike him, she was an equally ardent reader of books. Franklin had noticed some of the ills of society. Eleanor had studied to discover their remedies. While a student at a fashionable school in London, she had taken excursions into the slums to see how the poor lived. She had noted their hardships and she had listened to their grievances. And she had studied the literature of labor, of Henry George, of Karl

Marx. Once she had marched in a workers' parade. Her sense of obligation had been aroused. Something *must* be done to make the hard lot of the poor easier. "And you, Franklin, are the man to do it."

And thus it was through the road of social service that Roosevelt started upon his stony climb to political fame.

IV

In 1910 he entered upon his first political campaign—a Democrat running for the state senate in a Republican district. And he won. "The Roosevelt smile," said the voters, "is irresistible."

But, his colleagues in the senate soon discovered to their surprise, his independence was also irresistible. "That young Roosevelt has a mind of his own." "Yes, and a *dangerous* mind, too." He had set himself against the boss politicians of his own party—a bad precedent, they insisted, for a young upstart in public office. And the worst of it was that he couldn't be bribed. He was too well off. And he couldn't be ousted. He was too well liked. The bosses tried to fight him—in secret, in the open. But he couldn't be budged. "There is nothing," he laughed, "that I love as much as a good fight." What in the world were they going to do with this "fresh college kid?"

And the "fresh college kid" threw himself into another fight—for a reduction of the working week in New York State to fifty-four hours. And won.

It was in the same spirit of fighting independence that he went as an anti-Tammany Wilson delegate to the Democratic National Convention in 1912. At this convention, as one of the Tammany bosses put it, "the two educated guys"—Wilson and Roosevelt—"stole the show." Franklin Roosevelt played no unimportant part in bringing about the nomination and the election of Woodrow Wilson.

When Wilson was elected, he offered Roosevelt his choice of three posts. He could become either Collector of the Port of

FRANKLIN DELANO ROOSEVELT

New York, Assistant Secretary of the Treasury, or Assistant Secretary of the Navy. Without a moment's hesitation, Roosevelt decided to throw in his lot with the navy. For that was where his heart lay.

He immediately set to work advocating a larger and more effective American "patrol of the seas." For the world, as he had realized in his travels, is but a little cluster of trading posts, not *separated* but *connected* by the universal highway of the ocean. An easy road for the merchant, an equally easy road for the aggressor. A war in one continent, therefore, is a direct threat to the peace of the other continents. This elementary fact of modern geography Roosevelt recognized even before the First World War. America, he insisted, must have a navy big enough and strong enough to guard against any aggression from whatsoever source it might suddenly arise.

And he succeeded in strengthening the navy despite the opposition of those who couldn't see beyond the horizon. When America entered the war (in 1917), the young Assistant Secretary of the Navy had become, next to the President, perhaps the hardest working man in the government. "At times," Mrs. Roosevelt tells us, "sleep was practically eliminated for days." He personally scrutinized the repairing, the fueling and the arming of the ships, the building and the fortifying of adequate supply bases and arsenals and training stations, and the allocation of the necessary funds for the designated needs without any wasting of red tape or time. In his effort to generate action, and still more action, he broke enough laws, as he himself laughingly remarked, to send him to jail for nine hundred and ninety-nine years. Here, for example, is just one of his admirable though "illegal" transactions as related by the New York contractor, Elliot C. Brown, to Roosevelt's biographer, Ernest K. Lindley: On June 27, 1917, Roosevelt examined a site for a receiving-ship cantonment in New York City. On June 28, he gave the contractor an order to go ahead with the work. On June 29, the plans were on the way; on July 5, the ground was broken; on August 4, the work was completed; on August 11, breakfast was served at the new cantonment to 6800 men. And then, two months later, Roosevelt received from the government an official authorization to build that cantonment!

But Roosevelt was not content with his activities as a government official. He wanted to see action on the battlefield. He was young and healthy and eager to risk his life when so many other young Americans were risking theirs. He pleaded with the President to release him from his post. Wilson refused his plea—Roosevelt was too valuable a man where he was. The President did, however, allow his young subordinate to sail on an inspection tour of the fifty-odd American naval stations in the war zone. A dangerous job, but Roosevelt loved danger. He traveled over the submarine-infested Atlantic, visited the Azores, Corfu and the Orkney Islands, called on King George in London and on Clemenceau in Paris. On his return trip he contracted the flu and came home a very sick man.

But soon he recovered sufficiently to take another journey to France—this time in connection with the Peace Conference. Not as a member of the Conference, but as a supervisor for the demobilizing of the naval stations abroad. Again he had an opportunity to meet Clemenceau. And a remark that Clemenceau made to him on this occasion must have given Roosevelt much deep thought. "You wonder why we want to end this war with such a hard peace? Don't forget this tragic fact—that for the last century and a half every Frenchman who ever reached the age of seventy has been compelled to take part in a struggle against an aggressive Germany."

Roosevelt's return from this second trip was on the *George Washington,* the same ship that was bringing Wilson back a victor in the war and a victim of the peace. Roosevelt saw a great deal of his sad but still hopeful old prophet-chieftain on this trip. Someone pointed out to him the chair and the table on which Wilson had written the first draft of the League of Nations Covenant. Roosevelt asked his President for this

FRANKLIN DELANO ROOSEVELT

"memento of a great historic occasion," and the President graciously presented it to him.

And thus Franklin Roosevelt inherited the desk and the dream of Woodrow Wilson.

V

IN 1920 Roosevelt resigned from his post in the navy to run for the Vice-Presidency on the Democratic ticket. He conducted the campaign with his usual strength and sincerity and fire. He went on a speaking tour that took him into every state in the Union and kept him busy with an average of eleven speeches a day. The theme of his campaign was the perpetuation of Wilson's League of Justice. It proved too noble a message for too selfish an age. Roosevelt was defeated.

And then suddenly there came another and greater defeat. It was in the summer of 1921. A plunge into the ice-cold water of his summer home at Campobello, an hour of careless lolling in a wet bathing suit, a slight chill—and then years of silent suffering in the grip of a paralysis that seemed determined to kill. But Roosevelt was even more determined to live. He came out of this tragedy with weakened limbs and a strengthened soul. Illness is the best teacher of philosophy. The world offers many a curious angle to a man who is compelled to study it from an invalid's pillow. The ancient Greek philosophers had an apt saying—"Wisdom comes through suffering." Before his illness, Roosevelt had been an honest politician. After it, he became a devoted statesman.

While Roosevelt was making his fight for life, Alfred E. Smith had risen to the top of the Democratic Party. And now that Roosevelt had won his fight, he joined forces with Al Smith for the regeneration of the political life of America. It was a union between the poor little rich boy and the rich little poor boy—a combination of the Harvard and the Bowery accents into a new American dialect. A new though unnamed party arose as a result. This new party, which may be termed as the Aristo-democracy of 1928, cut deeply into both of the old parties. It united the progressive elements both in the Democratic and in the Republican camps. It fell short of electing Al Smith to the Presidency but it succeeded in sweeping Franklin Delano Roosevelt into the New York State House and, four years later, into the White House.

VI

ROOSEVELT came into the White House with a vision and he summarized this vision in four words—*the more abundant life*. As a convalescent at Warm Springs, in Georgia, he had witnessed physical suffering; and on his recovery he had devoted more than half of his fortune to the relief of such suffering. And now, in the midst of the depression, he witnessed economic suffering throughout the country and decided to devote all of his strength to the relief of *this* suffering.

When he took over the reins of the government, he found himself at the head of a hopeless, spiritless and strengthless nation. He revived its hope and its spirit and he began slowly to restore its strength.

His program at the outset was chaotic. But, in a crisis, deliberate planning is impractical. While the rescuer is trying to make up his mind as to whether to take a boat or to swim out to a drowning person, the poor victim is likely to die. What is needed in such an emergency is—first, quick action for survival; and only then, leisurely planning for recovery.

This is what President Roosevelt tried to do. The entire banking system, the heart that was pumping the economic lifeblood into the nation, was on the verge of collapse. He promptly performed an emergency operation. Declaring a bank holiday, he closed all the banks in the country, subjected them to a thorough examination, and then removed the unsound institutions and reopened those that satisfied the Treasury Department as to their soundness.

FRANKLIN DELANO ROOSEVELT

His next step was to try to provide food for the hungry. There were fifteen millions of them when he stepped into his executive office on March 4, 1933. The next morning, at breakfast, a friend asked him about his immediate plans. "I have seen," said Roosevelt, "the aged and the infirm, the poor and the helpless, standing for hours in breadlines waiting for their crust of bread and bowl of thin soup. The first thing I want to do is to take them out of those lines, rehabilitate them, feed them, make them happy once more. No nation can ever amount to anything while its people are in want."

This, throughout his first two terms in the White House, was his primary objective. To get the American people out of want. In order to accomplish this objective, he initiated his New Deal. This New Deal, to our contemporary and therefore limited point of view, resembles a labyrinth of wisdom and foolishness and compassion and justice and jumbles and contradictions and mistakes. Its general direction, however, appears to have been rightward and lightward—the conservation of the national resources for the common good; the harmonious balance of the various group interests in the United States; the reorganization of the spirit of the Supreme Court; the utilization of the federal subsidies for local needs; and the development of a policy of good neighborliness throughout the Western Hemisphere with a view to its ultimate fruition into a Pan-American League of Nations. Above all, the right of every American to enjoy the "four freedoms"—freedom of speech, freedom of worship, freedom from want and freedom from fear.

But a brief summary—indeed, *any* summary—is altogether inadequate to encompass the scope of the rapid kaleidoscope of intermingled permanent laws and emergency measures known as the New Deal. In an effort to answer the question, "What is the New Deal?" the editors of the London *Economist* wrote a thoughtful and factual book of a hundred and fifty pages—and confessed at the end that "the answer is still incomplete." For the blueprint of the New Deal was no less than an attempt to break the ground for a new road to ethical, social and economic fair play.

But hardly had the work begun when a horde of international brigands blocked the way. Roosevelt had to turn his attention from the establishment of national justice to the building of a national defense. Aware of his fitness as a pilot through dangerous waters, the country drafted him for a third term. And elected him, in spite of the unquestioned ability of his Republican opponent, Wendell Willkie.

And then, a year after his election, the storm broke. The treacherous attack on Pearl Harbor. Before the attack, our country had been divided—our enemy thought, *irreconcilably* divided—both on the domestic and on the foreign policy of President Roosevelt. The radicals complained that he was creeping too slowly on the road to salvation; the conservatives, that he was rushing too rapidly on the way to perdition. The employers insisted that he had allied himself with the labor agitators against honest enterprise; the workers, that he had united himself with the greedy exploiters against honest labor. The interventionists contended that he was giving aid and comfort to the aggressors with his policy of appeasement; the isolationists, that he was giving unnecessary provocation to one of the belligerents in a war that was none of our business.

But the attack on Pearl Harbor (December 7, 1941) produced a miracle. It united the country into a single passionate resolve for victory against the forces of evil. No more radicals or conservatives, employers or workers, interventionists or isolationists, Democrats or Republicans—but Americans all, eager and determined to follow the leadership of the Commander-in-Chief.

And Roosevelt is a commander in whom every American has the most implicit faith. For he is a master of world politics and a fighter of unconquerable grit. For him the word *defeat* simply does not exist. He has already fought a war, more terrible than Hitler's, and he has come off victorious. His attack of infantile paralysis, his doctors had declared, would either kill him or

FRANKLIN DELANO ROOSEVELT

leave him helpless for the rest of his days. But he stubbornly refused to die or to submit to a life of invalid despair. For many years he fought against destiny—and came out smiling at the top. In the darkest days of his illness he kept on encouraging his doctors who had not a single word of encouragement for him. Again and again he told them: "Never fear, I'll beat this thing yet!"

The man and the motto for a critical hour.

WITHDRAWN
UST
Libraries

DATE DUE			
DEC 15 1975			
MAY 15 1978			
GAYLORD			PRINTED IN U.S.A.